1/20/98

For Reference

Not to be taken from this room

Biography Today

**Profiles
of People
of Interest
to Young
Readers**

1997
Annual
Cumulation

Laurie Lanzen Harris
Executive Editor

Cherie D. Abbey
Associate Editor

Omnigraphics, Inc.

Penobscot Building
Detroit, Michigan 48226

Laurie Lanzen Harris, *Executive Editor*
Cherie D. Abbey, *Associate Editor*
Helene Henderson, Kevin Hillstrom, Laurie Hillstrom,
Sue Ellen Thompson, and John Wukovitz
Sketch Writers
Barry Puckett, *Research Associate*
Joan Margeson, *Research Assistant*

Omnigraphics, Inc.

* * *

Matt Barbour, *Production Manager*
Laurie Lanzen Harris, *Vice President, Editorial Director*
Peter E. Ruffner, *Vice President, Administration*
James A. Sellgren, *Vice President, Operations and Finance*
Jane Steele, *Marketing Consultant*

* * *

Frederick G. Ruffner, Jr., Publisher

Copyright © 1998 Omnigraphics, Inc.

ISBN 0-7808-0276-4

Indexed in
CHILDREN'S
MAGAZINE
GUIDE

Contents

3

Preface

Biography Today is a magazine designed and written for the young reader—aged 9 and above—and covers individuals that librarians and teachers tell us that young people want to know about most: entertainers, athletes, writers, illustrators, cartoonists, and political leaders.

The Plan of the Work

The publication was especially created to appeal to young readers in a format they can enjoy reading and readily understand. Each issue contains approximately 10 sketches arranged alphabetically; this annual cumulation contains 32 entries. Each entry provides at least one picture of the individual profiled, and bold-faced rubrics lead the reader to information on birth, youth, early memories, education, first jobs, marriage and family, career highlights, memorable experiences, hobbies, and honors and awards. Each of the entries ends with a list of easily accessible sources designed to lead the student to further reading on the individual and a current address. Obituary entries are also included, written to provide a perspective on the individual's entire career. Obituaries are clearly marked in both the table of contents and at the beginning of the entry.

Biographies are prepared by Omnigraphics editors after extensive research, utilizing the most current materials available. Those sources that are generally available to students appear in the list of further reading at the end of the sketch.

Indexes

To provide easy access to entries, each issue of *Biography Today* contains a Name Index, General Index covering occupations, organizations, and ethnic and minority origins, Places of Birth Index, and a Birthday Index. These indexes cumulate with each succeeding issue. The three yearly issues are cumulated annually in a hardbound volume, with cumulative indexes. The indexes also include references to individuals profiled in the **Biography Today Special Subject** volumes, explained below.

Our Advisors

This magazine was reviewed by an Advisory Board comprised of librarians, children's literature specialists, and reading instructors so that we could make sure that the concept of this publication—to provide a readable and accessible biographical magazine for young readers—was on target. They evaluated the title as it developed, and their suggestions have proved invaluable. Any errors, however, are ours alone. We'd like to list the Advisory Board members, and to thank them for their efforts.

Our Advisory Board stressed to us that we should not shy away from controversial or unconventional people in our profiles, and we have tried to follow their advice. The Advisory Board also mentioned that the sketches might be useful in reluctant reader and adult literacy programs, and we would value any comments librarians might have about the suitability of our magazine for those purposes.

New Series

In response to the growing number of suggestions from our readers, we have decided to expand the *Biography Today* family of publications. Five special subject volumes covering **Authors, Artists, Scientists and Inventors, Sports Figures, and World Leaders** have appeared thus far in the Subject Series. Each of these hardcover volumes is 200 pages in length and covers approximately 14 individuals of interest to readers aged 9 and above. The length and format of the entries is like those found in the regular issues of *Biography Today*, but there is **no** duplication between the regular series and the special subject volumes.

Your Comments Are Welcome

Our goal is to be accurate and up-to-date, to give young readers information they can learn from and enjoy. Now we want to know what you think. Take a look at this issue of *Biography Today*, on approval. Write or call me with your comments. We want to provide an excellent source of biographical information for young people. Let us know how you think we're doing.

And here's a special incentive: review our list of people to appear in upcoming issues. Use the bind-in card to list other people you want to see in *Biography Today.* If we include someone you suggest, your library wins a free issue, with our thanks. Please see the bind-in card for details.

And take a look at the next page, where we've listed those libraries and individuals that received a free issue of *Biography Today* in 1997 for their suggestions.

Laurie Harris
Executive Editor, *Biography Today*

Congratulations!

Congratulations to the following individuals and libraries, who received a free issue of *Biography Today* for suggesting people who appeared in 1997:

Sadia Ali, Springfield, VA
Champion R. Avecilla, San Jose, CA
Avondale High School,
    Auburn Hills, MI
Tiffany Bates, Machesney Park, IL
Caldwell Public Library, Caldwell, ID
Camden Fairview Middle School,
    Camden, AR, Marva M. Marks
Central Middle School Library,
    Dover, DE
Charlene Chan, Scarsdale, NY
City of Inglewood Public Library,
    Inglewood, CA
Joey Clark, Battle Creek, MI
Kayla Courneya, Bay City, MI
Rachel Anne Dymanski, Cleveland,
    OH
Monica Figueroa,
    Huntington Park, CA
Adam Finkel, Bloomfield Hills, MI
Floyd Light Middle School,
    Portland, OR, Linda Huynh
L.V. Freeman, East Orange, NJ
Tyler Gates, Hutchinson, KS
Jessica Gottschalk, Imlay City, MI
Sonia Gupta, Shoreview, MN
Haycock Elementary School,
    Falls Church, VA
Highland Park Public Schools/IMC,
    Highland Park, MI
J. David Kopp, St. Louis, MO
Lake Dolloff Elementary School,
    Auburn, WA
    Melissa Zastrow
Jody Langan, Litchfield, MN
Serena Liu, Rego Park, NY
Ha Ly, Charlotte, NC
Kathy Ly, San Jose, CA
Maharishi School, Fairfield, IA
McCune Attendance Center,
    McCune, KS
McCune Attendance Center,
    McCune, KS
    Martha Tilton

Ramsey Meitl, Oberlin, KS
Metcalf Junior High School,
    Burnsville, MN
Mt. Carmel High School, Saipan,
    Northen Mariana Islands
    Kim Minji
Angela Murray, Benton, AR
Mark Murray, Arnold, MD
Amy Ng, San Francisco, CA
Elisabeth Null, Fostoria, OH
Chad Passage, Adams Center, NY
Patrick Henry Junior Hill,
    Granada Hills, CA
    Marlene Alexander
Elise Patrick, Frederick, MD
Nicole Presutti, Indianapolis, IN
Paula Prindle, Erie, PA
Dana Reinoos, Milwaukee, WI
St. Clair Shores Public Library,
    St. Clair Shores, MI
    Rosemary Orlando
Shaw High School Library,
    East Cleveland, OH
    Jacqueline R. Avery
Rose Sibble, Ames, IA
Jessica Simmon, East Machias, ME
Spring-Ford Middle School,
    Royersford, PA
    Jeanne M. Havarilla
Moescha Steward, Smithfield, VA
Joanne Stewart, Saratoga Springs, NY
Rose Talbert, Laytonville, CA
Alyssa Tapp, Des Moines, IA
Jacinda Treadway, Nashville, TN
Billy Wagner,
    Chesterfield Township, MI
Washington Elementary School,
    Caldwell, ID
Korin Michelle Weber, Waterford, WI
Lisa Winger, Morrison, CO
David Xiao, New York, NY
Jared Yecker, Lancaster, PA
Alexandria Zarillo, Higginsville, MO

Madeleine Albright   1937-

Czech-Born American Secretary of State
First Woman to Serve as U.S. Secretary of State
Highest-Ranking Woman in U.S. Political History

BIRTH

Madeleine Albright was born Marie Jana Korbel on May 15, 1937, in Prague, Czechoslovakia. "Madeleine" was a nickname given to her by her grandmother when she was little, and the name stayed with her. Her parents were Josef and Mandula Korbel. Josef was a diplomat and Mandula, called Anna, was a homemaker. Albright has a brother, John, and a sister, Katherine, who are both younger.

YOUTH

Czechoslovakia

Albright's early life was defined by the history and politics of Europe during the 20th century. Her native country, Czechoslovakia, was formed in 1918 after the end of World War I. It was formerly part of the Austro-Hungarian empire, which covered a large section of what is now central Europe, including Austria, Bohemia, Moravia, Slovenia, and parts of Poland. This part of Europe had been ruled by monarchs of the Hapsburg family from the 13th century until World War I. The Treaty of Versailles, which ended World War I, broke up the empire and created many new nations, among them Czechoslovakia. The new nation contained Bohemia, Moravia, Silesia, and Slovakia. It was a democratic nation with strong, progressive political leadership. Albright's father, Josef Korbel, was a part of this political elite, and he raised his children to revere the democratic freedoms of their native land.

World War II

Czechoslovakia's freedom was short-lived. In 1938, the nations of Britain and France made an agreement with Adolf Hitler that allowed Germany to take over portions of Czechoslovakia, in return for a non-aggression pact with them. This agreement, known as the Munich Pact, was an act of appeasement. Historically, it has become a symbol of cowardice in the face of aggression. In essence, the Munich agreement allowed Nazi Germany, a nation with ambitions for invasion and destruction, to take control of another country, while France and England did not retaliate. But that certainly did not stop the Nazis. Just one year after the Munich Pact was signed, they invaded Poland. France and Britain declared war with Germany, and World War II began.

In 1939, when Albright was two, her family fled Czechoslovakia in the wake of the Nazi invasion. The Korbel family became war refugees in England, where they lived in London for the duration of the war. While they were there the German forces repeatedly bombed London, which she remembers well. She recalls a steel table in their kitchen, where they ate meals and hid during the bombing by the Nazis. "I spent a lot of time during the war in air-raid shelters or playing under a big steel table we had, so that if the house collapsed during a bombing I'd be all right." Josef Korbel served as part of the Czech government in exile in London throughout the war.

In 1945, when the war was over, the family returned to Czechoslovakia. Josef Korbel resumed his duties as a diplomat and was sent to Belgrade, Yugoslavia. Albright remembers that she would sometimes go with her father to greet other diplomats on missions. "The little girl at the airport who used to greet important visitors—that was me. I used to do it for a living." While the family lived in Yugoslavia, Madeleine was taught at home by a governess until she was 10, when her parents sent her to school in Switzerland. Being separated from family at such a young age might be hard for other children, but Madeleine was amazingly adaptable. "As a child, living in so many foreign countries made it easier for me to adjust to different situations and to make friends. My mother always taught me to be open and friendly with new people. She said I could learn a lot from them, and she was right."

Moving to the United States

Madeleine didn't stay in Switzerland very long. In 1948, the family once again became refugees, this time from the communist government that had taken control of Czechoslovakia. Josef Korbel was an outspoken foe of communism and therefore a potential enemy to the new government. So the family had to flee in secret. "My mother had to pretend she was taking our family from Czechoslovakia on a week's vacation, when we were really leaving for good," remembers Albright. They left their native country with just what their suitcases would hold; everything else had to be left behind. They settled first in New York, then moved to Denver, Colorado, where Josef became a professor at the University of Denver. Later, he created the School of International Relations at the University of Denver and was named dean.

Madeleine Albright has often said that her father was the greatest influence on her life. She was deeply inspired by his career as a diplomat and an academic, and by his fundamental beliefs in the dangers of totalitarian governments, like those of Nazi Germany and the Soviet Union. "My father was a strong influence on my life and what I have become," she recalled recently. "We talked about international relations all the time — the way some families talk about sports or other things around the dinner table." She and her siblings were encouraged to express their views and to learn as much as they could about the world.

EDUCATION

Albright's education was truly multicultural. By the time she was 10, she could speak three languages: her native Czech; English, which she learned during the war; and French, which she had to learn for school in Switzerland. When the family moved to Denver, she worked hard to speak English with an American accent. In Colorado, she attended Morey Middle School and then a private high school, the Kent School for Girls. And wherever she studied, she kept alive her interest in foreign affairs. "Wherever I went to school, I started an International Relations Club, and because I started it I'd become its president. I'm sure some of my friends found me very boring, but that was what I was interested in, so that's what I did." In high school, she won an essay contest sponsored by the U.N. She graduated from Kent in 1955.

Albright at age eight

After high school, Albright went to Wellesley College, an exclusive Ivy league school in Massachusetts. She studied political science and edited the school paper, bringing together her two great passions, politics and journalism. Commentators often remark on Albright's incredible capacity for hard work, which served her well during her student years, too. "In college, when everybody went skiing, I sat and studied."

During one summer off from school, she met Joseph Albright, the son of a wealthy newspaper family, while they were both working for the *Denver Post*. She graduated from Wellesley in 1959 with honors. Three days later she got married. Albright returned to school several years later, earning her Ph. D. from Columbia University in 1976.

MARRIAGE AND FAMILY

Madeleine and Joseph Albright were married in May 1959. Joe got a job with the *Chicago Sun-Times* soon after, and they moved to Chicago. Madeleine wanted to work as a journalist, too, but the prevailing sexism and discrimination against women of the time prevented her from doing so. As Albright recalls, her husband's boss asked her, "'Honey, what are you planning to do?' And I said, 'I am planning to be a reporter.' And he said, 'Guild regulations will prohibit you from having a job at the *Sun-Times* and our general feeling about a spouse working at a competitive newspaper will prevent you from getting a job at another newspaper, so honey, why don't you think of another career?'" "It made me mad, but not mad enough to fight, which I would do now, and I would expect my daughters to do," says Albright.

A year later, Joe got a job with a New York paper, and the couple moved to Long Island. In 1961, Madeleine gave birth to twins, Anne and Alice. The twins were six weeks premature and had to spend most of their early months in incubators. Albright was frantic; to take her mind off her concern, she took an intensive course in Russian, adding another language to her repertoire. Six years after the twins were born, Albright had another daughter, Katharine.

CAREER HIGHLIGHTS

By the mid-1960s, Albright was taking courses for her master's and doctoral degrees in international relations at Columbia University. She would get up at 4:30 in the morning, before the rest of the family, to get her studying done. She wrote her thesis on the role of the press in the 1968 Czech uprising against communist rule. Her thesis advisor at Columbia was Zbigniew Brzezinski, who would later become Secretary of State for President Jimmy Carter, and who would call on Albright to work for him at the White House.

Working for Edmund Muskie

Albright received her Ph.D. from Columbia in 1976, the same year she started her career in politics. The family had moved to Washington, D.C., where Joe Albright worked as a newspaper correspondent. Madeleine had worked as a fund-raiser for Senator Edmund Muskie of Maine, and after she finished her degree, he hired her as his chief legislative assistant. In that job, she researched and reported to Muskie on legislation that was being debated in the Senate.

Working for the Carter Administration

In 1977, Albright was hired by her former thesis advisor, Brzezinski, to work for him as a liaison between the White House and the Senate. That position lasted until 1980, when Carter was voted out of office.

Albright spent the years 1981 and 1982 as a Woodrow Wilson International scholar in Washington, where she worked on a book about the press and its role in modern Polish politics, published as *Poland: The Role of the Press in Political Change*.

In 1982, Albright's world was shattered when her husband told her he was leaving her for another woman. "It was a shock," Albright recalled. "I was very upset. I had been married for 23 years and I did not want a divorce. But life goes on. I'm over it." The divorce settlement left Madeleine Albright with a house in Georgetown, a farm in Virginia, and the financial resources to pursue whatever she wished. She began to teach at Georgetown University in Washington. She was a research professor of International Affairs and the Director of Women in Foreign Service Program in the School of Foreign Service. She taught courses in international affairs, U.S. foreign policy, Russian foreign policy, and Central and Eastern European politics. Albright has also worked actively for years to increase the opportunities for women in international affairs. She says that one of the things she taught her female students was to "interrupt. I found that as a woman, kind of working my way up in the government, that women often wait too long in meetings to make their views known. Then all of a sudden, some man says whatever it is that you were going to say and everybody thinks it's brilliant." She was a very popular professor and won numerous teaching awards.

During the early 1980s, Albright turned her home into a gathering place for Washington Democrats. After losing the White House to the Republicans in 1980, the Democrats needed an informal forum to meet and talk about foreign policy, and Albright's house became a kind of "policy salon." She was also a founder and president of the Center for National Policy, a democratic "think tank" that sponsored research, problem solving, and publications in the area of foreign affairs.

In 1984, Democratic Presidential candidate Walter Mondale named Geraldine Ferraro to be his running mate for vice president. As the first woman ever named to run for vice president for a major political party, Ferrarro was closely scrutinized in the press. To prepare her for statements and debates, the party hired Albright as Ferrarro's foreign policy advisor. "She was the perfect teacher," remembers Ferraro. "We'd discuss arms control, missile throw weight, geopolitics, you name it."

Albright was called on again in 1988 to act as foreign policy advisor for Michael Dukakis's campaign for the presidency. As she coached Dukakis for his presidential debates against George Bush, she met a young Democratic governor from Arkansas, Bill Clinton. Dukakis lost the election, but Clinton remembered Albright. He wrote to her asking for a recommendation for a spot on the council on Foreign Relations and she gave him a glowing one that helped him get the position.

Ambassador to the United Nations

In 1993, Clinton, who had been elected President of the United States in 1992, named Albright as the U.S. Ambassador to the United Nations. She was the first foreign-born American to hold the post, and one of only seven women in the entire 185-member body. As Ambassador to the U.N., Albright served as the Clinton administration's voice in international affairs. Clinton also elevated Albright's position to the level of a Cabinet post, and he made her an adviser to the National Security Council. The National Security Council, or NSC, is made up of the president, vice president, secretary of state, and secretary of defense. Its purpose is to coordinate national defense and foreign policy strategies. The NSC is advised by a group that includes the chairman of the joint chiefs of staff, the director of the CIA, the national security adviser, and in Clinton's NSC, Ambassador Madeleine Albright. As such, from the beginning of her job at the U.N. Albright was a prominent presence in both Washington, the political center of power for the U.S. and New York City, the site of the U.N.. She was a regular on the Washington-New York shuttle and maintained staffs and homes in both places. She was also the only woman on the U.N. Security Council, which is made up of representatives of 15 member nations and is considered the most powerful group within the organization.

Albright was a dynamic and outspoken ambassador. She proudly wore a pin in the shape of a snake after the Iraqi representative referred to her as a "serpent." She was known for her hawkish stance in the use of U.S. and U.N. military power. She often stated, "My mind set is Munich. Most of my generation's was Vietnam." By that she meant that she felt that not taking action in the face of aggression, as happened in the Munich Pact in 1938, would lead to oppression and totalitarianism. So Albright is likely to favor the use of U.S. military force in response to aggressive acts. Yet many American policy makers have a different frame of reference. For them, the U.S. military involvement in what began as a Vietnamese civil war in the 1960s and 1970s was a debacle. They see U.S. involvement in foreign affairs as something to be avoided.

Albright's hawkish stance led to triumphs and defeats for U.S. forces. During her first year, she fought for a U.N. peacekeeping mission in Somalia. The Somalia mission had been created to protect aid workers helping victims of the civil war that raged in that African nation. As part of the U.N. peacekeeping force, U.S. troops were sent to the Somalian capital of Mogadishu. The mission was a fiasco: 18 U.S. soldiers were killed, and rebel troops dragged the body of one soldier through the streets. American television audiences were horrified at the scene. U.S. opinion was immediate and negative; the U.S. forces soon came home.

Albright still believed in the power and ability of a U.S. military presence as part of U.N. peacekeeping missions. In her second year in the U.N., Albright persuaded other member nations to allow the U.S. to send troops to Haiti. Their purpose was to remove a military dictatorship from power and reinstate the democratically elected president, Jean-Bertrand Aristide. The action was highly controversial, but also very successful. Aristide was returned to power, and the U.S. forces were eventually replaced by U.N. peacekeepers.

Albright was also very involved in the U.N. role in keeping peace among the new nations of Europe. In 1989, the Soviet Union had collapsed, and the former communist nations of central and Eastern Europe regrouped, often along ancient ethnic lines. Ethnic fighting broke out in the former Yugoslavia between Serbian nationalists and Muslims. Albright fought for U.N. peacekeeping missions to be sent to the area and for the U.S. to use their Air Force to defend a "no-fly" zone in the besieged area of Sarajevo. Her actions were very controversial, particularly among the Serbian sympathizers at home and abroad. One day, as she was leaving the U.N., a Serbian woman shouted at her, in Serbian, "Why do you treat the Serbs like animals?" "Because they act like animals," shot back the Ambassador, living up to her reputation as someone who "tells it like it is." She was also an important figure behind the formation of the War Crimes Tribunal, formed to punish those guilty of war crimes in the conflict.

Albright made it her goal to appear as often as she could on television to explain what was going on at the U.N. and what the U.S. policy goals were. She said once that she considered the TV network CNN the "16th member of the Security Council."

When Bill Clinton won reelection in November 1996, his Secretary of State, Warren Christopher, announced he was leaving. Speculation ran rampant in Washington, as insiders and media wondered who would replace Christopher. Albright was considered a prominent candidate, and she had made it known she would love to have the job.

Secretary of State

On December 5, 1996, President Clinton nominated Albright to be Secretary of State. She was unanimously confirmed by the Senate and was sworn into office on January 23, 1997. She was the first woman to hold the rank and the highest-ranking woman in U.S. political history.

As Secretary of State, Madeleine Albright is responsible for outlining and executing the foreign policy initiatives of the Clinton administration. One of the reasons Clinton chose Albright was because she is able to outline policy problems and solutions clearly and succinctly. "She can go out there and explain in terms that people understand why stopping the war in Bosnia or famine in Africa or the sale of chemical weapons in the former Soviet Union should matter to them," said a White House source. One of her most important goals, she says, is to stress the importance of foreign policy to the American people. "We are in a period of foreign policy when all the rules are different," says Albright. "It's not easy to explain, because the media often do not allow you to have long conversations. But it's important to use whatever time one

Albright with her daughters Alice, Anne, and Katharine

has to talk to the public, because in a democracy you have to have public support for policy."

Albright's nomination was met with praise on both sides of the political spectrum. "I like this appointment better than anyone else," said Jeanne Kirkpatrick, who served as Ronald Reagan's U.N. ambassador in the 1980s. "This really represents a breakthrough." Albright was roundly praised for her hard work, dedication, and outstanding background in foreign affairs. And she is credited with breaking through the "glass ceiling," the barriers to women that continue to exist throughout the world of business and politics. "There is no harder glass ceiling," said Democratic insider Richard Moe. "Madeleine broke through it by working twice as hard as a lot of her male counterparts."

A Revelation about Her Background

In February 1997, just as she was settling in to her new job as secretary of state, Albright received some shocking news. A *Washington Post* reporter had been sent to her homeland to learn more about her early years. What he found undermined what she knew about her family history. The reporter, Michael Dobbs, discovered that Albright's parents had both been born Jewish. Like other Jews in Europe in the 1930s, they had converted to

19

Catholicism to escape the terrors of Nazism. Beginning in the 1930s, Hitler and the Nazis began a reign of terror against the Jews of Europe. As they extended their military and political control after the beginning of World War II, the Nazis began the systematic rounding up and extermination of Jewish people that is now known as the Holocaust. At least six million Jews died at the hands of the Nazis during World War II. Included among them, Albright learned, were three of her grandparents, as well as other relatives.

The news came as a shock to Albright. She and her siblings had been raised Catholic by their parents. They had never been told of their former Jewish background or that they had any relatives who had perished in the Holocaust.

The *Washington Post* story revealed that the reporter had interviewed a relative of Albright's family who had lived with the Korbels during World War II. This cousin claimed that she and other members of the Prague community had begun writing letters to Albright when she was Ambassador to the U.N. to tell her of her Jewish background. Albright said that she had indeed received letters when she was at the U.N., but that she thought they were false. When she met with Dobbs and examined the evidence, which included birth and death records of family members, she was convinced. Albright asked the press to allow her to deal with the revelation in her own time and in her own way. Discussing her parents' decision to renounce their Jewish heritage and to raise their children as Catholics, she told the *New York Times*, "I think my father and mother were the bravest people alive. They dealt with the most difficult decision anyone could make. I am incredibly grateful to them, and beyond measure." Other than that, she has not made a great deal of public comment on what she considers to be a deeply private matter.

Early Duties as Secretary of State

Albright's first major trip in her new job took place in February 1997. She visited 10 nations around the world, including France, Russia, and China. She spoke with European leaders, talked with Russian premier Boris Yeltsin, and arrived in China at the time of the death of Deng Xiaoping, one of the last of the Chinese communist leaders who date back to the revolutionary era under Mao Zedong. Albright was warmly welcomed by her hosts.

When asked to assess her strengths for her new office, Albright says, "I think I really am the embodiment of the turbulence of the 20th century, as well as of the tolerance and optimism of the United States." Her statements before the Senate during her confirmation hearings outlined her purpose and her stance. She vowed to "tell it like it is, here and when I go abroad. We must be more than an audience, more even than actors. We must be the authors of the history of our age."

HOBBIES AND OTHER INTERESTS

Albright has very little free time, but when she does, she enjoys spending time at her farm in Virginia. "Nobody would ever recognize me on the farm as I play around in my garden barefoot, and I go to the movies, and I knit," she says.

Albright is still close to her three daughters, who are now grown. They accompanied her to her swearing in as secretary of state and remembered what it was like growing up with their dynamic mom. "As a working mother, she's got fabulous juggling skills," says daughter Anne. "She knows how to pay attention to everything all the time." She said that when she and her sisters were growing up, "mom never told us, you should do this or you should do that. The one thing she really wanted to teach us was: do your best at your job, no matter what it is. She's said many times there's no such thing as luck. What you get you work for." The girls are all very proud of their mom, and she has said: "To my daughters, all I can say is that all your lives I've worried about where you were and what you were up to. Now you will have the chance to worry about me."

HONORS AND AWARDS

Woodrow Wilson Scholar: 1981-1982
Woman of the Year: 1995 (*Glamour* Magazine)

WRITINGS

Poland: The Role of the Press and Political Change, 1983

FURTHER READING

Books

Maass, Robert. *U.N. Ambassador: A Behind-the-Scenes Look at Madeleine Albright's World,* 1995 (juvenile)
Who's Who 1997

Periodicals

Boston Globe, May 13, 1988, p.47; Feb. 13, 1997, p.A10
Chicago Tribune, Dec. 8, 1996, p.A3; Feb. 5, 1997, p.A3; Feb. 8, 1997, p.A4; Feb. 23, 1997, p.A1
Glamour, Oct. 1995, p.161; Dec. 1995, p.72
Miami Herald, Mar. 22, 1996, p.A1; Feb. 12, 1997, p.D1
The New Republic, Aug. 22, 1994, p.19

New York Times, Dec. 6, 1996, p. A1; Jan. 6, 1997, p.A1; Jan. 9, 1997, p.A1;
   Feb. 5, 1997, p.A1; Feb. 22, 1997, p.A1
New York Times Magazine, Sep. 22, 1996, p.63
Newsweek, Feb. 10, 1997, p.23
San Francisco Chronicle, June 25, 1995, p.Z7
Time, Oct. 31, 1994, p.31; Dec. 16, 1996, p.32; Feb. 17, 1997, p.53
U.S. News and World Report, Feb. 13, 1995, p.60
USA Today, Apr. 8, 1993, p.A6; Dec. 6, 1996, p.A6
Washington Post, Jan. 6, 1991, p.F1; Dec. 6, 1996, p.A25; Feb. 9, 1997,
   Magazine Section, p.8; Feb. 13, 1997, p.A27

ADDRESS

U.S. State Department
Secretary of State
2201 C St. NW
Washington, DC 20520

WORLD WIDE WEB SITE

http://secretary.state.gov/www/albright/albright.html

Marcus Allen   1960-

American Professional Football Player
Running Back for the Kansas City Chiefs

BIRTH

Marcus LaMarr Allen was born on March 26, 1960, in San Diego, California. His father, Harold "Red" Allen, was a general contractor, and his mother, Gwen Allen, was a registered nurse. Marcus had three brothers—Harold, Damon, and Darius—and one sister, Michelle. He was the second-oldest among the Allen children.

YOUTH

As a child growing up in San Diego, Allen was part of a tight-knit family that was fairly well-off financially. His father, though a strict disciplinarian, also loved to indulge the children. Red Allen built the kids a basketball court, bought them Shetland ponies, and did whatever he could to keep them busy. He also played a very active role in his children's lives, managing one Little League team and sponsoring another. He believed that a strong family did things together, and he led by example.

Red Allen also taught his children the importance of being an individual—a leader, not a follower. Allen recalled that his father taught him to "depend on no one," to be "proud, dignified, and confident," and to present himself "as a winner." Gwen Allen also played a strong role in her son's development, insisting that he attend Baptist Sunday school, sing in the church choir, and become active in Boy Scouts. She once described Marcus as "Red on the outside, and me on the inside." It was a powerful combination that has served Allen throughout his life.

Allen was taught at an early age to respect adults and to maintain a strong belief in God. Those two values were very important in his early development, as well as in his later career. "God has blessed me," Allen stated. "And that is more important than anything. I really feel that everything I have done is because of Him. I feel He is guiding my life." Allen still remembers a plaque that hung on the wall of his parents' home: "Be careful of the words you say / So keep them soft and sweet / You never know from day to day / Which ones you'll have to eat." From that plaque, he learned to be thoughtful when he spoke, and always to be aware that how he said something was often as important as what he said. It was a lesson that stuck with him throughout his professional career.

EDUCATION

Allen displayed his talent for athletics throughout his years in the San Diego schools. By the time he reached Lincoln High School in San Diego, he was a star in basketball, football, baseball, and track. To this day, his mother is convinced that baseball was his best sport, and that Allen "could have been as good as Brooks Robinson" if he had stuck with the game. During his first two years at Lincoln, however, basketball was his main sport. He was the star of the team, but he quit in disgust his sophomore season when he felt that his teammates did not work as hard as he did and did not take the game seriously.

The basketball team's loss was the football team's gain. Allen started out as a defensive safety, and he was immediately the best player on the field. A devastating hitter, he also had a knack for making interceptions and turning them into big plays, often returning them for touchdowns. In one game, he made

30 tackles by himself. By Allen's junior season, Coach Vic Player knew that the young man was too talented to play only defense. He felt that Allen could dominate the game from both sides of the ball. But when Player asked Allen to also play quarterback, Allen resisted the suggestion. At one practice, he even intentionally fumbled the snap every time in the hopes that Player would end this experiment on offense. Instead, the coach became angry with Allen and kicked him off the team. Humbled, Allen came to practice the next day and begged the coach to take him back. It was an easy decision for Player. "If he hadn't come back, I would have gone to him and begged," the coach recalled. "But Marcus will never believe that."

Allen settled in at quarterback and quickly became a star at the position. During his senior season at Lincoln, he led his team to a 12-0-1 record and the city championship. He passed for 1,434 yards and nine touchdowns and rushed for 1,098 yards and 12 more touchdowns. On defense, he continued to make the big plays and hit everything that moved. He tallied 11 interceptions, returning four of them for touchdowns. He also made 94 solo tackles and assisted on an astonishing 217 more. He became the only player in Lincoln history to have his jersey retired. At the end of the year he received the Hertz Number One Award, which was given annually to the best high school athlete in California.

Needless to say, Allen was one of the most highly recruited football players in the country when he graduated from Lincoln High School in 1978. Coaches from all over the nation tried to convince him to attend their schools, but for Allen the decision was easy — he would attend the University of Southern California (USC). "It was always SC," he noted. "I first started watching them when O.J. [running back O.J. Simpson] played. From that point on, that was the school I wanted to go to." Allen spent the next four years at USC, studying public administration and playing football. He left USC in 1982, just one semester short of graduating.

CAREER HIGHLIGHTS

University of Southern California Trojans

Allen started his football career in college. He had been recruited to USC as a defensive back, and that is the position at which everyone thought he would become a star. Nick Canepa, a reporter who covered Allen's high school games, recalled that "the first time I saw Marcus, I was convinced he was going to be an All-Pro defensive back. I quit counting one day after he made 30 tackles." The entire USC coaching staff felt the same way, except for one man — head coach John Robinson. After just one week of practice, he decided to switch Allen to running back.

By moving him to running back, Robinson showed that he believed Allen could be one of the best runners in the country. At that time, USC was known

as "Tailback U" because it had produced one legendary running back after another—including O.J. Simpson, Ricky Bell, and Charles White. Robinson thought Allen could be next in that line of great backs. "Since the first time he put on our uniform," Robinson said, "it's been obvious that Marcus has three things you need to be a tailback at USC: the personal ambition, the magnetism, and that tailback look in his eyes." Allen himself was unhappy with the switch because it meant he would get almost no playing time in his first season. Playing behind junior tailback Charles White, who was the best in the country at that time, Allen gained only 171 yards his freshman year. He refused to get discouraged, though, and impressed his teammates and coaches by always working hard at practice.

In his sophomore season (1979-80), Allen faced the prospect of sitting on the bench again while White finished his USC career. Coach Robinson knew he had to find a way to get Allen into the lineup, so he asked the young player if he would move to fullback. Again, Allen was reluctant to make the switch. Playing fullback at USC meant doing the dirty work — blocking and clearing a path for the star tailback — and many (including Allen himself) thought he was too small for the job. But Robinson persisted. "Think about it, Marcus," the coach told Allen. "You're not going to play much at tailback."

That clinched it for Allen. He wanted to play. His nose was broken in his first practice at fullback, and he often found reasons to miss the physically punishing practices, but he stuck with it and became an excellent fullback. He was only six feet tall and 202 pounds, when players in that position are often several inches taller and 50 to 75 pounds heavier. Nevertheless, Allen became a ferocious blocker and managed to rush for 679 yards and eight touchdowns of his own. He claimed that his only worry was "if I played the position too well, Coach Robinson would make me stay there." But Robinson knew that the move was only temporary. Near the end of the season, the coach approached Allen and said, "Marcus, you sacrificed for the good of the team." Allen replied, "Yeah, I sacrificed my entire body!"

Allen was rewarded for his patience during his junior year (1980-81), when he became the starting tailback for the USC Trojans. He gained 1,563 yards rushing that season, second in the country to George Rogers of South Carolina, who won that year's Heisman Trophy (awarded annually to the best college football player). Allen also showed that he could do more than run with the ball, becoming an excellent pass receiver. In fact, he led all running backs nationally by averaging a total of 179.4 yards per game, running and receiving. For his efforts, Allen was named to the second-team All-American squad. The only bad thing about that season was that his team finished only 8-2-1, an off-year for the powerful Trojans.

In his senior season (1981-82), all of Allen's hard work and sacrifices finally paid off. He became the first running back in history to rush for more than 2,000 yards in a single season, finishing with an NCAA-record 2,342 yards to shatter the old record of 1,948 yards held by Tony Dorsett of the University of Pittsburgh. He averaged more than 212 yards per game and scored 23 touchdowns while winning every major college football award there was to win, including the Heisman Trophy and the *Sporting News* Player of the Year Award. For Allen, the stellar season was simply a matter of living up to his own high expectations. "You've got to think positively to achieve the impossible, to be what you expect to be," he explained. "I have a burning desire to be the best. If I don't make it, that's O.K. because I'm reaching for something so astronomically high. If you reach for the moon and miss, you'll still be among the stars."

By the time Allen's career at USC ended, he had set or tied 13 NCAA records. He rushed for 200 or more yards 11 times, including in 5 straight games, and he rushed for 100 or more yards in 20 of his 21 career starts at tailback. He totaled 4,682 yards rushing on 893 carries and added 801 yards receiving on 86 catches. Allen's only regret about his college years was that when he left school in 1982, he was one semester short of completing his degree in public administration. "I left school because I won the Heisman Trophy," he recalled. "I did a lot of traveling, and I missed the entire last semester. But I'm going back to school. What's important is that you get your degree."

Los Angeles Raiders

Despite Allen's great college career, pro scouts still had their doubts about his talents. They felt he was too slow to be a star in the National Football League (NFL), and they worried that he might turn out like Ricky Bell and Charles White—talented backs from USC who never made it big in the NFL. Those fears caused Allen to slip to the tenth position of the first round in the 1982 NFL draft, where he was selected by the Los Angeles Raiders. The Raiders, who had just moved from Oakland, were thrilled to land Allen. As team draft expert Ron Wolf explained, "If we had the first pick in the draft, it would have been Marcus Allen."

Allen fit in immediately on his new team. Even veteran Gene Upshaw, who was never known to like rookies all that much, was impressed by his new teammate: "The reason you never hear a bad word about him is because we all like him—because he's not like some other backs that come out of USC with big heads. He'll never be that way, either, because he's not that kind of kid."

Allen quickly made an impact on the field as well. In his first game, he ran for 116 yards on 23 carries, the most yards gained by a Raiders back in five years. After two weeks, the 1982 season was interrupted by the first players' strike in NFL history. The season resumed seven weeks later, but the number of remaining games was reduced from 16 to 7. But Allen did not let the strike distract him. He ended up rushing for 697 yards and led the league with 14 touchdowns. He also caught 38 passes for 401 yards and distinguished himself as a terrific blocker when he was not carrying the ball. "You can't drag Allen down with one arm," said Seattle Seahawks defensive player Manu Tuiasosopo. "I know, I had three or four missed tackles. You've got to hold him up and nail him. He just keeps coming at you." For his outstanding rookie season, Allen was named the *Sporting News* Rookie of the Year and was invited to the Pro Bowl. The Raiders had an excellent season as well, finishing 8-1. However, they were knocked out in the first round of the playoffs by the New York Jets, 17-14.

Super Bowl XVIII

To a man, the Raiders swore they would do better in the 1983 season playoffs. The team's coaches made some significant changes in strategy toward that end. Knowing that opposing defenses were set up to stop Allen, the Raiders decided to use a varied offense that distributed the ball among a number of players. This strategy was intended to make the offense more versatile and less predictable, as well as to keep the players fresher and healthier for the playoffs. But one of the main effects of the change was to limit the number of times Allen carried the ball. He felt frustrated by the Raiders' new offense, but he still managed to finish the season with 1,014 yards rushing and nine touchdowns despite missing three games with a hip injury.

The Raiders entered the playoffs primed to make a run at the Super Bowl. Thanks to his reduced role in the regular season, Allen entered the postseason with fresh legs, and it showed. He had his best games of the year in the first two playoff games, rushing for 121 and 154 yards in victories over the Pittsburgh Steelers and Seattle Seahawks, respectively. But the best was yet to come.

In the 1984 Super Bowl, the Raiders faced off against the Washington Redskins. Everyone expected a close game, but Allen had other ideas. He carried the ball 20 times for a Super Bowl record 191 yards and two touchdowns. His 74-yard touchdown run in the third quarter was a playoff record for longest scoring run, and it broke the spirit of the Redskins. The Raiders went on to win 38-9, and Allen was named Most Valuable Player of the Super Bowl. "I felt like I could run all day," he recalled of that special day. "I didn't know I set a record until I saw it on the scoreboard. My teammates were congratulating me. You dream of moments like this, but you never think they'll happen."

For Allen, who had always been close to his family, one aspect of the Super Bowl win stood out above all others: "The best thing was seeing the smiles on my parents' faces. I found my mother on the field after the game and gave her a big kiss. She had tears in her eyes. If I can give my parents this moment, that's my Super Bowl."

Winning it all in only his second season made it tough for Allen to reach new heights on the football field, but he kept trying. In 1984, he again topped the 1,000-yard rushing mark by carrying the ball for 1,168 yards and 13 touchdowns. The Raiders went 11-5 that year but were eliminated in the first round of the playoffs. In 1985, the Raiders' top two quarterbacks were injured, which caused Coach Tom Flores to scrap the balanced offense the team had been using and rely more heavily on Allen. He responded with one of the best seasons ever by a running back. He tallied 1,759 yards to become the first Raider ever to win the league rushing title. He also caught 67 passes for 555 yards, giving him 2,314 total yards from scrimmage. He tied a league record by rushing for more than 100 yards in nine straight games. The Raiders ended up losing in the playoffs to the New England Patriots, but Allen was rewarded for his spectacular season by being voted the league's Most Valuable Player by the Professional Football Writers Association.

That year would prove to be the highlight of Allen's career. In 1986, he started only 10 games because of a hamstring injury, although he did rush for more than 100 yards in the first two games of the season to set an NFL record for most consecutive games topping that mark (with 11 — nine from the previous season and two that year).

Contract Dispute

Allen's career changed dramatically in 1987, when the Raiders drafted flamboyant running back Bo Jackson. Suddenly, Allen was no longer the number one option in the backfield. His playing time was cut in half, and he was later asked to move to fullback. Always a team player, Allen did as he was asked. He still managed to lead the Raiders in rushing in 1987 and 1988, capping a string of seven consecutive seasons that he led the team in that category.

In 1989, Allen played in only eight games, and started just five, after suffering a knee injury. At the end of the season, he asked Raiders' owner Al Davis for a small raise. "I just wanted him to show me some appreciation for everything I had done for the organization," Allen explained. Davis, who had had a rocky relationship with Allen for several years, ignored the request. Allen did not know it then, but this was the beginning of the end of his Raiders' career. He continued to ask for a raise, and Davis continued to ignore him. Finally, Davis decided to punish Allen by cutting his playing time even further, forcing him into a backup role, and refusing to trade the still-talented runner.

After terrible seasons in 1990 and 1991 — in which he was used sparingly and rushed for only 287 and 301 yards, respectively — Allen had had enough. He sued the Raiders in court for the right to become a free agent, meaning that he would be free to sign with any team. He also decided to make his complaints public. During halftime of a *Monday Night Football* game in 1992, Allen was featured in a taped interview in which he blasted Davis and Raiders' Coach Art Shell. Because he knew he would win his court case and never have to play for the Raiders again, he took the opportunity to stand up for himself. "I felt it was time for me to speak out, and I don't apologize for that," he said of the controversial interview.

Looking back on those last years with the Raiders, Allen claimed that the experience made him a stronger person. "To me, it [was] all an education. It was a wonderful education," he noted. "Although I hated it, I didn't realize it at the time. When I was going through it, there was no light at the end of the tunnel for me, but when you look back at it and deal with everything, it was a tremendous experience."

Kansas City Chiefs

Allen won his court case just before the 1993 season, and he immediately signed with the Kansas City Chiefs — the Raiders' biggest rival. There, his career was reborn. He led the Chiefs in rushing his first season with 764 yards and led the AFC (American Football Conference) with 15 touchdowns. In 1994, he again led the team in rushing and touchdowns. During that season, he became only the ninth man in professional football history to rush for more than 10,000 career yards — and he reached the milestone in a game against the Raiders, which made the accomplishment even sweeter. In 1995, Allen was named the Chiefs team captain and led by example on the field. In addition to leading the team in rushing for a third straight year with 890 yards, he set two more career milestones: he became the first player in league history to record more than 10,000 yards rushing and 5,000 yards receiving, and he also became just the fourth player ever to score more than 100 touchdowns.

In 1996, the records continued to pile up. Allen passed the 11,000 yard mark in career rushing, broke Roger Craig's record for most receptions by a running back, and passed Walter Payton to become the player with the most career rushing touchdowns. Allen rushed for career touchdowns 111 and 112 during a game against the Detroit Lions, breaking Payton's old mark of 110. He moved into second place all-time in total touchdowns with 134 (trailing only Jerry Rice).

Many people thought that Allen would retire after the 1996 season, but he decided to return for one more year and will play his final games in 1997. "Physically and intellectually," he once said, "when my body tells me I've had enough, then I'll listen and step away from football." That time will soon come for one of the greatest running backs in NFL history. A certain Hall of Fame selection, Allen does not hesitate when asked in what team jersey he will be inducted. "To me, going in as a Chief, that's a no-brainer," he stated.

MARRIAGE AND FAMILY

Allen lives in Kansas City with his wife of four years, Kathryn. He and Kathryn are spokespersons for Ronald McDonald Children's Charities. Allen remains very close to his parents and siblings.

HOBBIES AND OTHER INTERESTS

Off the field, Allen has many hobbies. He participates in taekwondo, a Korean martial art, to improve his strength, flexibility, quickness, and balance. He even practices walking and kicking on a balance beam to improve his surefootedness. Allen also enjoys playing the piano—which he took up in 1984—collecting expensive automobiles, and playing and watching sports. In 1994, he opened an auto dealership, North Oak Toyota, in Kansas City.

After his playing career is over, Allen hopes to put his football knowledge to use in the broadcast booth or possibly even take up acting. "Oh, I think it would be great fun to get into acting," he admits. "But it's not solid and steady." No matter what post-football career he chooses, Allen says that one thing is certain: "I'm going to work very hard at it."

HONORS AND AWARDS

Heisman Trophy: 1981
Maxwell Award: 1981
College Football Player of the Year (*Sporting News*): 1981
NFL Rookie of the Year (*Sporting News*): 1982
Pro Bowl Team: 1982, 1984, 1985, 1986, 1987, 1993
Super Bowl XVIII Most Valuable Player: 1984
NFL Most Valuable Player (Professional Football Writers Association): 1985

NFL Player of the Year (*Sporting News*): 1985
Lifetime Achievement Award (Magic Johnson Sports Star Awards): 1994

FURTHER READING

Books

Allen, Marcus and Carlton Stowers. *Marcus*, 1997
Leder, Jane Mersky. *Marcus Allen*, 1985 (juvenile)
Lincoln Library of Sports Champions, Vol. 1, 1993
Who's Who among America 1996-97
Who's Who in America 1997

Periodicals

Current Biography Yearbook 1986
Detroit News, Feb. 2, 1997, p.D3
Ebony, Nov. 1983, p.145
Gentleman's Quarterly, Aug. 1988, p.222
Jet, Nov. 5, 1984, p.46; Feb. 3, 1986, p.46; Oct. 7, 1996, p.49; Dec. 16, 1996,
   p.51
Los Angeles Times, Feb. 2, 1997, p.C12
New York Times, Nov. 29, 1996, p.D:1
Sport, Nov. 1985, p.25; Oct. 1994, p.40; Feb. 1997, p.14
Sporting News, Oct. 30, 1995, p.45
Sports Illustrated, Dec. 13, 1982, p.18; Sep. 1, 1986, p.78; Dec. 11, 1995, p.90
Washington Post, Jan. 21, 1994, p.C1; Apr. 28, 1996, p.A6

ADDRESS

Kansas City Chiefs
Arrowhead Stadium
One Arrowhead Drive
Kansas City, MO 64129

WORLD WIDE WEB SITE

http://www.nfl.com

Gillian Anderson   1968-
American Actress
Star of "The X-Files"

[**Editor's Note:** *Anderson's mother, Rosemary, generously contributed extensive information to this entry, for which* Biography Today *extends its thanks and appreciation.*]

BIRTH

Gillian Anderson was born August 9, 1968, in Chicago, Illinois. Her mother, Rosemary, is a computer analyst. Her father, Edward, owns a post-production film company. She has a younger brother, Aaron (age 15), and a younger sister, Zoë (age 12).

YOUTH

After Gillian's birth, the family moved to Puerto Rico. When she was two, they moved to London, England, where her father attended the London Film School to study film production. The family lived in England for eight years before moving back to the United States. When they settled in Grand Rapids, Michigan, Anderson was ten years old and faced with culture shock. As her mother, Rosemary, told *Biography Today*, Gillian lost her British accent and acquired a Michigan one in about two weeks, but there were significant differences between her new American school and her English school. For example, English spellings of some words are not the same as American spellings, and the British have a different style of cursive handwriting and teach it much later than in the United States. American geography had not been taught in her English school, so Gillian had trouble with that as well. In addition, her new city proved to be very different from London.

Anderson was more inclined to be the class entertainer than a serious student. Her mother tells a favorite story about an interesting turn of events. When Gillian started seventh grade, her parents went to the school's open house and met her teachers. When they met her English teacher, he exclaimed, "That girl's going to be an actress," and listed examples of her classroom behavior, which her mother summed up as "showing off." Twelve years later, her younger brother started seventh grade at the same school and was assigned to the same English teacher. This was the first season that "The X-Files" was on the air. At the open house, Mrs. Anderson told the teacher, "I don't know if you remember it, but I can remember you're the first person who ever said, 'That's girl's going to be an actress'." So, at the end of the first season, Gillian came and visited his classroom and gave him an autographed picture, acknowledging that he was the first one to foresee her choice of career.

During her early teen years, Anderson developed interests in punk rock music, slam dancing, and experimenting with strange hair colors and styles — as well as acting. But, as her mother put it, Anderson "looked too weird to fit into" parts she auditioned for during that time. After going on auditions, Rosemary remembers people telling her that "[Gillian] did wonderful at auditions, but we just couldn't figure out how to fit her into that role." She also calls reports that Anderson had a Mohawk "an incredible exaggeration. . . . She did cut her hair down to about a quarter of an inch or an eighth of an inch on one side, and it grew in fairly quickly. . . . She always made sure her hair was different." About those years, Anderson has said, "I was angry and it was my way of keeping people at a distance."

Anderson's first role was in a middle school production of *Arsenic and Old Lace*; she played a policeman. During her junior year in high school, Anderson found a good acting teacher and a role in a community theater production. Rosemary recalls that during Gillian's senior year in high school, she produced and directed *The Real Inspector Hound*, a one-act play by Tom

Stoppard, and that Gillian engineered that production without any official sponsorship from the school. She gained recognition for her talent, focused more on her future, improved her grades, and developed goals which included going to acting school. "She was fortunate enough to get into an alternative high school for more highly motivated kids. It was quite a demanding high school, and she was not an academic star or anything, but they did require a great deal from her."

EDUCATION

Anderson had known for some time that, after high school, she wanted to attend the Goodman Theater School of DePaul University in Chicago. Her mother remembers holding her breath and wondering whether this was realistic. But Gillian went for the audition to get into the school, and they accepted her very quickly. So after graduating from City High School in Grand Rapids in 1986, Anderson entered DePaul. During her freshman year, Gillian was accepted into an intensive and prestigious three-week program with the National Theatre of Great Britain at Cornell University, which she attended during the summer. One of her former teachers at DePaul, Ric Murphy, remembers seeing potential in his now-famous student: "Gillian had an eight-line part in a French farce but turned it into a star role just by the attitude she brought to it. She has an incandescence." She earned her Bachelor of Fine Arts degree from DePaul in 1990.

CHOOSING A CAREER

Anderson had an early interest in science; she originally wanted to be a marine biologist or archaeologist. "I'm not exactly sure when that decision [to pursue an acting career] was made. It was something that I guess I always felt like I knew; it was just there." Just before graduation from DePaul, Anderson auditioned for the William Morris talent agency. The agency decided to represent her, and she moved to New York.

FIRST JOBS

Anderson's first professional acting job was a role in *Absent Friends,* an off-Broadway play by Alan Ayckbourn, for which she won a Theatre World Award. She went on to look for more acting roles while waitressing at two jobs. Later, she moved to Los Angeles, where "I swore I'd never do television. It was only after being out of work for almost a year that I began going in [to audition] on some stuff that I would pray I wouldn't get because I didn't want to be involved in it." Her ambition was to work in film. Nevertheless, she found herself auditioning for "The X-Files." As luck would have it, the day her final unemployment check came was the day she learned she won the part of Dana Scully.

CAREER HIGHLIGHTS

"The X-Files"

Since 1993 Fox Television's "The X-Files" has been commanding a growing cadre of fans—some of whom refer to themselves as X-Philes—with its weekly dose of strange story lines. Reminiscent of earlier TV shows like "The Twilight Zone" and "Outer Limits," "The X-Files" treats viewers to stories of the paranormal—but tries always to do so within the reach of "extreme scientific possibility." Anderson plays Agent Dana Scully to co-star David

Duchovny's Agent Fox Mulder. The two FBI agents explore such bizarre mysteries as UFOs and alien abductions, psychic phenomena, secret government experiments run amok, ghosts and evil spirits, marauding computers, genetically mutated beings of all kinds ranging in form from insect to human. Mulder and Scully also deal with the recurring theme of a government conspiracy hiding the truth about the presence of aliens.

The pilot show was only the third time Anderson worked in front of a camera, and she remembers it being very stressful."I was terrified. I didn't know what I was doing. . . . I learned slowly." The actress was chosen for the role despite the wishes of some who would have preferred to cast what she called "a typically marketable beauty," even though, as Anderson points out, "that was not how Scully was written." The show's creator, Chris Carter, noting that there are not many good female role models on TV, wanted to create one. "The people who hire me and pay me money, they were very concerned about Gillian Anderson. . . . I think how she might look in a bathing suit was what they were concerned about. It was very hard to convince them that she wasn't going to be in a bathing suit." He noticed immediately that Anderson "has an intensity that makes her perfect as Scully." Carter later said, "I feel blessed every day that I watch her work, because she gets better and better."

And Anderson has provided a good role model in Dana Scully, an intelligent, professional, independent woman with a strong moral sense. She has said that letters she receives from young girls indicate as much and that "this is probably one of the best compliments I could get as an actor. It's terrific because of what the character represents: honesty, justice, hard work and dedication and passion — and if that's what they're tapping into, that's fantastic."

Co-workers tend to remark on Anderson's lively sense of humor when asked to describe her — in contrast to Scully, who has rarely smiled on the show. As a continuing doubter of the paranormal, Scully provides a perfect counterpoint to Mulder and his willingness to believe in the paranormal. Scully's approach, Anderson believes, comes from her scientific background and training as a medical doctor. Though Anderson finds it frustrating that her character must be "skeptical all the time," that background "is always going to be the first thing that [Scully] turns to when she has to come up with explanations for situations . . . her rational mind will always be jumping to the forefront, before she accepts any idea or hypothesis of Mulder's. She is, I will say, more open-minded now and not so judgmental of Mulder and his ideas."

Working on a show with strange, often violent, story lines can be taxing, even when asleep. During the first season, Anderson told a reporter about a dream she had had in which she was shot by a gun. About a week later, she did a scene with a gun and remembered it looked like the gun in her dream. Then there was the time she put a live cricket in her mouth (she did not eat it). "I didn't even taste it," she recalls. "It was just kind of wriggling around in my mouth, and then I spit it out."

Fans of "The X-Files" relish the powerful relationship between Scully and Mulder, though creator Chris Carter continually assures everyone that the characters' relationship will never develop into a romance. As Anderson says, "There is an attraction between them that's physical, but it's primarily an attraction to each other's mind, and passion about the work. And that's enough."

According to very recent press reports, there is a significant difference in the amount of money Anderson and Duchovny are paid for their work on the show. The fact that there is a wage gap has become an issue for fans as well as her, and there is some speculation about how this will affect the future of the show. As Anderson notes, this wage disparity "gives a really bad image in our society in terms of what a woman's worth is in this world."

Success and Fame

Originally, Anderson's co-star, David Duchovny, garnered more attention, but her renown has been steadily growing. Recently she has been mobbed by thousands of fans at an Australian shopping mall and nominated for Emmy and Golden Globe awards. And in 1996, the Screen Actors Guild honored her with a best actress award. A World Wide Web site devoted to Anderson, the Gillian Anderson Testosterone Brigade, introduces itself as "a group of guys on the 'net who admire everything there is about Anderson . . . [who] is for many of us a personification of 'the real woman,' not yet another bimbo chasing after criminals in high heels."

When she and co-star Duchovny toured the FBI's headquarters and training center, real-life agents helped assess the stars' potentials as agent material. Agents deemed Anderson a promising prospect, and she later said she would not rule out the possibility, recalling that, as a child, "I'd go in the backyard and dig things up, because I loved investigating."

Anderson has felt a loss of privacy with fame, and she attempts to protect it. A sense of the foreign sometimes intrudes as well. She has remarked. "I'll be driving down the street in Canada and think, I'm in Canada. How did I get here?"

HOME AND FAMILY

What may also contribute to this sense of disorientation is the fact that so many changes occurred in Anderson's life in a relatively short period of time. During the first season of "The X-Files," Anderson fell in love with and married Clyde Klotz, an art director who worked on the set. They were married on New Year's Day, January 1, 1994, by a Buddhist priest in Hawaii. By the end of the first season, she was pregnant with their daughter, Piper, who was

born on September 25, 1994. "My feet were swelling and I was exhausted, sleeping between scenes. . . . It became almost like the crew's pregnancy, because everyone was pulling together to make it work," Anderson recalls. The writers and crew created ways to disguise her pregnancy and shoot stories around her delivery. Eleven days after a cesarean birth, she was back at work. The writers had written a story line in which Scully was in a coma, so that when she did return she had a less demanding workload.

Anderson and her family have a home in Vancouver, Canada, where "The X-Files" is filmed. She brings her daughter to the set every day. A nanny watches over Piper — though she has gotten into the props — and Anderson sees her during breaks. She says she is a happier person since having her daughter. "I'm much milder than I was before. When I became a mother, something inside me shifted. I have a little person who looks to me and depends on me. That's a big responsibility."

HOBBIES AND OTHER INTERESTS

Anderson would like to write a story for an upcoming "X-Files" episode, and plans are in the works. During her seasonal breaks, she enjoys vacationing with her parents and siblings as well as her husband and daughter.

She is also active in raising awareness of neurofibromatosis, a genetic disorder that afflicts her younger brother. She addressed a congressional luncheon in May 1996 to voice the need for research and public support.

Anderson, unlike Scully, is open to the existence of the paranormal in part because she has herself experienced a few episodes of unexplained phenomena. When she was about 14 years old, "I was dating somebody who lived an hour away. I had seen him the day before, found this black marble, and gave it to him. He said on the phone: 'Guess where I put it?' And I said, 'You took the lid off one of your cologne bottles and put it on the neck of the bottle.' He said, 'Oh, my God.' Because that's *exactly* what he had done."

When she and her husband moved into their new house in Vancouver, Anderson says she felt the presence of other spiritual beings. They learned that the house was built near a Native American cemetery, so they asked a Native American spiritual leader to perform a purification ritual. Afterwards, they felt the presences had gone. She also has seen psychics, one of whom predicted the birth of her daughter just after she was cast as Scully. Anderson believes that we all have spirit guides to help us through life, adding that "there is a natural order to things, and we are here to learn and to grow and to enrich our soul. All the information in the world is here with us and it's just a matter of tuning into it." She recollects that in high school she and the friends she hung around with were atheists, who believed that "religion was a crutch; but over the past few years I have grown to appreciate that feeling of safety or trust, that there is a light at the end of the tunnel and that there is a reason for us to be here."

SELECTED CREDITS

Television

"Class of '96," 1993
"The X-Files," 1993–
"Reboot," (guest voice) 1995

Theater

Absent Friends, 1991
The Philanthropist, 1992

HONORS AND AWARDS

Theatre World Award (*Theatre World*): 1991
Best Actress in Dramatic Series Award (Screen Actors Guild): 1996

FURTHER READING

Books

Genge, N. E. *The Unofficial X-Files Companion,* 1995
Lowry, Brian. *The Official Guide to the X-Files,* 1995

Periodicals

Calgary Herald, July 9, 1995, p.D12
Chicago Tribune, May 14, 1996, KIDNEWS, p.1; Sep. 27, 1996, FRIDAY, p.73
Entertainment Weekly, Mar. 18, 1994, p.58; Mar. 10, 1995, p.22
Los Angeles Times, Jan. 11, 1996, p.F1
McCall's, June 1996, p.52
Morning Call (Allentown, Penn.), July 7, 1996, p.T3
New York Times, Sep. 29, 1996, p.29
Oregonian, May 6, 1996, p.C1
People, Mar. 13, 1995, p.97; Oct. 9, 1995, p.72
Philadelphia Inquirer, Jan. 14, 1996, TV WEEK, p.6
San Francisco Chronicle, Feb. 20, 1994, TV WEEK, p.3
San Jose Mercury News, Oct. 2, 1994, West section, p.6
TV Guide, July 2, 1994, p.8; Mar. 11, 1995, p.8; Apr. 6, 1996, p.18; July 6, 1996,
    p.6
Yorkshire Post (England), Sep. 6, 1996, p.6

ADDRESS

"The X-Files"
P. O. Box 900
Beverly Hills, CA 90213

WORLD WIDE WEB SITE

http://www.TheX-Files.com

Rachel Blanchard   1976-

Canadian Actress
Stars as Cher in the Hit TV Series "Clueless"

BIRTH

Rachel Blanchard was born on March 19, 1976 in Toronto, in the province of Ontario, Canada. Her mother is a nurse who quit working to raise her kids, and her father is an economist. She has an older brother and a younger sister.

YOUTH

Blanchard grew up in Toronto, also spending time at her family's cottage in the country in northern Ontario. Anyone who's formed an impression of what she's like from watching Cher, her character on "Clueless," would be surprised. Blanchard's interests, in fact, are totally different from those of the character she plays. As a child, she loved spending time outdoors and playing sports, especially competitive hockey. "I never played with dolls," she recalls. "I had a tool set. I wasn't a girly girl. My dad was more like, 'Why don't you chop some wood?' or 'I'm renovating the basement today, Rachel. Can you help?'" Blanchard is also more practical when it comes to money. "I always earned my own money, and my dad put it away. I never had an allowance. If I wanted to go to a film, I'd ask my dad for $8 or $9. He'd give it to me but say, 'Well, the car needs to be washed tomorrow.' I paid for my own [private] high school. My dad would have paid, but I thought I should because I was the one who was attending."

CHOOSING A CAREER

Blanchard decided to become an actress when she was very young. "My family was at our country cottage, and I met the man who owns 'The Littlest Hobo' dogs. It was a Canadian show like 'Lassie.' He gave my mom the name of a casting director. I was five. I was always pretending I was on these shows, but it took me a couple of years to convince her to call the casting director."

But Blanchard's parents wanted to discourage her acting ambitions. "When I was six, my mom decided to let me be an extra because she thought I'd be really bored" and would decide to quit acting, remembers Blanchard. "But I loved walking up and down the street all day. I thought it was great. My sister tried it and hated it, so she quit."

Her mom confirms her early aptitude for acting. "People seemed to like her looks and her poise. And we let her act in bits and pieces—school had to come first and there were her hobbies she couldn't give up. But she took to it very naturally, no stage fright at all."

Blanchard started out doing commercials, and then worked on several (mostly Canadian) TV productions, including "The Campbells," "Katts and Dog," "Two for Joy," "War of the Worlds," "Chriss Cross," and "Glory Enough for All." She also appeared in two feature films, *Iron Eagle IV* and *Young Ivanhoe*. Her best known early work was her role on "Are You Afraid of the Dark?" the Nickelodeon hit series about the supernatural.

EDUCATION

Blanchard attended a private girls' school in Toronto, exclusive Havergal College, for several years. The experience proved to be good preparation for her current role as a wealthy, privileged teen. "I went to a private girls' school," she says. "The majority of people were down-to-earth, didn't care about clothes or makeup at all. But there was a small group who were extremely wealthy. They weren't snobby, but they were different."

After finishing high school, Blanchard enrolled at Queens University in Kingston, Ontario. She was finishing up her first year there when her education was interrupted by her acting career. She plans to continue her university courses between acting assignments.

CAREER HIGHLIGHTS

Blanchard landed her role on "Clueless" in a rather unusual way. The TV show, of course, derived from the 1995 hit movie starring Alicia Silverstone. Her performance as Cher made Silverstone an instant star and brought her a $20 million deal to appear in three movies, so she wasn't interested in working on the TV series. Blanchard was backpacking around Europe the summer that the movie *Clueless* came out, so she didn't get to see it. And when she got back, it wasn't yet out on video. So when her agent called to say that auditions were being held for the new TV show, she had no way to know what Cher's character was like. She also didn't have enough money to fly to Los Angeles for an audition that she was unlikely to pass.

But she still had a plan. She studied the script, and then with the help of her friends, she made an audition tape in the college video studio. "For my audition scene I wore bright yellow cords and a little blue V-neck T-shirt. [Director] Amy Heckerling wanted a follow-up tape and I remember she called me up and said, 'Maybe you could wear something a little more, uh . . . Cher is so together.' At my college people don't dress up, so I couldn't find a skirt in my closet. I had to borrow a different piece of clothing from all my friends." Soon after that, she was given an all-expenses paid trip to Los Angeles to audition in person. Of the hundreds of young actresses who had tried out for the part, there were only four finalists. After the audition, she flew back to Ontario to stay with her family at their cottage, where she got the big phone call saying she'd won the part. "Rachel won the role because of her innocence, optimism, wit, and charm," Heckerling said about her new star. "These are all qualities the character possesses, so it's important that our lead actress possess them as well. Rachel is a wonderful Cher."

"Clueless"

The cast of the TV series "Clueless" includes many of the actors who appeared in the hit film, including Stacey Dash as Dionne, Cher's friend; Elisa Donovan as Amber, Cher's rival; Donald Adeosun Faison as Murray, Dionne's boyfriend; Wallace Shawn as Mr. Hall, the beleaguered teacher; and Twink Caplan as Miss Geist, the disheveled guidance counselor (Caplan is also the co-executive producer). In addition to Blanchard, the newcomers are Michael Lerner as Cher's father and David Lascher as her step-brother, Josh.

Blanchard and actresses from "Clueless"

"Clueless" features the life and times of Cher Horowitz, who lives in Beverly Hills with her father and step-brother. It debuted in September 1996 in the Friday night TGIF lineup on ABC TV. As the *San Francisco Chronicle* describes it, "'Clueless' is a bubble-headed confection, . . . a brainless teenage cornucopia of blazing pink and lime-green fashions, doting parents, cellular phone calls in the classroom, personal acupuncturists, and cosmetic surgery. All at the age of 16." Others, though, have praised this flashy satire of the materialistic lifestyle of Beverly Hills for its fresh style, sharp writing, smart lines, and slyly disguised barbs.

Named after the actress and singer, Cher is a wealthy, materialistic, self-absorbed teen concerned with appearances and social standing. But for all that, she's also caring and good-hearted. Views of her character differed widely. This view was offered by the *New York Times*: "Cher is a consumer society's dream. Her world is a mindless whirl of clothes, cellular phones, and beepers. And boys, of course. Life as a joy ride. What a concept!" But Blanchard has this to say about her character: "Cher is a spoiled and rather sheltered, ignorant, rich Beverly Hills teenager. She's not stupid, but she doesn't know anything else. She can't relate to certain things because they can't be fixed with money. But she's innovative and good-hearted."

Blanchard is pretty quick to point out how she and Cher are different. "Ninety-nine percent of Cher isn't me," she says, "which is what's going to make her so much fun to play. I appreciate much simpler things, and I'm not a big shopper. You know, boys and clothes—that's not really my style." In fact, her style is really quite different. "When I'm in Cher's outfits, I feel more like her because they're restricting," she says. "But if I want to be reminded of who I am, I just look in my own closet. I have a lot of secondhand clothes—vintage clothes—and sports clothes likes sweats and shorts, rather than up-scale, trendy dresses. In my outfits I can go and do anything.

"I'd rather spend my money on new roller blades or hockey stuff or a plane ticket home to Canada. I like to think I dress with style, but I don't spend a lot of time on it. How many clothes do you really need?"

HOME AND FAMILY

Blanchard, who is unmarried, still considers Toronto her home, and she returns there whenever she has the chance.

HOBBIES AND OTHER INTERESTS

Blanchard's interests today reflect her activities growing up. She enjoys mountain climbing, camping, and roller blading. She still enjoys playing hockey, and she recently played—and scored a goal during warm ups—in the celebrity hockey all-star game. Going shopping, collecting clothes, and beauty regimes are pretty far down on her list of fun things to do.

CREDITS

"Clueless," 1996-

FURTHER READING

Periodicals

Chicago Tribune, Dec. 23, 1996, Tempo Section, p.7
Entertainment Weekly, Oct. 25, 1996, p.98
Glamour, Nov. 1996, p.92
People, Sep. 2, 1996, p.52
Toronto Star, Sep. 21, 1996, p.SW42
TV Guide, June 15, 1996, p.9

ADDRESS

Paramount Television
5555 Melrose Avenue
Modular Bldg., Suite 213
Los Angeles, CA 90038

WORLD WIDE WEB SITE

http://www.abctv.com

Zachery Ty Bryan 1981-

American Actor
Plays Brad Taylor on the TV Series "Home
Improvement"

BIRTH

Zachery Ty Bryan was born in Aurora, Colorado, on October 9,
1981. His mother, Jenny Bryan, and his father, Dwight Bryan,
help manage their son's acting career. Zachery has one younger
sister, Ciri.

YOUTH

Zachery was only five years old when he decided he wanted to become an actor. He did some modeling for print ads and acted in television commercials in Denver. When he was 7, he was selected from more than 200 children who tried out for a Burger King commercial in New York. For the next two years, he would fly into New York from Colorado when he got commercial work. Then, at age 9, he asked his parents if they would take him to Los Angeles so he could try out for a television series. They agreed to go, but only for five weeks. After auditioning several times for the pilot of "Home Improvement," Zachery was given the role of Brad Taylor, the oldest son. His parents both put their careers on hold and moved the family to a small community near Pasadena.

EDUCATION

Since starting on "Home Improvement," Zachery works on the series from June through April and is tutored on the set five hours a day. "It's better than school because there's only me, so I'm usually ahead of my class," Zachery says. Between taping the show and doing his schoolwork, he puts in a nine-and-a-half hour day.

In the future, Zachery hopes to attend college. He is an excellent student, and he says that math and foreign languages are his favorite subjects.

CAREER HIGHLIGHTS

Since 1990 Zachery has played Brad Taylor, the oldest of Tim and Jill Taylor's three sons on "Home Improvement." The show features Tim Allen as Tim "The Toolman" Taylor, the host of a local TV do-it-yourself show, his wife Jill (Patricia Richardson), their three sons, Brad (Zachery), Randy (Jonathan Taylor Thomas), and Mark (Taran Smith), their neighbor, Wilson (Earl Hindman), and their friend Al Borland (Richard Karn), Tim's assistant on his cable TV show, "Tool Time." For some viewers, its classic family values are its greatest appeal, "a comedy where the father is a hero," according to executive producer Matt Williams, "a dad who has a good relationship with his sons."

Over the years, Zachery has watched his character grow from a precocious, freckle-faced kid to a teenager with an eye for girls. He especially enjoys working with Tim Allen, whom he describes as "a very funny guy." His biggest problem working with Allen is staying in character and keeping a straight face. "Home Improvement" began its seventh season in the fall of 1996 and continues to be a favorite with young viewers.

Zachery has also starred in the Disney film, *First Kid*, about a Secret Service agent (played by comedian/actor Sinbad) who is assigned to protect the son of the president of the United States. Zachery's character is a bully who is

jealous of all the attention the "first kid" is receiving. He has also had starring roles in the family adventure films *Big Foot: The Unforgettable Encounter* and *Magic Island*. He spent the summer of 1996 in Vancouver, British Columbia, acting in the independent film, *True Heart.*

In addition to his work in films, Zachery has made guest appearances on other television series, such as "Picket Fences," "The Fresh Prince of Bel Air," and "Thunder Alley." He hosted the "Sea World/Busch Gardens Party for the Planet" for CBS and appeared in "Mickey: Reeling Through the Years" and "Disney's Runaway Train" for The Disney Channel.

Soccer

Zachery's major interest aside from acting is soccer. He started playing the game when he was only four years old. In 1995 he beat out hundreds of other young soccer players to win a place on the southern California Olympic Development Program team for boys under 14, which trains athletes to compete for the United States at the Olympic and World Cup levels.

Zachery still devotes many hours each week to perfecting his skills and playing competitively for his local soccer club, the Claremont Stars. The Stars took second place in the 1996 Dallas Cup, America's most prestigious amateur international soccer tournament. Serving as a youth ambassador for the World Cup in 1994 gave Zachery a taste of what it would be like to play on the U.S. World Cup team some day. For now, he finds that heading off to soccer practice after leaving the set helps him get rid of stress and make new friends. Steve Hoffman, head coach for the southern California Olympic Development Program team, believes that Zachery's devotion to soccer is closely tied to his life as an actor: "When he assumes the role of a soccer player, he assumes that role totally," Hoffman says.

Zachery recently hosted a soccer video produced by ESPN, the sports network. The video tells the story of a boy who plays soccer and misses an important penalty kick. After being coached by real-life soccer stars John Harkes and Mia Hamm, he gets a chance to make a goal in the World Cup competition and succeeds. Zachery says the video is geared to those who are competitive players, not beginners.

HOME AND FAMILY

Zachery lives in Los Angeles with his parents and his younger sister. He says that fame hasn't changed him or his family very much. He still has the same friends that he had before, he still plays soccer, and his parents still treat him more like their child than the family breadwinner.

MAJOR INFLUENCES

Zachery is well aware of the pitfalls involved in being a star at such a young age. "I think the reason a lot of kids get burned out on acting is because they don't realize they have to have other things to focus on until it's too late," he says. He cites Ron Howard, who played Opie on "The Andy Griffith Show," and Jodie Foster, who starred as a young girl in the film *Alice Doesn't Live Here Any More,* as examples of child stars who made a successful transition to adult careers in the film business.

But it's Tom Hanks that Zachery admires most. Not only has Hanks turned out to be an award-winning actor, producer, and director, but he has portrayed a wide range of characters. Zachery considers himself a dramatic actor rather than a comedian, and he hopes to follow in Hanks's footsteps after completing his university education.

HOBBIES AND OTHER INTERESTS

When he isn't acting or playing soccer, Zachery enjoys going to the movies and "just hanging out" with his friends. He likes rap music — especially the Fugees, 2-Pac, and Dr. Dre — and is also a fan of Mariah Carey and Boyz II Men.

Zachery has been involved in a number of charity projects. He has made public appearances on behalf of the Emily Anderson Center, the D.A.R.E. program, The Starlight Foundation, and the Jimmy Fund.

CREDITS

"Home Improvement," 1990-
Big Foot: The Unforgettable Encounter, 1995
Magic Island, 1995
First Kid, 1996

FURTHER READING

Boys' Life, Nov. 1995, p.8
Cleveland Plain Dealer, Feb. 6, 1996, p.9E
Newsday, June 16, 1996, Kidsday Section, p.1
Toronto Star, Apr. 24, 1995, p.C4

ADDRESS

Innovative Artists
1999Avenue of the Stars
Suite 2850
Los Angeles, CA 90067

WORLD WIDE WEB SITE

http://www.abc.com

Adam Ezra Cohen 1979-

American Student
Winner of the 1997 Westinghouse Science Talent
Search

EARLY LIFE

Adam Ezra Cohen was born May 30, 1979, in New York City. His parents are Joel and Audrey Cohen. Joel is a population biologist at Rockefeller University and Columbia University. Audrey is a professor of business at Baruch University. Adam has a sister, Zoe, who is a student at Harvard University. He is currently a

Cohen with his exhibit at the Westinghouse Science Talent Search

senior at Hunter College High School in New York City. He lives on the Upper East Side of New York in an apartment with his family.

MAJOR ACCOMPLISHMENTS

Adam has been inventing scientific objects for several years now. In fact, he has created 152 inventions to date, although he hasn't had any of them patented. In 1992, he developed a car windshield with elastic springs that would give a little on impact. This invention could help prevent injury to passengers in a car accident. In 1995, he created a new type of hard drive for a computer, which won top prize in the New York Science and Technology Expo. He has also created a computer cursor that can be moved solely with a person's eyes. That invention could help paralyzed people use computers.

Adam entered the Westinghouse Science Talent Search with another invention linked to computers. He created what he calls an "electrochemical paintbrush" that can print extremely small characters on a microchip. It would allow 50 words to be printed on a space the width of a human hair. His invention has potential commercial value, because it could change the way that information is encoded on microchips used in computer processors.

One of the most remarkable things about Adam is that he has created his inventions using his tiny bedroom as his lab. The key component in his invention is the microscope he created that is needed in his intricate, microscopic process. According to *The New York Times*, his microscope was made of "Legos, modeling clay, and a pile of electronic circuits suspended from his bedroom ceiling by bungee cords." Using this device, Adam puts incredibly small deposits of copper on a transparent electrical conductor. The microscope is suspended from his bedroom ceiling to avoid any vibration that could alter the process.

Adam claims he is motivated by "curiosity. I just sort of followed down this tree of possibilities. I was just doing whatever looked coolest until I ended up with this."

The Science Talent Search

The Science Talent Search is an annual contest for high school seniors. It is sponsored by Westinghouse Electric Corporation and Science Service, a non-profit organization that encourages the study of science. The Science Talent Search is the oldest high school competition in the country, and it offers the largest unrestricted science scholarships. From a group of 1,652 seniors, Adam was one of 40 finalists in the final competition, and he was declared the winner on March 10, 1997. His award includes a college scholarship worth $40,000.

Adam isn't too fond of rock groups, sports, or most popular entertainment. "I think most of popular culture is dumb," he says. In his spare time, Adam likes to hike, ice skate, jog, read, collect mushrooms, travel, and play soccer.

Asked whether his outstanding academic credentials made him a nerd, Adam said, "Well, maybe nerds have more fun. But I am not a nerd. I have a lot of friends. Just because I'm interested in science doesn't mean I'm not socially acceptable."

His dad, Joel Cohen, seconds this. "Adam is a normal and well-adjusted youngster. The forty finalists [in the Westinghouse competition] unanimously elected him to be their leader. I think this is the first time an elected leader has also won the top prize." Joel Cohen describes his son as a "delight. The only thing we have to watch is what he puts into our refrigerator—bottles filled with blue stuff and desiccated rats. It's his stuff, and we don't touch it."

Adam plans to go to college in the fall, at either Harvard University or the Massachusetts Institute of Technology. He will major in physics.

FURTHER READING

Associated Press, Mar. 11, 1997
Boston Globe,, Mar. 12, 1997, p.A6
New York Times, Mar. 11, 1997, p.C23
Newsday, Mar. 13, 1997, p.A4
Philadelphia Inquirer, Mar. 11, 1997

ADDRESS

Science Talent Search
Science Service
1719 N Street NW
Washington, D.C. 20036

WORLD WIDE WEB SITE

http://www.westinghouse.com

Claire Danes   1979-

American Actress
Star of the Acclaimed Hits "My So-Called Life,"
Little Women, and *Romeo and Juliet*

BIRTH

Claire Danes was born in New York City on April 12, 1979. Her father, Chris Danes, used to work as an architectural photographer, but more recently has worked as a computer consultant. Her mother, Carla Danes, was a textile designer and painter who also ran a school for toddlers; she currently helps manage her daughter's career. Claire has one older brother, Asa, who works for a non-profit organization in New York.

YOUTH

Danes had an interesting childhood. She grew up on Manhattan (in New York City) in a stimulating and creative household. Both of her parents were artists, and the family lived in a loft in Soho, a hip and funky neighborhood known for its vibrant cultural life. She was very young when she first decided that she wanted to be a performer. "When I was five, I remember my parents got a video camera and that weekend I just exploded." She also talks about seeing Madonna for the first time at about that age. "Madonna was on TV, and I just started jumping up and down along with her. I knew, there and then."

Soon, Danes was working hard to reach that goal. She started dance lessons at age six, and three years later she enrolled in the Lee Strasberg Theatre Institute. There she studied Method acting, an approach created by Constantin Stanislavsky and further developed by Lee Strasberg. A Method actor tries to identify fully with the character and to use natural movements and voice. "They had us do these weird exercises," Danes explains, "like 'Pretend an egg was cracked on your head and feel all the places on your body the yolk touches.' I loved it." Even at such a young age she was very serious. All the other kids were just trying to have fun, while Danes was trying to "feel the moment."

EDUCATION

Danes started out attending the city's public schools. For middle school, she attended the Professional Performing Arts School, a magnet school in New York, where she studied acting for two hours a day. After that she went to Dalton, a prestigious private school in New York. Being in school wasn't easy for her, as she recalls here. "I hated the cliques. You couldn't be friends with just one cheerleader, you had to be friends with all of them. I never wanted to be part of just one group. I wanted to hop around. But I couldn't. So I got isolated. I tried to pick one friend to get by with, but that didn't work either. I couldn't find anyone I liked, so I wasn't friends with anyone. That sounds really down."

It was while she was a student at Dalton that Danes started working on "My So-Called Life," in a Los Angeles studio. She had a tutor on the set there, and she completed her assignments from Dalton by mail. After a while she transferred to Le Lycee de Francais, a private high school in Los Angeles. Danes graduated from high school in 1997. Education is very important to her family, and she has promised her parents that she will eventually attend college, although she has no current plans to do so. Danes has also said that when she does go to college, she will continue to act during her school vacations.

From "My So Called Life"

FIRST JOBS

Danes's earned her first professional acting jobs when she was quite young, including small parts in off-Broadway theatrical productions and a few short films. Then she was cast in an independent film about child abuse called *Dreams of Love* (1992) at the age of 11.That was when, Claire says, "I got hooked." Soon after, she got some help breaking into the business. Her parents had rented out studio space in their loft to a photographer, who didn't have enough money one month to pay the rent. Instead, the photographer offered to produce 8 x 10 head shots of Claire. Her parents agreed, and they sent the photos out to 35 agencies. Five immediately wanted to sign her. Claire chose the agency Writers & Artists, which helped her find work. She

61

filmed a TV pilot with Dudley Moore that was never picked up, and appeared in an episode of "Law and Order."

CAREER HIGHLIGHTS

"My So-Called Life"

Danes got a very early start on her professional career. She was only 13 when she tried out for "My So-Called Life" in December 1992. The series was being created by the same team that had produced "thirtysomething," a critically acclaimed series from the late 1980s, and their new show was generating a lot of interest throughout the industry. Danes, still living in New York, flew to Los Angeles for the audition. Although she was only the second actress to audition for the part, the producers were immediately convinced that she was the one. The pilot for the show was shot in early 1993, and Danes and the rest of the crew assumed that it would be shown shortly thereafter. Instead, ABC said that they didn't have an appropriate time slot for the series and delayed it for about a year and a half, until fall 1994.

"My So-Called Life" focused on the life of Angela Chase, a confused, earnest, realistic teenager who recounts her experiences with family, friends, high school, and her first big crush. Often dark and depressing, the series was intense, with no neat solutions to crushing problems and no unrealistic happy endings. "My So-Called Life" was set in a fictional town near Pittsburgh, and it included all the social problems of modern life. But its real focus was not this external world, but instead Angela's inner emotional world, which she revealed through introspective interior monologues. These describe a teenage girl's emotional journey from adolescence toward adulthood. In this way, Angela is seen by the viewers as charming and original, by her parents as headstrong and sullen, by her peers as young and malleable, and by herself as confused and alone.

Danes immediately proved herself up to meeting the demands of this series. It was an immediate critical success, earning Danes widespread acclaim for her heartfelt portrayal. Many considered it ironic, though, that she should so movingly portray the angst of high school life when she didn't even attend school — the scheduling demands of "My So-Called Life" required that Danes be tutored on the set. "Here I am on this show, being this symbol of a high school person in angst, and I haven't even been to high school yet," she said. "I have had those feelings, though, about not fitting in, not knowing if anyone else in the world feels the way you do." This lack of direct experience didn't seem to affect her performance. Praised as luminous and compelling, Danes was widely hailed by reviewers for her maturity, self-possession, grace, poise, and, above all, her honesty and sincerity. She wowed her peers in the industry also. Her performance inspired Winona Ryder to pursue her for a part in *Little Women*. And Steven Spielberg was so impressed that he called her "one of the most exciting actresses to debut in ten years. I don't really understand why she's captured my heart. She just has an amazing honesty in her presence. She represents a lot of what we parents like in our kids."

Despite such high praise, "My So-Called Life" did very poorly in the ratings. It won a very devoted, but very small audience. The show was canceled after just one season, although it currently appears in reruns.

Getting Started in Films

Following "My So-Called Life," Danes went on to a succession of small but important roles in feature films. She started out in *Little Women* (1994), based on the novel of the same name by Louisa May Alcott. Set in Massachusetts in the 1860s during the Civil War, the story shows us the lives of the four March sisters, Meg, Jo, Beth, and Amy, and their mother, called Marmee. Danes played Beth, who, in one of the film's most affecting scenes, dies of scarlet fever. Her performance in *Little Women* brought her accolades from critics and led to roles in future films. It also brought her a new friend and mentor in Winona Ryder, who played Jo.

From Little Women

After that, Danes went on to *Home for the Holidays* (1995), in which she played the daughter of Holly Hunter. Danes was directed in the film by Jodie Foster, an acclaimed actress, director, and producer who, when younger, had left a thriving acting career to attend college. She successfully returned to film after she graduated, making a smooth transition in the process from child star to adult actress. While directing Danes in *Home for the Holidays*, Foster became her mentor and role model, encouraging her to take a break from acting to attend college. Foster had this to say about Danes: "She's got a movie-star quality, yet she's a real actress. Usually you only get one or the other."

Danes next appeared in *How to Make an American Quilt* (1995), a film about a young graduate student, played by Winona Ryder. While trying to make a decision about getting married, she spends the summer with her grandmother (played by Ellen Burstyn), great aunt (played by Anne Bancroft), and the women in their quilting circle. Flashbacks show scenes from their youth, with Danes playing the younger version of the Anne Bancroft character. Danes followed that with *I Love You, I Love You Not* (1996), in which she played a Jewish girl who visits her grandmother, a Holocaust survivor, played by of Jeanne Moreau. Next up was *To Gillian on Her 37th Birthday* (1996), in which she played an only child, struggling in a family where the mother has died in a tragic accident and the father is overwhelmed by grief.

William Shakespeare's Romeo and Juliet

Danes next went on to her first starring role in a feature film. She played Juliet to Leonardo DiCaprio's Romeo in *William Shakespeare's Romeo and Juliet* (1996), a contemporary version of this classic. The film is an updating of the romantic tragedy about true love gone awry when the son and daughter of two warring families fall in love. The families intervene, with tragic consequences. The film retains Shakespeare's Elizabethan language, but moves the setting to the present time. The action takes place in fictional Verona Beach, a violent resort town that looks like Miami. The two families, the Capulets and the Montagues, are warring street gangs.

With its quick-cut editing, designer costumes, violence, hip soundtrack, and speedy pacing, the film was described as Shakespeare for the MTV audience. Some viewers objected to this contemporary approach, saying that it undermined the beauty of the language and the drama as a whole. Yet others hailed it as risky, bold, experimental, radiant, and passionate. No matter what their view of the movie as a whole, critics routinely praised Danes's performance, and many called it her best ever. DiCaprio, from the very start, was quick to compliment his colleague and praise her talent. "When we were auditioning Juliets, she was the only one who came right up and said the

From William Shakespeare's Romeo and Juliet

lines directly to me. She was right there, in front of my face, saying every single line with power." Danes was equally smitten with DiCaprio, saying "He's brilliant. He's so smart and perceptive, and he's also wild and out of control. I love that about him."

Current Projects

Danes has recently been at work on several projects that are scheduled to be released in the near future. Next up is *U-Turn*, directed by Oliver Stone and due out in October 1997. In this film, co- starring Sean Penn, Nick Nolte, and Jennifer Lopez, a hoodlum's car breaks down in a small town, with tragic consequences. Danes will also be appearing in fall 1997 in *The Rainmaker*, based on a novel by John Grisham and directed by Francis Ford Coppola. She co-stars with Virginia Madsen, Danny DeVito, Jon Voight, and Matt Damon in this thriller about a young lawyer who takes a case for a poor family whose deceased son was denied medical treatment by an insurer. In *Polish Wedding*, due to be released in 1998, Danes plays a young unmarried woman, Hala, who gets pregnant by the son of a local police officer. The film also stars Gabriel Byrne and Lena Olin as her Polish-American parents. She is also said to be considering the role of Cossette in the upcoming film of *Les Miserables*, playing opposite Liam Neeson, Geoffrey Rush, and Uma Thurman.

HOME AND FAMILY

Danes has been just a teenager throughout most of her acting career, so she has lived with her parents at their homes in New York City and Santa Monica, California. She and her mother are especially close, since her mother has accompanied her to all of her acting jobs and stayed on the set with her at all times. But now that Danes has turned 18, she has said that she will be getting her own apartment and starting to move off on her own.

MAJOR INFLUENCES

When asked about what actors have inspired her, Danes is always quick to answer. "Meryl Streep," Danes reports. "She is so brilliant. She's the epitome of what acting is. As for his work, River Phoenix was also great."

HOBBIES AND OTHER INTERESTS

Danes mentions drawing, modern dance, movies, reading, and shopping as some of her interests.

CREDITS

Dreams of Love, 1992
"My So-Called Life," 1994-95 (TV series)
Little Women, 1994
Home for the Holidays, 1995
How to Make an American Quilt, 1995
To Gillian on Her 37th Birthday, 1996
I Love You, I Love You Not, 1996 (released in Europe)
William Shakespeare's Romeo and Juliet, 1996

HONORS AND AWARDS

Golden Globe: 1995, for Best Actress in a Drama in "My So-Called Life"

FURTHER READING

Periodicals

Entertainment Weekly, Sep. 6, 1996, p.26
Interview, Jan. 1995, p.68
Los Angeles Times, Oct. 27, 1996, Calendar section, p.3
New York Times, Aug. 14, 1994, Section 2, p.30; Nov. 1, 1996, p. C1; Nov. 5, 1996, p.C13

People, Oct. 3, 1994, p.131
Premiere, Oct. 1996, p.89
Sassy, Aug. 1994, p.68; Mar. 1995, p.54; Dec. 1995, p.32
Seventeen, Sep. 1994, p.155; Sep. 1995, p.211; Nov. 1996, p.132
TV Guide, Aug. 27, 1994, p.20

ADDRESS

Baker Winokur Ryder
405 South Beverly Drive, Suite 500
Beverly Hills, CA 90212

Celine Dion   1968-
Canadian Singer

BIRTH

Celine Dion was born on March 30, 1968, in Charlemagne, a small town in Quebec, Canada. The province of Quebec is French-Canadian, and the Dion family spoke only French while Celine was growing up. Her parents had a small restaurant, Le vieux baril, where her mother, Therese, cooked the meals, and her father, Adhemar, tended bar. He also, at various times, worked as a lumberjack and as a prison guard. Celine, the last of their 14 children, is six years younger than her closest sibling and 22 years younger than the eldest. She has 8 sisters (Denise,

Claudette, Liette, Louise, Ghislaine, Linda, Manon, and Pauline) and 5 brothers (Clement, Michel, Jacques, Daniel, and Paul).

YOUTH

Music was an integral part of Dion's life from the very start. Her mother played violin and her father played accordion, and all the children learned to play instruments also. On many weekends, the family appeared throughout Quebec as the Dion Family, performing folk songs and top-40 material for a French-speaking audience. Back home at the family restaurant, everyone helped out. The children took turns cooking, serving customers, clearing tables, and singing. By age five, Celine was standing on top of the tables, belting out French songs. Soon, customers started calling in advance to make sure she would be singing.

EDUCATION

Dion was not much of a student. She readily admits that she often fell asleep in class because she stayed up late each night singing in her family's restaurant. "At school I was sleeping and dreaming all the time. I didn't learn anything," she says. "For me, singing was the *real* life, not two plus two equals four." The other kids made fun of her; they called her "the vampire" because of her buck teeth. Dion dropped out of high school at about age 14. She has said that she has no regrets about leaving school: "it was taking me away from music, from my happiness, from my dreams."

GETTING STARTED IN MUSIC

The story of how Dion got started in music is legendary. In 1980, at age 12, she made a cassette tape of a song written by her mother, "Ce n'etait qu'un reve" ("It Was Only a Dream"). Her mother wrapped up the tape with a red ribbon and added a note that said, "This is a 12-year-old with a fantastic voice. Please listen to her." Then she sent the tape to a famous Canadian record producer, Rene Angelil. He wasn't really interested, so it lay unopened on his desk until Celine's brother Michel called a few weeks later to remind him about the tape. Angelil listened to it, amazed. "I couldn't believe the voice," he later said. "It was a shock. I had to see if it was for real." He immediately called Dion and asked her to come in for an audition, so she and her mother went to his office that afternoon.

At first she didn't make much of an impression. She was skinny, gawky, frumpy, and shy, with buck teeth. But then he asked her to sing. She hesitated at first, and said that she usually sang with a microphone. "I said, 'Okay,'" Angelil recalls. "I took my pen like this and I said to her, 'Pretend it's a microphone and there are a thousand people here in the room.' So she took the pen, started singing — and became another person. You couldn't believe the voice for a 12-year-old." Angelil also admits "I had goose bumps listening to that voice, so full of feeling, and older than her years." Her singing moved him so much, in fact, that it brought tears to his eyes. Despite Dion's youth and her awkward appearance, Angelil signed her on the spot to a five-year contract, beginning a professional and personal partnership that has now lasted over 15 years.

CAREER HIGHLIGHTS

Early Career

Although Angelil believed in Dion's talent, he soon discovered that the rest of the recording industry wasn't interested. He couldn't convince any of the major labels to allow this 12-year-old singer to make a recording. So he mortgaged his house to finance the project himself. Her very first single became a No. 1 hit record both in France and Quebec, selling 700,000 copies and making her the first Canadian ever to achieve a gold record in France. During the next six years, Dion made a series of French records and became a huge hit in Quebec, selling some $10 million in albums there and in Europe. She was known as "la p'tite quebecoise" (the little Quebecer), a term of affection as the people of Quebec took the young singer into their hearts. She toured throughout Canada and Europe and won several international awards. She even sang for the Pope during his 1984 visit to Montreal.

By 1987, Angelil had convinced a major label of Dion's talent. Sony Music released *Incognito,* her ninth French-language album. The recording soon went double platinum, selling 2 million copies. That same year, she appeared at the Juno Awards, the Canadian version of the Grammy Awards. That night, she sang a song in English. Here, an executive from the music industry talks about that night. "We'd heard her sing in French, but we were a bunch of Anglos, right? We kind of went, yeah, nice, but I don't get the words. And then she came out at the Juno Awards that year and did this song by Aldo Nova called "Just Have a Heart" and blew everybody away. There was not a piece of flesh in the audience that did not have goose bumps on it."

Despite this success, she gradually began to chafe a little bit at some of the limits of public opinion. As Dion grew older she wanted to mature and to change, and she felt that her image was restricting her. "When you're in show business when you're 12 or 13, people know you like you're their child," she explained. "The province of Quebec is very small, and I was on every TV show and every newspaper. It was too much. People are used to seeing you one way, and then you become 18 years old, and they don't want to accept that change."

Image Makeover

The best way for Dion to change her image, she and Angelil believed, was to drop out of sight for a while. So in the late 1980s she dropped out for about a year and a half. During that time she did several things to change both her physical image and her approach to her music. She cut her hair, had her teeth fixed, updated her makeup, and changed her wardrobe to feature more tight, sexy, sophisticated clothes. She also decided that she wanted to learn English to increase the size of her audience and to increase her chances of becoming a star. Before that time she had learned a few songs in English phonetically, without really understanding the meaning of all the words. So Dion took an intensive Berlitz course to learn English, practicing every day from 9:00 in the morning unitl 5:00 at night for several months.

The decision to learn to speak and sing in English was a risky one for Dion. The preservation of the French language is very important in Quebec. This French-speaking province is surrounded by the rest of Canada, where English is the major language. Many Quebecers view their language as a crucial part of their cultural identity. And Dion was attempting to make the crossover from French to English at a time when political tension on this issue was high. Many people in Quebec, known as separatists, have been fighting for the province to secede from Canada and become an independent country. They might have viewed her new English skills as a repudiation of her heritage. Dion had good reason to worry that singing in English would alienate her Quebec fans.

Becoming an International Star

Still, Dion continued her steady climb to the top of the entertainment world. In 1990 she released her first recording in English, *Unison,* which featured a mix of soaring ballads and dance tunes. The record company, Sony Music, launched a massive promotional campaign that included music videos, concert tours, and appearances by the singer on American TV talk shows. One of the ballads, "Where Does My Heart Beat Now," caught the attention of radio stations and the public. Its success brought Dion the opportunity to sing a duet with Peabo Bryson for the title song of the Disney animated film *Beauty and the Beast.* This Top 10 hit won for Dion an Oscar and a Grammy, as well as worldwide attention. She also continued to record in French during this time, including her acclaimed album, *Dion chante Plamondon* (1991), which featured songs by the noted French lyricist, Luc Plamondon.

Many view 1992 as her breakthrough year. That year she released *Celine Dion,* her first gold record in the United States. Its first single, "If You Asked Me To," spent three weeks at the top of the pop charts. In addition, 1992 was the year that Dion and Peabo Bryson sang "Beauty and the Beast" at the Academy Awards. This performance, with two billions viewers around the

world, cemented her image as a new star. Her next album, *The Colour of My Love* (1993), was another big breakthrough for Dion. It featured two top singles, "The Power of Love" and "Think Twice," as well as "When I Fall in Love," a duet with Clive Griffin that was the theme song for the hit film *Sleepless in Seattle*. *The Colour of My Love* sold over 11 million copies, including one million in Canada. Dion next went on to *The French Album* (1995; also titled *D'eux*), which was widely considered her most artistically satisfying effort to date. This recording sold five million copies, making it the best-selling French language album ever. Dion had succeeded in winning new American admirers without sacrificing her longstanding Quebec fans, who flocked to her concerts and bought up each new album.

Dion's most recent release is *Falling into You* (1996). It features the hit single "It's All Coming Back to Me Now" as well as her covers of Eric Carmen's "All by Myself" and Tina Turner's "River Deep, Mountain High." But the highlight of the album is the chart-topping "Because You Loved Me" from the movie *Up Close and Personal*, an uplifting song ideally suited to Dion's soaring, dramatic style. It's no wonder that *Falling into You* has sold over 22 million copies. Sales have been so strong, in fact, that the album was on the Top Ten list for over a year. The phenomenal success of *Falling into You* has certified Dion as a true superstar.

Keys to Her Success

There are several different elements that people mention when they analyze Dion's success. First and foremost is her vocal talent. "What she's got is a spectacular pop voice," Susan Semenak wrote in the *Montreal Gazette*, "that can skip to a thundering crescendo from a whisper in a beat." Dion's five-octave range is perfectly suited to the big, bold, sentimental epics that she sings with conviction and intensity, what Alan Jackson of the *Times of London* called "her soulful, pitch-perfect voice and dramatic interpretive style." Her specialty is grand, melodramatic ballads, but she can sing every mainstream style, from remakes of hits from the 1960s and 1970s to pop-gospel and dance-pop. In concert, she delivers her material with a gutsy and emotional stage presence that her fans find riveting. Some critics have lamented that she has wasted her beautiful voice on slickly produced, formulaic, superficial pop songs. They also regret her lack of subtlety. As Patrick MacDonald wrote in the *Seattle Times*, "Every song she does is like a finale, with swelling orchestral arrangements and at least one glass-shattering crescendo." Her millions of admirers clearly disagree.

But voice and talent, both Dion and Angelil believe, are only about 20 percent of what it takes to be a star. "The rest," he says, "is the discipline, determination, how much you want to be a star, how many sacrifices you are willing to make." And Dion has been willing to do whatever it takes. Ever since she was a little girl she has been determined to be a singer and to be rich and famous, and she has worked ceaselessly to reach this goal. In the early years she toured constantly, always trying to reach out to more fans around the world. In addition to the demands of preparing for concerts and recording albums, she has always made herself available to the press for interviews, photo shoots, and appearances on TV. She has also been relentless in taking care of her voice. At one point in 1990 she lost her voice completely, and her doctor advised her to remain silent for three weeks. She complied perfectly—she didn't say a word the entire time. Since then, she has been extremely careful. She tries not to speak on the day of a performance, always travels with two humidifiers, does vocal exercises every day, and abstains from alcohol and tobacco. She has been willing to do whatever it takes to be a star. According to

Angelil, "When Celine stopped singing for the sheer joy of it in the car, in the plane, wherever she was, I knew she had what counted to be a star." For Dion, now a best-selling, superstar singer, all her hard work and determination have paid off.

For the future, Dion is said to be planning upcoming albums in both English and French. But there has also been some conjecture that she would like to try something new. Several years ago, in 1991, she appeared in a Canadian television miniseries as an abused teenager, and she received praise for her convincing and understated performance. She has said in the past that she would like to act again at some point, although she has no current plans to do so. Many admirers believe she has the talent to do whatever she wants. According to one music manager, "She's one of the most moving singers I've ever seen. That's probably why acting is the natural thing for her to do. I can't see any reason for her career to slow down. She's really young. She has only her imagination to limit her."

MARRIAGE AND FAMILY

Dion and Angelil have been professionally involved since she was 12. By the time she turned 20, Dion has said, their professional respect had turned to love. They were engaged in March 1993 and were married on December 17, 1994, at Notre Dame Basilica in Montreal, Quebec. She called it "the ceremony of my dreams, what I had always hoped for. It was magic." She has often said that she and Angelil hope to have children eventually.

Although Dion spends much of her time living in hotels on tour, she and Angelil have a home in Montreal, and they are also building an $8 million complex on Jupiter Island, Florida. The complex will include a recording studio and a guest house big enough for her whole family. Dion has also bought several homes for her parents over the years. When she was 18 she bought them their first "new" house, with all new furniture and appliances, and she later bought them a ski chalet in the Laurentian mountains of Quebec. Recently, Dion bought a $3 million mansion for her parents in Palm Beach, Florida.

MAJOR INFLUENCES

Dion is often compared to Barbra Streisand, whom she reveres. "She's definitely the person I look up to the most in show business," Dion says about Streisand. "She has so much class and is so talented. I love her and love every movie she's done. If I can have a little bit of her career, I'd love it." In addition, Dion credits the artists Anita Baker, Terence Trent d'Arby, Michael Bolton, the Neville Brothers, and Whitney Houston as being her most important musical influences.

HOBBIES AND OTHER INTERESTS

With her constant touring schedule, Dion hasn't had time for many hobbies, although she does admit to a passion for shopping, especially for shoes. But the one thing that she does make time for is the Cystic Fibrosis Foundation in Canada. Dion has been promoting public awareness of CF since 1982, and Dion became the group's national Celebrity Patron in 1993. Cystic fibrosis is a genetic disorder that affects breathing and digestion. Her niece, Karine, died of the disease when she was 16.

SELECTED RECORDINGS

La voix du Bon Dieu, 1981
Celine chante Noel, 1981
Tellement j'ai d'amour, 1982
Chants et contes de Noel, 1983
Les chemins de ma maison, 1983
Melanie, 1984
Celine Dion en concert, 1985
C'est pour toi, 1985
Incognito, 1987
Unison, 1990
Dion chante Plamondon, 1991 (titled *Des mots qui sonnent* in France)
Celine Dion, 1992
The Colour of My Love, 1993
Celine Dion a l'Olympia, 1994
The French Album, 1995 (titled *D'eux* for international release)
Falling into You, 1996
Live a Paris, 1996

HONORS AND AWARDS

Yamaha World Song Festival: 1982 (2 awards), Gold Medal for Best Song and Musician's Award for Top Performer
Eurovision Song Contest: 1988
Juno Awards (Canadian Academy of Recording Arts and Sciences): 1991 (2 awards), Female Vocalist of the Year and Album of the Year, for *Unison*; 1992, Female Vocalist of the Year; 1993 (four awards), Female Vocalist of the Year, Single of the Year, for "Beauty and the Beast," Best Selling Francophone Album, for *Dion chante Plamondon*, and Best Dance Single, for "Love Can Move Mountains"; 1994, for Female Vocalist of the Year; 1995 (2 awards), Album of the Year and Best Selling Album (Foreign or Domestic), both for *The Colour of My Love*; 1996, Best Selling Francophone Album, for *D'eux*; 1997 (three awards), Best Selling Album (Foreign or

Domestic), for *Falling into You*, Best Selling Francophone Album, for *Live a Paris*, and Female Vocalist of the Year

World Music Awards: 1992, Best Selling Canadian Artist; 1996, Best Selling Canadian Artist; 1997 (3 awards), Best Selling Canadian Artist, World's Best-Selling Pop Artist, and World's Best Selling Overall Artist, all for *Falling into You*

Academy Award: 1993, Song of the Year, for "Beauty and the Beast"

Grammy Awards: 1993, for Best Pop Performance by a Duo or Group with Vocal, for "Beauty and the Beast"; 1997 (2 awards), Best Album of the Year and Best Pop Album, both for *Falling into You*

Medaille des arts et lettres (French Medal of Arts): 1996, to recognize her has the best-selling French language artist in history

International Achievement Award (Canadian Academy of Recording Arts and Sciences): 1997 (a joint prize won by Celine Dion, Alanis Morissette, and Shania Twain)

FURTHER READING

Periodicals

Chatelaine, Aug. 1991, p.51; Sep. 1996, p.44
Entertainment Weekly, Mar. 29, 1996, p.34
Maclean's, June 1, 1992, pp.40, 44; Dec. 28, 1992, p.36
New York Times, Feb. 23, 1997, Section 2, p.34; Apr. 14, 1997, p.C14
People, June 13, 1994, p.57; Mar. 3, 1997, p.73
Time, Mar. 7, 1994, p.71; Aug. 12, 1996, p.
Times of London, Apr. 29, 1995
TV Guide, Feb. 22, 1997, p.26
Us, Dec. 1993, p.71

ADDRESS

Epic Records
550 Madison Avenue
New York, NY 10022

Celine Dion International Fan Club
P.O. Box 551
Don Mills, Ontario
Canada M3C 2T6

WORLD WIDE WEB SITE

www.music.sony.com

Jean Driscoll 1966-
American Wheelchair Athlete

BIRTH

Jean Lynn Driscoll was born on November 18, 1966, in Milwaukee, Wisconsin, to Angie and James Driscoll. The second of five children, Jean grew up with older sister, Fran, brother Jacques, and twins Ron and Ray. Her father worked as a laborer while her mother earned a living as a nurse.

At the time of Jean's birth, doctors immediately realized that the newborn had improperly developed. As her mother recalled, Jean "was born at 9:15 in the morning and I didn't see her until

10 o'clock at night. Next morning they whisked her off to Children's [Hospital], kept her there on observation for a week." Physicians diagnosed the problem as spina bifida, a birth defect in which the bony spine that protects the spinal cord develops abnormally.

Spina Bifida

Spina bifida is a congenital disorder that affects one out of every 1,000 babies born in the U.S. In spina bifida, the spinal column does not close completely in a developing baby. The condition can leave a portion of the spinal cord protruding from the back at birth. Because the spinal column is the nerve center of the body, spina bifida often results in nerve damage or even paralysis. In some cases, the nerves that control muscles, the bowels, and the bladder may be affected. Often, as in Jean's case, a child with spina bifida has difficulty developing the ability to walk. Jean needed braces and crutches, and later a wheelchair, to get around.

Jean's physical problems were compounded by a cleft palate—a separation in the roof of her mouth—which made eating difficult, but surgery later corrected that problem.

YOUTH

Physical disabilities like spina bifida often have a great impact on a child's emotional and social development. From a very young age, Jean was unable to walk without assistance, and it bothered her. She was unable to play sports or games like other children. Driscoll recalls being pulled to church in a wagon and finding it "very humiliating." Instead of being happy about her siblings' accomplishments, she resented them. "I was always real jealous of my sister when she brought home her volleyball trophies and my brothers when they brought home basketball trophies." She once tried out for the grade school cheerleading squad but left in embarrassment when, in the middle of her routine, she lost control of her bladder, a condition that often plagues those with spina bifida.

For Driscoll, it seemed that all of her choices in life were limited by her condition. Some physicians and friends told her she would never walk normally, never complete her education, have only a menial job, and have to depend on her parents for the rest of her life. "When I was growing up," says Driscoll, "I was the kid who hid behind my mom's legs. I never felt like I quite belonged." Driscoll lashed out in anger at family members, friends, and God. "When I was a kid, I was constantly angry at God. I was always asking, 'Why me? Why me?' You just don't understand why things like this exist when you know there is a loving God who seems to be taking care of everyone else, not you."

Fortunately, Driscoll had the love, support, and more importantly, the prodding of her family. They always "tried to get me to be as independent as possible," she explains. "They'd have me take the laundry basket from the basement to my bedroom, which was on the second floor. I wasn't happy about this, because I was wearing leg braces and it was difficult. But they kept telling me, 'What are you going to do when we're gone? You can't always rely on us'." Rather than yield to her disability, Driscoll started to develop her own style of handling situations. She learned to walk in a sideways shuffle and challenged friends to races, even though she knew she could not keep pace. Sometimes, she stretched out on the ground, cast away her braces, and dared anyone to outcrawl her. She didn't accept what other people thought about her. Instead, Driscoll reacted with a stubbornness that has served her well. "I got tired of people saying, 'You can't do this,'" she explains. "I always thought, 'I'm gonna prove you wrong!'"

EDUCATION

Driscoll attended Mother of Perpetual Help Grade School in Milwaukee. Though she compiled impressive grades, she had difficulty getting along with the other students because she felt out of place. The angry young girl had not yet accepted her disability and desperately wanted to be like other students in her class.

Her determination could not slow the debilitating effects of spina bifida, however. Through her grade school years she was able to walk with braces covering the lower half of her legs. But when she was 14 and a freshman at Custer High School, Driscoll fell during a bicycle ride and dislocated her hip. She required five hip surgeries, none of them successful. She spent an entire year in a body cast, gazing through the living room window from the hospital bed set up at home as life went on outside. When the body cast was removed, Driscoll needed crutches to walk short distances. For longer stretches, she had to use a wheelchair. This change deeply affected the active youth. As she says, "I was devastated because of all the negative connotations our society puts on a chair. I wasn't real sure what my life was going to be like." This situation lasted until 1989, when Driscoll was about 22. The muscles and tendons in her knees wore out, and her doctors told her she would have to permanently use a wheelchair.

After losing an entire year because of her bicycle accident, Driscoll returned to Custer High in her wheelchair, a situation that deeply upset her. Driscoll explains that "At school, people seemed freaked out by the wheelchair. I just wanted to scream, 'I'm still the same person!'" She wanted classmates to understand that "Riding a chair is like learning to walk: At first it's a big deal, but when you get the hang of it, you forget it."

One individual who understood was fellow student Jim Ratzburg. Like Driscoll, he had been confined to a wheelchair because of spina bifida. His attitude made all the difference. Whereas Driscoll had allowed self-pity and anger to destroy her life, Ratzburg wasted no opportunity to accomplish things. He pushed Driscoll to participate in such wheelchair sports as soccer, basketball, softball, tennis, hockey, and track. Slowly, Driscoll began to notice that a whole new world existed for her. "At first I wasn't sure I wanted to hang out with all these other chair people and be stereotyped with only having those types of friends. But after I went there [Custer High School], I got hooked."

For the first time in her life, Driscoll actively participated in team events and individual athletic competitions, and she relished the chance to pit her strengths against those of others. One of her close friends, Debbie Richard-son, mentioned to Driscoll that "the best thing that ever happened to her is being in a chair. In crutches, she could never have done anything in sports." Driscoll agreed, and though she still retained some anger and frustration, she at least now had an outlet for her talent. As she later recalled, "I was always on the sidelines in sports until I started using a wheelchair. That's the irony of my life. I was the scorekeeper and manager and one of the best fans, but I was never able to get in there and get dirty. Then, all of a sudden, I went from being able to walk and ride a bike to using a chair, and that was my opportunity to get in there." Driscoll graduated from high school in 1984.

College Years

Her college years started in rocky fashion. She entered the nursing program at the University of Wisconsin at Milwaukee in 1987, but flunked out that first year. Still bitter over her disability, Driscoll also watched in quiet turmoil as her parents battled through a divorce. The combination proved more than Driscoll could handle, as she faced losing two parts of her life that had given her stability—the comfort of a united family and the happiness of performing well in school. As she explains, "School was the only thing that had given me self-esteem, and all of a sudden I had lost that, too. I was at a rock-bottom point in my life. I was suicidal, and I didn't think I had anything to offer this world."

Fortunately, two men spotted Driscoll playing basketball one day and were impressed with her skill and competitive fire. Marty Morse, a paraplegic, and Brad Hedrick operated the University of Illinois's Rehabilitation and Educa-tion Center in Champaign, Illinois. First opened in 1948, the center boasted the nation's finest program for disabled individuals, and it offered wheelchair athletes the chance to compete at the highest level, particularly in track, basketball, and swimming. Morse and Hedrick convinced Driscoll to enter the University of Illinois in 1987, and her world suddenly expanded. Instead

of being different from all the other students, Driscoll was simply one more person in a wheelchair. Rather than wallowing in anger, she met men and women who accepted the challenge of being in a wheelchair and tried to achieve new heights. "I didn't like myself at all until I was about 20 years old," she says.

At Illinois, she decided that a person can adopt either a disabled frame of mind, in which the individual waits for things to happen, or a non-disabled frame of mind, in which the person actively seeks out new tests and fields of opportunity. Although her body needed to rely upon a wheelchair to get around, Driscoll realized there were no limits upon how far she could go if she put her mind to it. "All of a sudden I was around all of these people, who despite all these chairs were very proactive, who were pursuing masters and doctorate degrees. They were getting married, having children. I started to realize I could deal with my disability." At Illinois, Driscoll tossed off the self-imposed shackles that had prevented her from accomplishing all that she could and embarked upon the road that eventually led to personal triumphs.

She combined an outstanding career as an athlete with her studies in rehabilitation administration, earning her bachelor's degree in 1991 and her master's degree in 1993. Driscoll began her athletic career in earnest during these college years. With Marty Morse's encouragement, she entered her first wheelchair race in 1986. She became a vital contributor to the University of Illinois's women's wheelchair basketball team, which won two national championships in 1990 and 1991 with Driscoll as a starter.

CAREER HIGHLIGHTS

Early Races

Driscoll first entered wheelchair racing more as an activity than as a determined competitor whose goal was to win races and garner world records. She mentions that "I was a nobody in this sport when I first started in 1986, when the Derse Sign Co. sponsored me. I knew it was something I wanted to try, and I didn't start training seriously until 1987." Her first race—a five-mile event in Milwaukee—so drained Driscoll that she later said, "[I] swore I'd never do another road race." She adds that "I didn't really have a lot of confidence in my ability and didn't see as much potential in myself as Marty [Morse] saw in me." However, Morse nurtured the raw talent in his athlete and constantly pestered her to enter marathons. In 1989, while Driscoll was still a student at the University of Illinois, she won her first national race by edging Candace Cable in a 12-kilometer duel in Spokane, Washington. Cable had not lost a road race in five years, and that made Driscoll start taking her sport more seriously.

Though still reluctant to compete in marathons, Driscoll finally entered the 1989 Chicago Marathon, more as a way of pleasing her coach than herself. A long-distance endurance test that challenges top-notch athletes, marathons wind through city streets and up and down area hills for 26 miles, 385 yards. For those in wheelchairs, marathons pose formidable tests of athletic talent. Muscular arms and strong hands are needed to turn the wheels on level streets or up steep grades, and knowledge of the marathon's course is imperative so the athlete can avoid cracks in the pavement or holes. Surprisingly, Driscoll finished second in the women's division in that first marathon, even though she had hated the arduous training. When Morse informed her after the race that she had qualified for the 1990 Boston Marathon—the ultimate for marathon racers—Driscoll acted as though she had swallowed something bitter. "I don't want to do the Boston Marathon," the exhausted athlete barked at her coach. "I don't want to do any more marathons. I met this goal, I did the marathon distance. I didn't die out there. But I don't want to do any more marathons." Morse would not let her relax, though, and prodded her into going to Boston.

Unconvinced that her future rested in the select world of marathoners, Driscoll headed for Boston "not wanting to be there, not believing that I belonged in this race. I thought the hills were going to eat me up." Besides, only two weeks earlier she had helped the University of Illinois women's wheelchair basketball team capture its first of two national championships, so she hadn't been able to practice for the marathon. In spite of these obstacles, Driscoll not only placed first among all female wheelchair competitors in the 1990 Boston Marathon but set a new world record and earned $25,000 for her efforts. However, she remained unconvinced about the sport. "The first time I won Boston, I didn't think I even belonged in the race. I couldn't help thinking it was a fluke." She quickly proved otherwise by winning the next year (1991), even though she again lost training time because the Illinois wheelchair basketball team captured a second national crown. In 1992, Driscoll topped her previous two marathons when she registered another world record time of one hour, 37 minutes to win her third straight Boston Marathon.

Despite her success in Boston, Driscoll experienced difficulties and heartbreaks elsewhere. During the 1990 Los Angeles Marathon she was cruising along in the lead when one wheel fell off her chair and knocked her out of contention. As Driscoll remembers, "I had to pull into a gas station for repairs. It took them 15 minutes to find the right tool to put the wheel back on the axle, and then it rained." She had better success at the 1992 Paralympics, in which 3,500 physically challenged athletes from 127 nations competed against each other. There, she won gold medals in two different relays: the 4 x 100 meters, and the 4 x 400 meters. She suffered one of her biggest disappointments at the 1992 Summer Olympics, when she placed second in the 800 meter wheelchair exhibition race.

Like a true champion, however, Driscoll used the poor showing as incentive and immediately set a goal of winning the gold medal in the next Olympics. Her reaction surprised no one who knew her, for Driscoll is a driven individual. Marty Morse claims that she is a "very goal-oriented person," and her brother Ron, adds, "What she puts her mind to, she accomplishes."

Driscoll methodically prepares for each race. She travels the race course at least twice beforehand and takes notes about the location of rough spots, potholes, cracks, and other factors that might affect the outcome. She frequently divides races into segments. For instance, she splits the Boston Marathon into two distinct portions. The first 10 miles mainly wind downhill, "which I don't like because my competitors routinely outroll me without having to do any work." She hopes to keep pace with the leaders here, because she normally outdistances her competitors in the remaining 16 miles, a series of torturous uphill challenges for which she loves to prepare. Driscoll normally trains from two to five hours each day, six days a week, logging as many as 150 miles, often into stiff headwinds. Driscoll uses special gloves, which look like small, flat boxing gloves. She meticulously records her training sessions in a journal, which she frequently consults before each race. She also lifts weights three times every week, which has so increased her upper arm strength that the 110-pound athlete can bench press 200 pounds.

Later Races

Driscoll maintained her tight grip on the Boston Marathon by winning the 1993, 1994, and 1995 events. Following the 1995 marathon she and the other victors were invited to Washington for a morning jog with President Clinton, who took one look at Driscoll's powerful arms and exclaimed, "You have the best-looking arms in America."

Driscoll, who is deeply religious, claims that "God has a plan for each and every one of us." She frequently cites her two favorite biblical passages — Romans 12:12 which admonishes people to "Rejoice in your hope, be patient in tribulation, be constant in prayer"; and 2 Timothy 4:7, which proclaims "I have fought the good fight, I have finished the race, I have kept the faith." She turned to that faith in the summer of 1995 when she was involved in a serious water tubing accident. She broke one leg and missed four months of racing — a span she labels "the worst four months" of her athletic life. Placed on the sidelines for the first time, Driscoll turned the incident into a positive. She missed racing's excitement while she recovered and claimed "I didn't like watching other women win the races that I was used to winning." As a result, she roared back into the sport with a renewed determination to climb back on top. In the first 11 races of her busy 1996 schedule, for instance, she won eight events in her specialty of long-distance races and placed second or third in the other three, which happened to be shorter events, such as the 800 meter race. In the 1996 Paralympics, Driscoll triumphed in the 10,000 meters, smashing the world record and snaring her first gold medal. She went on to win a second gold medal in the marathon as well as a silver medal in the 5,000 meters and a bronze medal in the 1,500 meters. In the 1996 Olympics, she took a silver medal in the 800 meter wheelchair exhibition event.

The following year she lost the Los Angeles Marathon by one second. She used that as incentive for the 1997 Boston Marathon, where she attempted to record her eighth straight victory. In a close race, Driscoll kept pace with Louise Savage, who had defeated her at Los Angeles. When the pair approached the 23-mile mark, the wheels of Driscoll's chair became caught in a trolley track and spilled the champion to the ground. She knew her chances of victory disappeared with the mishap, but Driscoll would not give up. She got back in her chair and sped off, determined to take second in spite of a damaged tire. She stated later "I knew I couldn't finish first, and I wanted to finish second. I didn't train so hard for this race not to finish." Over the race's final three miles she kept repeating to herself, "I can't give up. I've lost first. I

can't win. But I've got to get second. I've got to get second. I can't get third."
Driscoll dramatically finished the race in second place.

True to form, Driscoll accepted full blame for the accident. "I know all about those tracks," she told the press. "I raced over them seven times and won, and I drove on them many times checking over the course. I was very much aware of what was there. I had decided to be aggressive, and that's why it happened. It was my fault." Though disappointed in not winning, Driscoll saw her accident as sending a positive message to the nation about her sport. "I think it was a good thing, actually. I mean, I'm not happy that I crashed. But the way things turned out, it was good because the public saw that, yeah, this is sport!" She added that "it was important for people to see that yeah, we go down, but we get up like any other athlete."

Educating the Public

As determined as Driscoll is to win, she is even more determined to enlighten the public. She feels that she and other athletes in her sport are precisely that — athletes, not disabled people. She shudders at being labeled handicapped or physically challenged. "That makes it seem everything I do is a challenge. Well, brushing my teeth and brushing my hair [are] not a challenge. Most of us hate 'physically challenged'." She claims that "There are a lot of cutesy terms out there. What you are is a person first, a person with a disability. And you are an athlete. The disability is secondary. I am not helpless against my legs. And I'm not wheelchair-bound. I am not tied to that wheelchair." Driscoll attempts to educate people that she is no different than they are. "This chair is like a pair of glasses. It offers independence, just like your glasses. You get up in the morning and put them on and forget about them. That's what I do with this chair."

Above all, she hopes people understand that there is far more ability than disability for those in wheelchairs and that being in a wheelchair "is a characteristic, like hair color. My sport doesn't require legs, it requires arms and my chair. I'm not a disabled athlete, I'm an athlete." She points out that many sports fans erroneously equate wheelchair sports with the Special Olympics, which is held for those with mental disabilities. Whenever anyone made that assumption during the 1996 Paralympic Games, she quickly corrected them with the statement she was in Atlanta, Georgia, for the "Summer Olympics, just like Jackie Joyner-Kersee."

To promote the cause of wheelchair athletics, Driscoll books numerous speaking engagements before high school and junior high school students. She hopes they leave the speech with a new attitude. "I love turning lightbulbs on. I always leave my speaking engagements on an emotional high." She explains that "When people first see me, they see the chair" and that "when somebody sees somebody in a chair, their heart goes out to them and they pity them and feel sorry for them and they don't know how they could ever live a life if they had to spend it in a chair. I love to go out and tell people that my chair is a characteristic, like hair color or height. It's not a defining principle." Afterwards, when she signs autographs for the teenagers, Driscoll writes, "Dream big and work hard" because she wants to encourage youth to rise up to tough challenges, just as she has done. While making the major leagues may be a distant dream, she contends that "if you are committed enough and make the sacrifices, it can happen."

Driscoll has seen positive changes in attitudes about her sport. Stories about Driscoll and other wheelchair athletes now show up with baseball and golf on the sports pages of newspapers rather than as human interest stories in the feature section. Technology has transformed the wheelchair into a sleeker, lighter, faster implement. More and more, she and her compatriots are viewed as top-caliber athletes instead of individuals who have overcome their adversity. One of her main sponsors, Ocean Spray, has created the $10,000 Jean Driscoll Award, which annually awards money to four female wheelchair athletes to further their training.

Always a goal-setter, Driscoll will achieve full satisfaction only when female wheelchair athletes compete equally with their male counterparts. "Genetically, men have little advantages, but I'd like to see us continue scaring them, coming close to them."

Right now, Driscoll plans to continue racing until about the year 2000. Then, she plans to develop a career in speaking.

HOME AND FAMILY

Driscoll travels year-round to compete in her sport. Her home base is in Champaign-Urbana, Illinois, where she coaches the wheelchair track/road racing team for the University of Illinois. She is also the Director of the Illinois Wheelchair Classic, and Director of the American Sports Effectiveness Program. She is single. I'm starting to think about life after racing," she said recently. "I'd love to have a family someday."

HOBBIES AND OTHER INTERESTS

Driscoll loves singing, and in 1991 she set as a goal to sing the national anthem at a sporting event. In February 1992 she sang before a University of Illinois home game, and two months later she performed before 53,000 people at the Milwaukee Brewer home opener. As she asserts, "Sometimes I think you need to set goals that may seem unrealistic, but I was real shocked at how quickly I reached this goal." With a grin, she states of the Brewer game, "That was a rush. I am not missing out on anything in life."

Driscoll is also a composer. One of the songs she wrote was used in a television documentary about her life, "Against the Wind" which was broadcast on public television in 1996.

HONORS AND AWARDS

Wheelchair Athlete of the Year: 1987
Boston Marathon (Women's Wheelchair Division): 1990-96 (seven years), first place
Women's National Championship Wheelchair Basketball Team: 1990, 1991, with the University of Illinois
Sportswoman of the Year (Women's Sports Foundation): 1991
Olympic Wheelchair Exhibition, 800 meters: 1992, 1996, silver medal

Paralympic Games, 4 x 100 meter relay: 1992, gold medal
Paralympic Games, 4 x 400 meter relay: 1992, gold medal
Paralympic Games, 10,000 meters: 1996, gold medal
Paralympic Games, marathon: 1996, gold medal
Paralympic Games, 5,000 meters: 1996, silver medal
Paralympic Games, 1,500 meters: 1996, bronze medal
Gene Autry Courage Award: 1997

FURTHER READING

Periodicals

Boston Globe, Apr. 16, 1993, p.33; Apr. 16, 1993, p.37; Apr. 16, 1996, p.42; Apr. 22, 1997, p.F1; Apr. 22, 1997, p.F6
Chicago Tribune, May 2, 1990, p.1; June 18, 1992, p.1; Apr. 16, 1996, p.3; Apr. 22, 1997, p.4
Fresno Bee, July 13, 1996, p.B8
Los Angeles Times, Feb. 27, 1997, p.1; Mar. 3, 1997, p.10
Milwaukee Journal Sentinel, Apr. 13, 1996, p.C1; Aug. 1, 1996, p.C1; Dec. 5, 1996, p.C2
Runner's World, Apr. 1996, p.70
St. Louis Post-Dispatch, Apr. 20, 1991, p.4C
Washington Post, Aug. 21, 1996, p.B3
Women's Sports & Fitness, Jan/Feb. 1992, p.46

Video Documentary

"Against the Wind," 1996

ADDRESS

Ocean Spray Cranberries
One Ocean Spray Drive
Lakeville-Middleboro, MA 02349

Louis Farrakhan   1933-

American Religious Leader
Head of the Nation of Islam
Organizer of the 1995 Million Man March

BIRTH

Louis Haleem Abdul Farrakhan, as he is known today, was born
Louis Eugene Walcott on May 11, 1933, in the borough of the
Bronx in New York City. His mother was Mae Manning Clark, a
domestic worker who had emigrated to the United States from
St. Kitts, a British colony in the West Indies, in the Caribbean.

The beginning of Farrakhan's life was stormy. Mae Manning
married a Jamaican man, Percival Clark, who left her soon after-

ward. She then got involved with Louis Walcott, from the West Indies. They had a son, Alvan Walcott, who was Farrakhan's older brother. Then her husband, Percival Clark, briefly returned, and she became pregnant by him. Percival Clark soon left again. Mae was upset about the pregnancy because of her ongoing relationship with Walcott. She and Alvan were both dark-skinned, and she worried that the new baby would be light-skinned like Clark and would reveal her infidelity. She decided to try to abort the baby herself — at that time abortion was illegal. Three separate times she tried to abort the pregnancy. "After the third time," Farrakhan says, "she decided she would go ahead and have the baby and face the consequences." That baby was Louis Eugene Walcott, later Louis Farrakhan. Louis Walcott, Farrakhan's de facto step-father, later abandoned the family also.

YOUTH

When Farrakhan was just three, the family moved to Boston. He grew up in the Roxbury section of the city, long a Jewish enclave that was just becoming a flourishing West Indian neighborhood. It was a poor area, but families there emphasized hard work, education, and pride in their heritage. Mae Manning Clark, along with many of her relatives, was a follower of Marcus Garvey. A Jamaican who came to the United States in the early 1900s, Garvey founded the Universal Negro Improvement Association, which endorsed dignity, self-reliance, and economic independence for African-Americans. Garvey championed the "Back to Africa" movement, which called on blacks to return to Africa and create an all-black homeland where they could be free of white domination. Many see echoes of these views in those espoused by the Nation of Islam, of which Farrakhan is now the leader.

In addition to this emphasis on their racial heritage, religion also played a dominant role in Farrakhan's early family life. They were active in St. Cyprian Episcopal Church, where he was a choirboy. Their church was, at that time, the spiritual center of their immigrant neighborhood, and young Farrakhan always made an excellent impression there. As one neighbor recalled, "My family particularly loved Gene (his childhood nickname) because he was a warm, smiling, obedient, well-directed young man."

Early on, Farrakhan showed a rare musical talent. He began seriously studying violin at the age of five, practicing several hours a day. His mother chose the instrument, and at first he hated it. "I didn't want to play any violin. I thought it was an instrument for sissies, but she intended for me to play that instrument. And, certainly, if I didn't practice, I would get whipped. My mother said she didn't believe in psychology. She used 'slapology,' 'stickology,' and 'broomology,' and one of those 'ologies' always worked, at least with me." With time, though, Farrakhan grew to love the violin. He liked to practice in the bathroom, he once said, because "the violin seemed to resonate better there." He later learned to play the guitar and the ukulele also.

EDUCATION

Farrakhan's academic and musical abilities won him admittance to Boston Latin, a prestigious public high school. He felt uncomfortable in the predominately white school, and after one year he transferred to English High School. He was a track star and an honor student, particularly excelling in music and drama. He also worked hard to overcome a stuttering problem. He graduated from English High school in 1950.

After high school, Farrakhan hoped to attend Juilliard, the famed music school in New York. But because of the school's distance and his family's poverty, he didn't even apply. Instead, he earned a track scholarship to Winston-Salem Teachers College, an all-black school in North Carolina. He attended college for about three years. In 1953, his sweetheart, Betsy Ross, now known as Khadijah Farrakhan, got pregnant. Louis Farrakhan dropped out of college, returned to Boston, and got married.

FIRST JOBS

With a new wife and a baby on the way, Farrakhan needed to go to work. Earlier, he had appeared on the *Original Amateur Hour,* a popular network show hosted by Ted Mack that showcased new talent. After that experience, Farrakhan believed he could make it as a musician. He had long been a fan of calypso music, as had his mother, who had invited many performers to their home while he was growing up. He especially liked the music's political edge, which incorporated sharp insults to the political powers into the beat. Farrakhan went on the road as a calypso singer, using the names "Calypso Gene" and "The Charmer," touring nightclubs around the country. People say he was as good as Harry Belafonte, who had made his start singing calypso.

In 1955, though, Farrakhan's whole life changed. While touring clubs in Chicago, he attended a meeting of the Nation of Islam and heard Elijah Muhammad speak. Farrakhan decided to convert to the Nation of Islam. Because Elijah Muhammad didn't allow members to be entertainers, he left his nightclub act behind. He discarded his "slave name" of Wallace and became Louis X; years later he renamed himself Louis Farrakhan.

THE NATION OF ISLAM

Since that time, Farrakhan's life has been intimately tied up with the Nation of Islam. To understand his career, some background on the group's history is essential.

The historical reputation of both the Nation of Islam and its leader, Farrakhan, is complicated and controversial. The Nation of Islam is just one of a number of groups whose members are called Black Muslims. The Nation of Islam combines religion with the black nationalist movement. Despite the name, the group is not considered part of the Islamic religion, and the Nation of Islam's adherents, though called Muslims, are not considered orthodox Muslims. As explained here by Mustafa Malik, director of the American Muslim Council, "To be a Muslim, you have to believe that there is only one God and Muhammad is his last Prophet. The Nation of Islam people believe that Elijah Muhammad is the last Prophet. There is nothing in common except that we call ourselves Muslims and they call themselves Muslims." Another difference is that the Islamic faith, unlike the Nation of Islam, does not judge people on the basis of race.

The Nation of Islam was founded in 1930 in Detroit, Michigan, by Wallace Dodd Fard, also known as W.D. Farad Muhammad, a door-to-door salesman who sold silks. While selling, Farad also spread his message that Black Americans should return to the Islamic faith, which was taken from them when they were driven from Africa as slaves. In 1934, he disappeared and was never heard from again. His assistant, Elijah Poole, took over, changing his name to Elijah Muhammad.

Elijah Muhammad

Elijah Muhammad led the Nation of Islam from 1934 until his death in 1975. He claimed that Farad Muhammad, the founder of the Nation, was an incarnation of Allah (God) and that he, Elijah Muhammad, was Allah's divine messenger, a prophet. Blacks were Allah's chosen people, according to Elijah. He said that black people were part of the tribe of Shabazz, which came from an explosion in space 66 trillion years ago. White people were created 6,000 years ago by a mad black scientist named Yacub. Through genetic manipulation, Yacub created the white race, which proved to be defective and inferior — "devils," in Elijah's view. These surprising theories about Yacub and the creation of the races were first proposed by Elijah Muhammad, and they have been embraced by Louis Farrakhan and modern-day Black Muslims as well.

Elijah Muhammad rejected the call for integration and equality that characterized the Civil Rights Movement in the 1950s and 1960s. Instead, Muhammad espoused black nationalism, arguing for the complete separation of the races and the creation of a new nation just for blacks. He drew on Marcus Garvey's "Back to Africa" movement from the early 1900s. Muhammad also advocated black self-sufficiency, saying that blacks should learn to take care of their own community and not expect help from white individuals or the white government. To that end, he created a multi-million dollar business organization, based in Chicago, that included a bank, a publishing house, a fish import company, apartment complexes, small businesses, schools, and temples.

Elijah Muhammad emphasized self-respect, racial pride, personal responsibility, respect for family, and avoidance of drugs and alcohol. He recruited, in particular, in poor neighborhoods and in prisons, places where his message of self-help was most needed. Members of the Nation became known for their moral behavior, upright bearing, and neat appearance. The young women donned modest clothing and joined the Muslim Girls Training Class to learn how to be proper wives and homemakers. The young men wore their hair cropped short, dressed in suits with white shirts and bow ties, and joined the Fruit of Islam. This group served several purposes for the Nation of Islam. It was a way for young men to break away from their previous life on the streets, but it also served as a security contingent for the Nation. At various times in the group's history, it has even functioned as a paramilitary force.

Stanley Crouch, a prominent black critic of African-American music and cultural life, reflected on that era in the *Village Voice.* By the 1950s, "Suddenly here were all these clean-cut, well-dressed young men and women — men mostly," Crouch wrote. "You recognized them from the neighborhood. They had been pests or vandals, thieves or gangsters. Now they were back from jail or prison and their hair was cut close, their skin was smooth, they no longer cursed blue streaks, and the intensity in their eyes remade their faces. They were 'in the Nation' and that meant that new men were in front of you, men who greeted each other in Arabic, who were aloof, confidant, and intent on living differently than they had."

Malcolm X

One of those "new men" was Malcolm X. Malcolm Little, as he was originally known, had been a pimp and a drug dealer before converting to the Nation of Islam while in prison. He became a minister in 1952. In 1955, when Farrakhan left his singing career and nightclub tour to join the Nation, Malcolm X was the minister of the Nation of Islam temple in Boston. He later became the national spokesman for the Nation of Islam as well. The best known and most respected of the Nation's ministers, Malcolm X recruited thousands of new members. For the next few years, Farrakhan and Malcolm X were intimately tied together. Farrakhan, in fact, called Malcolm the father he never had.

In 1957, Malcolm X moved to New York to become minister of the Harlem temple. His star on the rise in the Nation, Farrakhan became minister of the temple in Boston. He wrote a song called "A White Man's Heaven Is a Black Men's Hell," which became a Black Muslim anthem, and he wrote two plays about the movement that gained him widespread attention.

But by the early 1960s, he and Malcolm X were growing apart. Malcolm was changing his beliefs, developing an interest in orthodox Islam and rejecting racial separatism. He learned that the Nation had been involved in financial improprieties that benefitted his idol, Elijah Muhammad, and that Muhammad had been involved in a series of extra-marital affairs with women from the Nation of Islam — in direct violation of their moral teachings. Malcolm X left the Nation of Islam and became an orthodox Muslim. A rift divided the Nation, and Farrakhan sided with Elijah Muhammad. In December 1964, Farrakhan wrote this in a Nation newspaper, *Muhammad Speaks*: "Only those who wish to be led to hell, or to their doom, will follow Malcolm. The die is set and Malcolm shall not escape. . . . Such a man is worthy of death." Two months later, on February 21, 1965, Malcolm X was shot to death during a speech in a hotel ballroom. Three Nation of Islam members were convicted of the assassination. Farrakhan has expressed regret that he may have contributed to the violent environment in which the slaying took place, but he has denied that he had any role in the actual murder. Thirty years later, some people still question that assertion.

Farrakhan continued to work his way up in the Nation of Islam chain of command. In May 1965, just three months after Malcolm's death, Farrakhan was named to replace him in the important position of head minister of the Harlem mosque. He later became national spokesman as well, traveling around the country to speak on behalf of Elijah Muhammad and the Nation of Islam. For the next ten years, he continued preaching like this.

Then in 1975, Elijah Muhammad died. He named as his successor his son, Wallace Deen Muhammad, who later changed his name to Warith Deen Mohammed. But Mohammed, who had been educated at an Islamic university in Cairo, Egypt, favored traditional orthodox Islam. Almost immediately, he started moving the group in that direction. He changed the group's name to World Community of Al-Islam in the West (later the American Muslim Mission), disbanded the Fruit of Islam, dissolved the financial operation, and rejected the ideology of racial separation that his father had supported. In 1977, Warith Deen Mohammed called Farrakhan to the temple in Chicago to keep a closer eye on him, it's been said. Soon afterward, Farrakhan broke away from Warith Deen Mohammed's group. With his followers, he returned to the name Nation of Islam and the beliefs of Elijah Muhammad.

Farrakhan Leads the Nation of Islam

Since then, the Nation of Islam under Louis Farrakhan has been headquartered in Chicago. His belief in black separatism, economic independence, and self-respect has remained virtually unchanged. Through the Fruit of Islam, which Farrakhan reinstated, the Nation has continued to recruit men from prisons, inner-city streets, and other tough circumstances, helping them to clean up their lives with discipline, orderliness, and purpose. Women in the Nation, on the other hand, are expected to be subservient: to remain at home, wear modest clothing, and take care of home and family.

For many years Farrakhan shunned publicity and was virtually unknown to whites. But at the same time he was well known to many in the African-American community, particularly on black college campuses, for his electrifying speeches. A charismatic preacher, Farrakhan can lecture for several hours at a time without notes, "mesmerizing audiences with his alternate use of gravity and humor, compassion and anger, fact and hyperbole," according to Ian M. Rolland in *Vital Speeches*. "He easily covers a huge range of subjects in his lectures. The need for strong families, black economic empowerment, education, morality, the media, self-worth, and the white conspiracy against blacks are all common themes."

In addition to public speaking around the country, Farrakhan has headed up several other projects over the years. In about 1985, he received a $5 million, interest-free loan from Muammar el-Qaddafi, the leader of Libya, to create POWER, People Organized and Working for Economic Rebirth. This company, which is headquartered in Chicago, produces soaps, detergents, and personal-care products. He also built a large restaurant complex in Chicago. The goal of these enterprises is to further African-American independence and self-reliance by empowering blacks to create jobs in their own communities. But they have been criticized by some as poorly run businesses that serve mostly to enrich the highest-ranking members of the Nation of Islam. Farrakhan also organized the Fruit of Islam as a quasi-paramilitary group to fight crime and provide security. Some members of inner-city neighborhoods have praised this disciplined group for cleaning up their streets and getting rid of drug dealers and gang members. In other places, though, people have complained that the Fruit did nothing except hassle community members.

Controversial Views

Farrakhan and the Nation share beliefs that are questionable to many Americans. Early on, when he was not very well known, some of his comments passed unremarked in the national media. For example, in 1980 he gave what he called one of his first major speeches. This is what he had to say: "The white man is our mortal enemy, and we cannot accept him. I will fight to see that that vicious beast goes down into the lake of fire prepared for him from the beginning, that he never rise again to give any innocent black man, woman, or child the hell that he has delighted in pouring upon us for 400 years. And I'm home to stay!"

In 1984 Farrakhan first started to gain national media attention. Jesse Jackson was running for president that year, and Farrakhan publicly supported him. Jackson made a comment in which he referred to Jewish people as "Hymies," an ugly ethnic slur. A black reporter named Milton Coleman overheard Jackson's comment and reported it in *The Washington Post*, a major newspaper. Afterward, Farrakhan had this to say: "We're going to make an example of Milton Coleman. . . . We're going to punish the traitor and make the traitor beg for forgiveness. . . . One day soon we will punish you with death! . . . This is a fitting punishment for such dogs."

Jews have been a frequent and recurring target of Farrakhan's. Many Jewish people are sensitive to ethnic slurs because of their history. During the Holocaust, 6 million Jewish people were systematically killed. This happened only 50 years ago, during World War II. There are many people still alive today who remember the horrors of their experiences in concentration camps, and they rightly fear that it could happen again. A climate of intolerance, hate speech, and anti-Semitic remarks is frightening, and many feel that Farrakhan's comments have helped to create such a climate.

Farrakhan has said that Jews are "bloodsuckers" who became rich by exploiting blacks; he called Judaism a "gutter religion" and a "dirty religion"; and he said that Adolf Hitler was "a great man." Referring to the Holocaust, he said that "Little Jews died while big Jews made money. Little Jews were being turned into soap, while big Jews washed themselves in it." In 1985 he made a comment that referred to the phrase "Never again," which Jewish people say about the Holocaust, and referred also to the ovens, in which Jewish people were killed during the Holocaust. Here is what Farrakhan said: "The germ of murder is already sewed into the hearts of Jews in this country. Some person is going to think they're doing God a favor and seek my death. . . . The Jews talk about 'Never again.' Well, I am your last chance, too, Jews. Listen, Jews, this little black boy is your last chance, because the Scriptures charge [you] with killing the prophets of God. But if you rise up to try to kill me, then Allah promised you that he will bring on this generation the blood of the righteous. All of you will be killed outright. You cannot say 'Never again' to God, because when He puts you in the oven, 'Never again' don't mean a thing." Such comments are deeply offensive to many people, both Jews and non-Jews.

Farrakhan has made other comments that are surprising or astonishing to many Americans. He believes that there has been a white conspiracy to introduce drugs into the black community to destroy it. He also believes that there is a giant spacecraft, which is called the Mother Wheel, orbiting some 40 miles above the Earth. The Mother Wheel contains bombs that will rain down on Earth to destroy all the whites. He says that he once had a vision in which he was taken aboard a small spacecraft to the Mother Wheel, where he heard the voice of Elijah Muhammad.

Because these beliefs are controversial for mainstream America, many people have tended to discount Farrakhan's importance. Yet commentators universally acknowledge his appeal to many young black men, especially those from difficult economic circumstances. He gives voice, they agree, to their frustration with a system that has failed them. "No one but Farrakhan so effectively addresses the anger of young black men," William A. Henry III said in *Time* magazine. And Farrakhan also gives them a moral foundation, self-discipline, and a way to improve their lives.

Million Man March

It was against this background that Farrakhan called for the Million Man March, which took place on October 16, 1995, in Washington, D.C. The March was intended to address a crisis in the black community: among black men, statistics tell of high unemployment and low wages, high rates of prison incarceration and low rates of college attendance. The march was to be a day of "atonement and reconciliation" for African-American men, a chance to recognize and make amends for their past mistakes and to dedicate themselves to "moral and spiritual renewal." Men were asked to pledge responsibility for themselves and their families. They were also asked to take a leading role in helping to protect their communities from violence. Approximately 400,000 men from around the country filled the nation's capital, listening to a day of speeches. The mood of the crowd was somber, disciplined, relaxed, and friendly, a day of camaraderie and fellowship.

Certainly, not all were followers of Farrakhan. Many said that they had come not to support Farrakhan, but instead to share in the work of renewing the black community. Others felt a deep ambivalence and debated the significance of their decision, wondering whether attending the march expressed tacit approval of its organizer, Farrakhan. But many agreed, according to Stanley Kauffman in the *New Republic,* that "it's better to have a galvanizing, aggressive, challenging leader, whatever his faults, than to have no such figure at all."

The event elicited a national debate on the current condition of race relations in the United States. President Bill Clinton gave a speech in Texas that same day where he discussed the current state of race relations in America and his view of the march: "[Some] of those in the march do have a history that is far from its message of atonement and reconciliation. One million men are right to be standing up for personal responsibility, but one million men do not make right one man's message of malice and division. No good house was ever built on a bad foundation. Nothing good ever came of hate." As R.W. Apple, Jr., wrote in the *New York Times,* "Whatever its other effects, the immense throngs that washed across the Mall for today's Million Man March helped to thrust questions of racial division and deprivation back to the forefront of American politics, and it is unlikely that they will soon recede."

It's unclear whether Farrakhan will even let those questions recede. With the Million Man March, Farrakhan moved to the forefront of the national political agenda. Many observers believe that he would like to stay there. They wonder what his intentions are for future political involvement, and they doubt whether he will be content to remain on the sidelines for long. "The pivotal question," according to William A. Henry III in *Time* magazine, "is whether the appeal of the Nation of Islam — and of Farrakhan — is separable from his invective of hate." Observers wonder whether he will be able to modify the hate-filled invective that often fills his speeches. If he does not, many question whether Farrakhan can become a leader for all African-Americans.

Recent Activities

In the months following the Million Man March, Farrakhan made an extended "world friendship tour," making stops in 20 countries in Africa and the Middle East. On the tour he visited many countries whose leaders are considered among the world's most repressive, corrupt, and authoritarian

tyrants, despots responsible for terrorism and serious human-rights abuses. He visited Nigeria, Sudan, Libya, Iran, and Iraq, where he met with Saddam Hussein, against whom the United States fought the Gulf War. At several stops, Farrakhan made anti-American remarks. In Iraq, he said that "God will destroy America by the hands of Muslims"; in Iran, he condemned the United States as the "Great Satan" and predicted that he would be jailed when he returned to this country.

At the time, Farrakhan said that his world tour was intended to spread the message of personal responsibility from the Million Man March. According to Benjamin Chavis, former head of the NAACP who helped organize the march, "I think the purpose of the trip was a good-will tour to take the spirit of the Million Man March—which is a spirit of atonement and reconciliation—to nations that need atonement and reconciliation." Others, though, saw a different purpose. Critics noted that several businesses of the Nation of Islam are experiencing serious financial difficulties, and they concluded that Farrakhan's tour was an effort to raise money to fund the Nation. The press agency of Libya appeared to confirm this when they reported that Libyan leader Muammar el-Qaddafi had promised $1 billion to the Nation of Islam to expand its role in electoral politics. But Libya later denied any promise of support. Farrakhan was further criticized, especially by black leaders, for his apparent support for African regimes that oppress their black citizens. In particular, many were outraged by his support for Sudan, whose government has been charged with allowing the practice of slavery. Whatever Farrakhan's motives for his world tour, it had a major effect on his public profile. One year after the Million Man March, many felt that Farrakhan had undercut the support generated by the march and compromised his efforts to move into the mainstream of American public life.

MARRIAGE AND FAMILY

Louis Farrakhan married Betsy Ross (now Khadijah Farrakhan) on September 12, 1953. They have nine children, over 20 grandchildren, and several great-grandchildren. They live in Chicago in an elegant mansion that used to belong to Elijah Muhammed.

HOBBIES AND OTHER INTERESTS

Farrakhan still loves to play the violin, often playing at home between 1:00 and 3:00 a.m.

WRITINGS

A Torchlight for America, 1993

FURTHER READING

Books

Haskins, Jim. *Louis Farrakhan and the Nation of Islam,* 1996 (juvenile)
Magida, Arthur J. *Prophet of Rage: A Life of Louis Farrakhan and His Nation,*
   1996
Who's Who in America, 1996

Periodicals

Chicago Tribune, Mar. 12, 1995, p.1; Mar. 13, 1995, p.1; Mar. 14, 1995, p.1;
  Mar. 15, 1995, p.1 (4-part series)
Current Biography Yearbook 1992
Emerge, Feb. 1996, p.36
Esquire, May 1989, p.89
Essence, Nov. 1996, p.95
Nation, Jan. 21, 1991, p.37; Jan. 28, 1991, p.86
New Republic, Oct. 28, 1985, pp.11 and 13
New York, Oct. 7, 1985, p.16; Oct. 21, 1985, p.22; Nov. 6, 1995, p.24
New York Times, Mar. 3, 1994, p.A1; Mar. 4, 1994, p.A1; Mar. 5, 1994, p.A8
  (3-part series); Oct. 15, 1995, Sec. 1, p.22; Oct. 16, 1995, pp.A1 & B6;
  Oct. 17, 1995, pp.A1, A18, A19, and A20
New Yorker, Apr. 29 and May 6, 1996, p.116
Newsweek, June 28, 1993, p.30; Oct. 30, 1995, pp.28, 32, 36, and others
People, Sep. 17, 1990, p.111
Philadelphia Inquirer, Feb. 29, 1984, p.A1
Time, Feb. 28, 1994, pp.11, 20, 24, and 28
Times of London, Aug. 3, 1992; Feb. 3, 1996
U.S. News & World Report, Apr. 23, 1984, p.13
Vital Speeches, Apr. 1, 1995, p.376
Washington Post, Apr. 3, 1984, p.A6; Oct. 26, 1989, p.B4; Mar. 1, 1990, p.A16;
  Mar. 2, 1990, p.A23

ADDRESS

Nation of Islam
734 West 79th Street
Chicago, IL 60620-2424

OBITUARY

Ella Fitzgerald   1917-1996
American Jazz Singer

BIRTH

Ella Jane Fitzgerald was born April 25, 1917, in Newport News, Virginia. The legendary singer known as the "First Lady of Song" had a voice that was sweet, swinging, and could soar three octaves. A dominating force in jazz music for some 60 years, Fitzgerald was known as a sublime interpreter of some of the greatest songwriters of the 20th century.

Fitzgerald was very private about many personal details of her life, most of which came to light only several years before her death. For her own reasons, she preferred to allow her public relations people to invent a story about a loving and secure early life for her and to give little verifiable information on her real life. Much of what we now know about her early years comes from a recently published and much-praised biography by Stuart Nicholson, *Ella Fitzgerald: A Biography of the First Lady of Jazz.*

Ella was the only child born to William Fitzgerald and Temperance (called Tempie) Williams Fitzgerald. Ella's birth parents were never married, but her father acknowledged that she was his daughter. Her father left her mother when Ella was two. After that, Ella's mother Tempie began living with Joseph Da Silva, a Portuguese immigrant. Ella and her mother moved to Yonkers, near New York City, with Da Silva when Ella was three. In Yonkers, Tempie and Da Silva had hoped to find good jobs and a decent place to live. But it took them both a while to find work, and they lived in one room in housing provided by a local religious agency. Later Tempie found work as a laundress and Joe worked in a sugarhouse. Tempie and Joe had a daughter in 1923, Frances, who became very close to her half-sister, Ella.

YOUTH

Ella grew up in a racially mixed neighborhood in Yonkers. Her friends were black and immigrant Italian, Irish, and Greek children, who got along and played together. As a child, Ella was a shy, gawky girl, but she already knew she wanted to perform and be famous. "Someday you're going to see me in the headlines. I'm going to be famous," she said, according to one old friend from childhood.

She loved to sing and dance. She started singing at her church, the Bethany African Methodist Episcopal Church, when she was in elementary school. At the same time, she started dancing with Charles Miller, the brother of her friend Annette Miller. "It was just that she loved to sing and dance," Annette Miller recalled years later. Ella and Charles would make up dance numbers and perform in the streets in front of their houses. "She would get up and sing and dance," remembered Annette Miller. "It was then that we'd say 'Ella was going to go places, as a dancer.'"

EDUCATION

Ella started school at Public School 10 in her Yonkers neighborhood in 1923. Later, she went to Benjamin Franklin Junior High School. She was an excellent student, and was remembered by her student friends for her love of dancing and singing. One recalls: "It would be at lunchtime or in the morning when we were outside the building. She would be standing against the wall, and she would be popping and shaking and swaying, dancing to herself."

Ella had favorite singers, whose records she loved to listen to and try to imitate. Early favorites included Louis Armstrong, Bing Crosby, and the Boswell Sisters, especially lead singer Connee Boswell. "She was tops at the time," remembered Fitzgerald. "I was attracted to her immediately. My mother brought home one of her records, and I fell in love with it. I tried so hard to sound just like her."

Early Tragedy and Life on the Streets

In 1932, when Ella was only 15, her mother died of a heart attack. This tragedy set into motion the most difficult time in Ella's life, a time she refused to talk about publicly. After her mother's death, her stepfather became abusive, and she left his home and went to live with an aunt in Harlem. She'd done well in school up to that point, but she dropped out to try to make some money. She ran "numbers"—an illegal lottery game—for a local racket and worked as a lookout to keep the police from raiding a local brothel. Fitzgerald's biographer Stuart Nicholson believes that she got caught at this point and was put in the Colored Orphan Asylum in Riverdale, New York. She ran away. When she was caught again, she was placed in the New York State Training School for Girls in Hudson, New York, where she was treated like a prisoner. According to Nina Bernstein of the *New York Times*, Ella and all the black girls in the facility were segregated into broken-down, overcrowded buildings, where they were often beaten by staff.

Thomas Tunney, who headed the institution from 1965 to 1976, tried to get Fitzgerald to return to talk to the current residents in the 1970s. Fitzgerald understandably refused. "She hated the place," Tunney recalled. "She had been held in the basement of one of the cottages once and all but tortured. She was damned if she was going to come back."

After her release, Ella lived on the streets of New York City, scrounging to make enough to live. "You ask me how did she eat," says Charles Linton, who later sang with Ella in Chick Webb's band. "She lived with people she talked to, and she ate with them, she slept wherever she could." It was Linton who helped Ella get her first big break, with the Webb band.

CAREER HIGHLIGHTS

Debut

Ella Fitzgerald first appeared on the stage on November 21, 1934, at Harlem's famed Apollo Theater. She entered an amateur contest and sang two songs, "The Object of My Affection" and "Judy." She had originally planned to dance, but when she got up on stage she was so scared all she could think of to do was sing. She sang both songs imitating her idol, Connee Boswell, and she won the contest. As the winner, Ella was supposed to get a week's work at the Apollo. But because of her appearance, Ralph Cooper, the show's emcee, didn't give her the work. Ella performed wearing a ragged dress and men's boots; she was dirty and unkempt from living on the streets. According to Charles Linton, "she lived in such a way that Ralph wouldn't give it to her . . . how she was dressed and everything that goes with not being clean because she didn't have a place to live."

Jazz great Benny Carter had seen Ella, and brought her to the attention of band leader Fletcher Henderson. But Henderson, too, declined to have Ella sing with his band because of the way she looked. Ella continued to perform in local amateur events, and she won first prize at the Harlem Opera House's amateur contest, winning a week-long engagement with Tiny Bradshaw's band.

In early 1935, Charles Linton mentioned to his boss, Chick Webb, that he had found a girl singer for the band. Like Henderson and others, Webb was at first put off by Ella's appearance. But he agreed to give her a chance, and to see how the crowds reacted to her. Linton found her a place to live and offered to pay for regular meals in a restaurant. And members of Webb's band helped with clothes. The hat check girl at the club she worked at taught her the basics — to bathe regularly, to comb her hair — the routine of personal hygiene that had gotten lost after months of living on the streets.

Ella took the opportunity and ran with it. She quickly became a favorite with fans, critics, and fellow musicians. The audiences at the Savoy Ballroom in Harlem loved the new young singer, so Webb had to take notice. Music critics, too, were struck by her talent. George T. Simon of the *Metronome* remembered that he was "knocked out by her, knocked out not only by the way she sang but the spirit and the way she would lead the band by throwing kicks on the side of the bandstand." And the other musicians in Webb's band were in awe of her ability. "I don't know where she learned it, but she read music," remembered Mario Bauza. "She could sight-read better than any of the singers," recalled Teddy McRae. Ella's ability to hear and repeat a tune with ease was always remarkable, as was her talent to work with a piece of music, taking apart the rhythm and melodic line, rework it, and make it her own.

Thus Fitzgerald began her six-decade career in show business. Her ability and versatility mark these 60-plus years in music, as she made the transition from the Big Band era of the 1930s and 1940s, to jazz and bebop in the 1940s and 1950s, to the era of the popular song, a career that won her the name as "the first lady of song."

Singing with the Big Bands

With Chick Webb's group Ella sang songs typical of the "Big Band" era in music. The Big Band era was characterized by full orchestrations of popular songs, often called "Swing" music, because of its danceable rhythms and tunes. These groups often had a major composer and director as their leader, such as Duke Ellington or Count Basie, and a major vocalist to perform solo sections. Other premier vocalists of the Big Band era include Sarah Vaughan, Joe Williams, and Billie Holiday. In 1935, Fitzgerald began her recording career with "Love and Kisses," which she performed with the Webb band. In 1938 she had her first big hit with a recording of "A-Tisket, A-Tasket," which she co-wrote.

With a growing list of recordings and a blossoming performing career, Fitzgerald came to the attention of other big names in music, including Benny Goodman and Jimmie Lunceford, who offered her recording and per-forming dates. A measure of her early success came in 1937 when *Down Beat* and *Melody Maker* magazines announced that their readers' polls had voted Ella the Number One Female Vocalist.

In 1939, Chick Webb died. By this time, Ella was enough of a star that she was named the head of the band. She had no experience with the business aspects of running a band, so those duties were taken by other members, and she basically was the star of the group. The band recorded and toured for several years as Ella Fitzgerald and Her Famous Orchestra, then broke up in 1942. Ella began a new phase of her career, as a singer with a wide variety of ensembles.

"Scat" Singing

During the 1940s Fitzgerald began to develop as a jazz singer, learning to take apart a melody and improvise small solos around the melodic line. She also began to improvise with singing nonsense syllables to the tunes she would make up—what is called "scat" singing. The famous jazz trumpeter Louis Armstrong is credited with developing scat in the 1930s, but Ella was surely one of its finest practitioners.

One of the most remarkable elements of Fitzgerald's talent was her sense of pitch—she rarely if ever sang out of tune. In the opinion of one of the greatest singers of the modern era, Mel Torme, who is also one of Fitzgerald's greatest fans, this aspect of her extraordinary talent was especially evident in her scat singing. "Anyone who attempts to sing extemporaneously—that is, scat— will tell you that the hardest aspect of that kind of singing is to stay in tune. You are wandering all over the scales, the notes coming out of your mouth a millisecond after you think of them. . . . A singer has to work doubly hard to emit those random notes in scat singing with perfect intonation. Well, I should say all singers except Ella. Her notes float out in perfect pitch, effortless, and most important of all, swinging."

Ella Fitzgerald in 1952

Bebop

In one of her greatest recordings of the 1940s, "Flying Home," Fitzgerald showed what she had learned and made her mark as a jazz singer. As her biographer Stuart Nicholson notes, "'Flying Home' was a watershed in Ella's career. It was the product of over two years' experimentation in extending the boundaries of jazz singing and remains among the finest jazz vocal records of all time. In it she harnesses scat singing for its musical potential. . . . Ella was aligning herself with the new thing in music: bebop."

"Bebop" is the name given to a type of jazz developed mainly by jazz giants Dizzy Gillespie and Charlie Parker in the 1940s. Unlike the swing style of jazz played by the Big Bands, bebop was music to listen to, not to dance to. Its complex chords were too unusual for some who were used to the easy harmonies of swing. Bebop was influenced in part by the musical theories of such classical composers as Igor Stravinsky and Paul Hindeminth, and the musicians who developed bebop had spent years talking, thinking, and playing out their own interpretations. Improvisation has always been a part of jazz, but even in this area bebop offered something new. Bebop explored the harmonic qualities, especially the chord progressions, rather than the melodic possibilities of a piece. This gives the music its distinctive and often dissonant flavor.

Gillespie was one of the many musicians that Ella performed with during the 1940s and 1950s, and their collaborations were memorable. Fitzgerald remembered that when they performed together and "the band would go out to jam, I liked to go out with Dizzy because I used to get thrilled listening to them when he did his bebop. That's actually the way I feel I learned what you call bop. It was quite an experience, and he used to always tell me, 'Come on up and do it with the fellas.' That was my education in learning how to really bop. We used to do 'Oo-Bop-Sh'Bam-a-Klook-a-Mop." When I felt that I could sing that, then I felt like I was in."

By the late 1940s Ella was an established artist performing with some of the biggest names in jazz and making a very comfortable living from her recordings and concerts. In addition to Gillespie and Parker, some of the musicians she played with at the time include Louis Armstrong, Louis Jordan, Ellis Larkins, and pop groups like the Ink Spots.

Norman Granz

Fitzgerald's career took a major turn in 1953, when Norman Granz became her manager. A musical entrepreneur and founder of the legendary Verve label, Granz wanted to bring jazz to people around the country. He developed a performance platform and recording outlet for the finest jazz artists of the era, starting with live concerts at the Los Angeles Philharmonic, which were broadcast and recorded. Billed as Jazz at the Philharmonic, and known throughout the jazz world as JATP, they were a smash hit all over the country. Granz featured such stars as Ella, Nat King Cole, Duke Ellington, and Count Basie, and they, too, became even better known; their concerts and recordings became anticipated events across the nation. Another ground breaking feature of Granz's arts management was that he refused to allow racial prejudice in the booking, seating, or conduct of his concerts. Under his direction JATP presented the first concert before an integrated audience ever played in Charleston, South Carolina.

Granz was able to lure Ella from her manager at the time, Moe Gale, and took over her career. In the opinion of Fitzgerald's biographer Nicholson, "With his JATP concert tours, Norman Granz almost singlehandedly made the presentation of jazz on the concert platform a commonplace. In so doing he would elevate the status of both Ella Fitzgerald and Oscar Peterson to that of international concert artist." Mel Torme is quoted by Nicholson as saying, "I give credit to Norman Granz for saying to Ella, 'You are far more than a cult singer. You should be a national treasure, and you should be able to draw people in Las Vegas and the biggest nightclubs in New York.' And that's what he did for her." Around this time, the phenomenal Ella Fitzgerald received an award from Decca records, for whom she had sold 22 million records to date. Several of Fitzgerald's signature recordings date from this era, including "How High the Moon" and "Lady Be Good."

But despite being on top of the music world, Fitzgerald faced a humiliating instance of racial prejudice at the peak of her fame. In 1954, en route to Australia with her maid and pianist John Lewis, she was bumped off a flight in Hawaii so that their first-class seats could go to white people. Fitzgerald's new manager, Granz, took his client's situation to court, where he filed suit on her behalf to protest the discriminatory act. The suit was settled out of court, but Granz and Fitzgerald had made their point.

The Songbooks

In the 1950s, under Granz's direction, Fitzgerald began to record the music of some of the most popular composers of the 20th century, including George and Ira Gershwin, Cole Porter, Harold Arlen, Irving Berlin, Duke Ellington, Jerome Kern, Johnny Mercer, and Rodgers and Hart. Some of these songs had been popularized in Broadway shows, some as popular hits on the radio. But in the hands of Ella Fitzgerald, they became American music classics. Granz had notable conductors and arrangers for the Songbook series score the pieces, and Ella interpreted them with her characteristic fluid phrasing and magnificent vocal shadings. Her voice conveyed the exuberant variety of the songs, from lively upbeat tunes to ballads, in turn sweet, yearning, wistful, or witty. One of the most famous quotes about the series came from Ira Gershwin, who said, "I never knew how good our songs were until I heard Ella Fitzgerald sing them." Each of the songbooks has its fans, but the general consensus is that the Gershwin recordings, arranged and conducted by Nelson Riddle, are the finest. In the opinion of many, Fitzgerald elevated the songs of these composers to the level of art song.

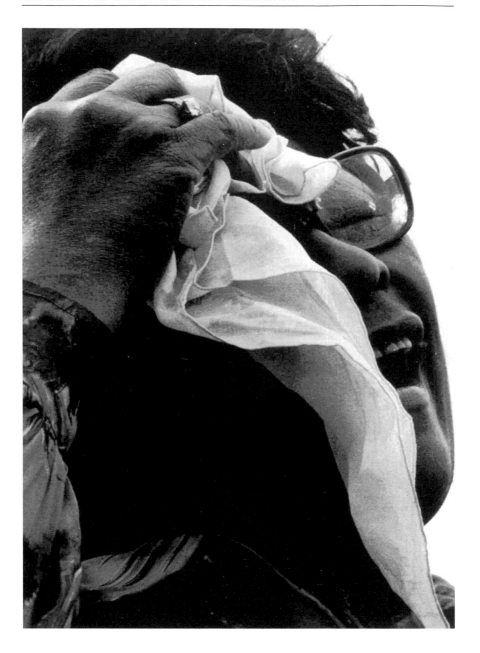

Jazz critic Whitney Balliett of the *New Yorker* provides an insight into Fitzgerald's achievement in the Songbooks. He believed that "in many ways the Ellington Songbook is the best, particularly her version of Billy Strayhorn's 'Lush Life,' which she does ad lib, accompanied only by Oscar Peterson. The song itself is an uneasy combination of delicacy and crudeness, yet she threads her way through easily, using little improvisation and making the music float, a trick Ella at her most relaxed could always do."

In 1955, Granz got Ella a small part in a Hollywood movie, *Pete Kelly's Blues*, in which she had a small role as a singer. She did a great job, according to the *New York Times*: "The wonderful Ella Fitzgerald . . . fills the screen and soundtrack with her strong, mobile features and voice."

Fitzgerald was as big a hit in Europe as she was in the U.S. Once, on tour in Berlin, she made a mistake—and music history—in singing "Mack the Knife," a song made popular by Bobby Darin and Louis Armstrong. Midway through the song, she forgot the lyrics, and began to scat about it: "Aw, Bobby Darin and Louis Armstrong/They made a record, oh, but they did/And now Ella, Ella and her fellas/We're making a wreck, what a wreck of 'Mack the Knife'." The recording of the performance was a hit all over the world.

In the mid-1960s, Fitzgerald was still keeping up her breakneck recording and performing pace when she collapsed from exhaustion while touring Europe. While recovering, she granted an interview to well-known jazz critic and composer Leonard Feather. Fitzgerald was notoriously shy and didn't like talking about herself. But with Feather she opened up with several interesting comments about how she did what she did. "You can tell whether a singer really likes a song or not—no matter how hard they try with something they do for commercial reasons, it's a song they are enthusiastic about you can just feel them putting that little extra something into the performance," she told Feather.

About her own favorite songs to perform at that time, she told him "I still like songs with changes, songs that present some kind of a challenge and make you say to yourself, 'What are you gonna do with this?'" It was for just this kind of selfless service of her voice to the music that made Fitzgerald such a favorite of musicians and fans alike. Feather talked about her talent as an interpreter of his compositions: "You realize instantly that she knew just what you meant by a certain phrase, that she dug your chord changes or sensed what lyrical point you were trying to make. You know at once that your few hours of effort had been sublimated by the touch of genius."

Fitzgerald was soon back to touring and recording, and she also appeared on most of the television variety shows popular in the 1960s and 1970s. She shared the concert stage with the bands of Count Basie and Duke Ellington, and other masters of song, like Frank Sinatra. She also made a foray into the popular music of the time, including the songs of Bert Bacharach and the Beatles, which are generally regarded as less successful than her handling of jazz classics.

In the later 1970s, Fitzgerald's health began to fail, largely as a result of the onset of diabetes. This debilitating disease can affect the eyes, kidneys, heart, and circulatory systems. Ella began to lose her eyesight around this time, and the beautiful, velvety voice began to sound a little rough around the edges. In 1986, she had bypass surgery, but was up and performing within a year. Her many recordings had garnered honors for years, and in 1991 she won her final Grammy, for a collection entitled *All That Jazz*. Gradually, however, Fitzgerald had to give up the stage because of declining health. She gave her final performance in 1993 in West Palm Beach, Florida. As a further result of diabetes, she suffered circulatory problems and her legs had to be amputated below the knee in 1993. After suffering a stroke in early June, she died at her home in Beverly Hills, California, on June 15, 1996.

MARRIAGE AND FAMILY

Fitzgerald was married twice. Her first marriage was to Benny Kornegay, a shipyard worker whom she met while performing with the Webb band in 1941; the marriage was annulled in 1942.

In 1947 Fitzgerald was married for the second time, to world-renowned bassist Ray Brown. They adopted the son of Fitzgerald's half-sister, Frances, and raised him as Ray Brown, Jr. They had no other children. The marriage ended in divorce in 1953; in the opinion of many friends and colleagues, the demands of two music careers took its toll on the relationship. But Fitzgerald and Brown remained friends and continued to perform together for years after their divorce. Brown performed at a tribute to Fitzgerald at Carnegie Hall in New York one month after her death.

HOBBIES AND OTHER INTEREST

Fitzgerald was involved in children's charities from the late 1940s until the end of her life. She was the national head of Foster Parents Plan, which was started after Word War II to provide orphanages for children in Europe. In this country, she started the Ella Fitzgerald Child Care Center in Los Angeles to help disadvantaged children. In her spare time, she liked reading and cooking, and she was an avid soap opera fan.

FITZGERALD'S LEGACY

Fitzgerald was the favorite singer of many musicians of many generations. Mel Torme, Benny Goodman, even Bing Crosby called her the best. "Man, woman, or child, Ella is the greatest," Crosby declared. "She showed me the way," claimed Torme. "She was the pathfinder. She was the best singer on the planet." To singer Rosemary Clooney, Fitzgerald "sang every song as if it were the first time." "She was the last of the first team," said composer and arranger Quincy Jones. "I'm talking about Ellington, Basie, the ones who invented this music." "She was my favorite singer," said Tony Bennett, predicting "her recordings will live forever. She'll sound as modern 200 years from now, no matter what techniques they come up with."

For Frank Rich of *The New York Times*, her passing meant the passing of an era."It's not just that her singing is beautiful. It is also liberating, transporting us into a realm of pleasure beyond all barriers, whether of race and age, of jazz and pop, of high art and low, or even, when she floats into scat, of language. That timelessness will never fade. It's when you start to wonder if our increasingly Balkanized and contentious country could ever again produce a voice as unifying in spirit and universal in appeal as Ella Fitzgerald's that you realize a glorious time in our culture's history, not just a remarkable woman, has passed."

SELECTED RECORDINGS

Chick Webb and His Orchestra, 1935
The Cole Porter Songbook, 1956
Ella Fitzgerald Sings the Rodgers and Hart Songbook, 1956
Ella and Louis [with Louis Armstrong], 1956
Jazz at the Philharmonic, 1957
Like Someone in Love, 1957
Porgy and Bess [with Louis Armstrong] , 1957
Duke Ellington Songbook, 1958
Ella Fitzgerald Sings the Irving Berlin Songbook, 1958
The George and Ira Gershwin Songbook, 1959
The Intimate Ella, 1960
Mack the Knife: Ella in Berlin, 1960
Ella and Basie: On the Sunny Side of the Street, 1963
Take Love Easy [with Joe Pass], 1973
Fine and Mellow, 1974
Fitzgerald and Pass . . . Again [with Joe Pass], 1976
A Perfect Match: Basie and Ella [with the Count Basie Orchestra], 1979
All That Jazz, 1991
Ella Fitzgerald: 75th Birthday Celebration, 1992

HONORS AND AWARDS

Grammy Awards: 1958, Best Vocal Performance, Best Jazz Performance, for
    Duke Ellington Songbook; 1960, Best Vocal Performance, Best Vocal
    Performance Album, for *Mack the Knife: Ella in Berlin;* 1976, Best Vocal
    Performance Album, for *Fitzgerald and Pass . . . Again;* 1991, for *All That Jazz*
Kennedy Center Award: 1979
National Medal of Art: 1987
Ordre des Arts des Lettres (France): 1990

FURTHER READING

Books

Colin, Sid. *Ella: The Life and Times of Ella Fitzgerald*, 1986
Nicholson, Stuart. *Ella Fitzgerald: A Biography of the First Lady of Jazz*, 1993
Who's Who in America, 1996

Periodicals

Billboard, June 29, 1996, p.9
Chicago Tribune, June 19, 1996, Tempo Section, p.1
Current Biography Yearbook 1990
Down Beat, June 1993, p.22; Sep. 1996, p.16
Independent, June 17, 1996, p.16
Jet, July 1996, p.58
New York Times, Apr. 25, 1993, Section II: p.31; June 16, 1996, p.A1; June 16, 1996, p. A23; June 23, 1996, Section II: 34, Section IV: p.4; July 12, 1996, p.C3
Newsday, July 1, 1996, p.B4
Newsweek, June 24, 1996, p.80
People, July 1, 1996, p.42
Time, June 24, 1996, p.83
Times of London, June 17, 1996
Variety, June 24-30, 1996, p.124
Washington Post, June 16, 1996, p.A1; June 17, 1996, p.C1

WORLD WIDE WEB SITE

http://jazzcentralstation.com

Harrison Ford   1942-

American Actor
Star of Such Popular Films as the Star Wars Trilogy,
the Indiana Jones Movies, and *Air Force One*

BIRTH

Harrison Ford was born on July 13, 1942, in Chicago, Illinois. His father, Christopher Ford, came from an Irish-Catholic background, while his mother, Dorothy Ford, came from a Russian-Jewish family. Growing up, Ford and his younger brother Terence, who is also an actor, were exposed to both faiths, although they weren't raised with a strong religious background.

Ford's ties to the entertainment world go back several generations. His namesake, his grandfather, Harrison Needleman, worked in vaudeville before deciding on more steady work with the Brooklyn streetcar line. When Harrison was young, his father was an advertising executive. At that time, Chicago was a center of radio advertising, and Christopher Ford both wrote and performed in radio commercials. He was also active in television. "He was a pioneer of television commercials," Ford recalls. "He invented the concept of the see-through washing machine to demonstrate the suds, and he was the first to use stop motion photography. He certainly seemed to have a lot more interesting job than a lot of the other guys' dads. This may sound silly, but it encouraged me not to want a real job." Years later, after Harrison was grown, his parents opened an antique shop.

YOUTH

Ford is an intensely private man who resists disclosing information about his personal life. He considers himself an actor, not a movie star, and says that he doesn't want to be turned into a celebrity. In interviews Ford refuses to talk about his own life, preferring instead to focus on his work. Over the years, he has disclosed very few details about his childhood experiences.

Still, some facts are known. Ford grew up in financially comfortable circumstances in a succession of affluent suburbs around Chicago, including Park Ridge, Morton Grove, and Des Plaines, Illinois. "I had a basic Midwestern upbringing," Ford recalls. "I came from a home where I felt supported and encouraged. I had a pretty normal childhood. It was only in the outside world that I felt uncomfortable." Ford has said that he felt different from his classmates. He didn't fit in. Quiet and unathletic, he didn't participate in sports or games with the other kids.

EARLY MEMORIES

It's hard to imagine today, but the boy who would grow up to be a famous action hero was constantly picked on by bullies as a kid. "I was kind of a runty thing. And I liked to hang out with the girls. That annoyed the boys. So every day after school, they would throw me over the edge of the parking lot and roll me into the weeds. Eventually, my beatings were so inevitable that I'd just go to the lot and wait," Ford recalls. "The entire school would gather to watch this display. I don't know why they did it. Maybe because I wouldn't fight the way they wanted me to. They wanted a fight they could win. And my way of winning was to just hang in there."

EDUCATION

Ford attended elementary and junior high school in the Chicago suburbs; he finished up at Maine Township High School in Park Ridge, Illinois (the school that Hillary Clinton later attended). There, he was the president of the Social Science Club and the Model Train Club, a representative of the Boys' Club, and a member of the Model Radio Club. Ford was a shy kid with few friends. "I never set out to be held in esteem," he says now. "I just wanted to be able to hold my head up in private. I couldn't even find a niche in high school. My classmates considered me an oddball, and they were probably right. Not that I cared much for what my classmates thought. I didn't know my classmates then. I don't know them now. I've never been to a reunion."

By high school, also, his academic performance was falling apart. Although his grades were good when he was young, they began to slip during high school. "The problem was I didn't have any goal," he explained years later. "I didn't believe in careers and thought holding down a nine-to-five job was a monumental task. I just wanted excitement in life." But his family expected him to go to college despite his poor grades. He got only one offer—from Ripon College in Wisconsin. He often jokes that he probably got in there only because his high school advisor went skiing with their admissions officer. Ford graduated from Maine Township High School in 1960.

College Years

Ford's decision to attend Ripon College, a small liberal arts school, proved to be a disastrous choice. "I did not fit in," he says, "and I did not want to fit in." For the most part, he was miserable there. "When I look back, I suspect I was in a clinical depression. I would sleep for four or five days at a time. There was one class that I never went to. I remember once when I slept for several days and finally roused myself, got myself out of bed, managed to get dressed— this seemed to be taking an intense effort—and actually made it to class. All of this seemed to be happening in slow motion. I even put my hand on the door of the classroom, but I seemed to be unable to turn the doorknob. So I let it go and went back to sleep."

Ford studied English literature and philosophy while at Ripon. In his junior year, needing an extra elective course, he signed up for a drama class. From his first performance, as Mr. Antrobus in the Thornton Wilder classic *The Skin of Our Teeth*, Ford loved it. With white powdered hair, a big moustache, and several pillows to pad out his middle, Ford loved the sense of freedom he felt when disguised as someone else. "I'd never had the courage to do that sort of thing before," he recalls, "and I had real fear facing people. Now I had more responsibility—just for knowing my lines—than I'd ever faced in my life! It was my first experience of working with a group of people on a clearly defined goal." Finally, it seemed, Ford had found that sense of purpose that had been missing throughout his school years.

Unfortunately, though, that sense of purpose came too late to save Ford's college career. Not attending his classes, skipping the exams, failing to turn in assignments — it all finally caught up with him just three days before his 1964 commencement, when school authorities informed him that he lacked the requirements to graduate. To earn his degree, he would need to spend another semester at Ripon. Instead, Ford decided that it was time to leave school to become an actor.

BECOMING AN ACTOR

Ford recently reflected on how and why he decided to become an actor. "My decision to go into acting was mostly a reaction to my friends and college classmates who knew what they were going to do with their entire lives. They were all going off to work in the same office year after year, in the same job — maybe until they got a gold watch. That would be the limit of their life experience. Maybe they'd be doing fantastic things and would be very successful, but I just couldn't imagine doing that — the same thing year after year. I thought acting would give me the opportunity to confront new and interesting challenges, to work with certain people on a finite problem within a finite period of time and then do it again with another set of problems, different people. You would travel to interesting places and meet interesting people. All of it turned out to be essentially what I've gotten."

FIRST JOBS

But it would be a long, hard road to get there, one that Ford couldn't possibly have envisioned when he decided to leave college in 1964. He started out acting in summer stock in Wisconsin. Ford was married by this time, to his college sweetheart Mary, and they soon decided it was time to move. But where — New York, the center for live theater, or Los Angeles, the center for movie and TV work? After loading all their things in their Volkswagen bus, he flipped a coin to decide between the two. The first flip came up heads, for New York. After thinking about it, Ford flipped again — and again — until it came up tails, for California. "I knew I'd probably be poor and hungry," he says. "I didn't plan on being cold as well."

Arriving in Laguna Beach, south of Los Angeles, Ford started out doing a variety of odd jobs. He worked as a pizza chef, a yacht broker, a department store assistant buyer, and a paint store employee. It was during this time that he got the scar on his chin. Driving on a winding road, he reached back to put on his seat belt and hit a telephone pole. He ended up with a bad gash on his chin. While working odd jobs, Ford got involved at the Laguna Beach Playhouse. He was in the show *John Brown's Body* when he was "discovered" by a talent scout from the New Talent program at Columbia Pictures. Soon he was offered a contract and was earning $150 per week.

The Studio System

When Ford joined the motion picture industry, it still operated under the old studio system. Today, an actor is totally independent, free to pursue a role on any movie put out by any movie studio. But at that time, many actors—as well as directors and others in the industry—were under contract to a single studio. They drew a weekly salary, but in exchange they were, for the most part, assigned to specific roles and pictures. Actors had very little say over these assignments—the studios had almost complete control. Always trying to develop the next generation of stars, the studios groomed their young hopefuls accordingly, offering acting classes, fashion tips, and even advice on which date to take to the next big function. "They called me an actor," Ford says. "They gave me enough to pay my rent, but the attitude that they could manufacture a star from raw material was silly. Styling your hair, dressing you—it was all so deadly wrong, calculated to remove all those particularities which made you interesting in the first place."

At Columbia Pictures, Ford won his first movie role in *Dead Heat on a Merry-Go-Round* (1966), which starred James Coburn. Ford had a very small part as a bellboy who delivers a telegram. Afterward, a studio executive called him in to criticize his work. Here is their exchange, as recounted by Gerald Clarke in *Time* magazine. "'Sit down, kid, I want to tell you a story,' the executive said to Ford, who played a bit part as a bellboy. 'The first time Tony Curtis was in a movie he delivered a bag of groceries. We took one look at him and knew he was a movie star. But you ain't got it, kid, you ain't got it. I want you to go back to class and study.' At which point Ford leaned across the desk and replied, 'I thought you were supposed to look at him and say, There is the grocery boy.' That was the beginning of the end of Ford's career at Columbia, but the beginning of the beginning of his life as an actor. Though the Columbia executive did not recognize it, Ford was demonstrating a talent that was later to become his trademark: the ability to deliver a fast, funny, and sometimes devastating comeback."

That cocky attitude didn't win Ford any friends at the studio, though, so after 18 months and several other small roles, Columbia canceled his contract. He went on to a contract with Universal Studios, where he didn't last long either. In the meantime he had had several small parts: in the films *Luv, A Time for Killing, Journey to Shiloh*, and *Getting Straight*, and in the TV series "The Virginian," "Ironside," "The F.B.I.," "Love American Style,"and "Gunsmoke."

Turning to Carpentry

By this point Ford had also taken up carpentry. After buying a house that was in need of extensive renovations, he started teaching himself to do the repairs just by reading books on the subject. Soon, he started doing carpentry work to help support his family. His first job was to build a $100,000 recording studio for musician Sergio Mendes. Although self-taught, Ford did such a good job that Mendes started recommending him to others. Ford soon went on to other jobs for other celebrities, including Sally Kellerman, Joan Didion and John Gregory Dunne, James Caan, Richard Dreyfuss, and James Coburn. Carpentry gave Ford the financial security to become picky about his roles, so he could afford to turn down small or boring parts while waiting for something better to come along. And it also gave him a feeling of pride, confidence, and self-respect, as he auditioned for various roles, because he knew he didn't need the work.

American Graffiti

While Ford was working as a carpenter, one of his friends from his days at Columbia, Fred Roos, was working as a casting director. Roos was selected by George Lucas to do the casting for his upcoming film, *American Graffiti*, a nostalgic look at teen life in California in the early 1960s and a paean to those summer nights of cars and cruising. At this point Lucas was a young director just getting started; no one knew that he would go on to make the Star Wars and Indiana Jones movies and become one of the top film makers of his generation.

When Roos tapped his friend Ford for a part in the movie, Ford had no idea what an important part it would be. At first he was put off by the salary— only $485 a week, when he could make $1,000 a week working as a carpenter—so he turned them down. But then Lucas offered Ford an increase of $15, all the way up to $500 a week, so he took the job. Ford appeared in *American Graffiti* (1973) in a supporting role as Bob Falfa, an older hot-rodder who challenges one of the film's main characters to a drag race. His scene provides the climax to the film. Ford enjoyed the process of making the movie, because it was the first time he felt that he could make suggestions and that his opinions would be respected on the set. "It was as if the whole world had changed," he later recalled. "For the first time people had listened and for the first time I was in the company of people who cared enough about things to do them the right way." *American Graffiti* proved to be a huge success with both critics and viewers, although Ford's performance was not usually singled out for notice. So he stuck with carpentry for a bit longer, taking just a few small roles in films he believed in and waiting for something big to come along.

CAREER HIGHLIGHTS

As it turned out, Ford didn't have long to wait. Within several years he went on to make *Star Wars*, the top-grossing movie of all time. With the sequels to that film, as well as the Indiana Jones movies and his later roles, he has

From Stars Wars

become one of the most popular actors working in Hollywood today. His films have also made more money than those of any other star. During the 20 years since the initial release of *Star Wars*, Ford's films have grossed over $2 billion in the United States alone, making him the most successful actor in the history of the business. Yet Ford consistently says he has no desire to be a celebrity, and he avoids the trappings of stardom. He says that he has always viewed acting as a craft and himself as a craftsman. Being a good actor, for Ford, means disappearing into a role so the audience sees only the character. To that end, he is very reticent about his private life, saying that the more the audience knows about him, the harder it is for them to believe that he is somebody else.

For Ford, the essence of his success is his convincing screen persona. Despite their different stories, many of his on-screen characters have shared certain similarities. The *New York Times* called them "restrained, modest, life-sized heroes." They are ordinary guys, perhaps a bit cynical and aloof but with great honesty and integrity, who overcome their troubles through determination, hard work, and luck. And as the audience, we root for them all the way. As

121

Ford himself describes it, "The struggle to do the right thing, whatever the circumstances, is really the only interesting part."

THE STAR WARS MOVIES

Ford's first role of this type was in *Star Wars*. Although it's hard today to imagine anyone but Harrison Ford as Han Solo, at the time it was no sure thing. When director George Lucas started casting for *Star Wars*, he didn't want to hire anyone from *American Graffiti*—he wanted all new faces. Coincidentally, though, Ford happened to be doing some carpentry work around the production offices when casting took place. Lucas asked him to come in and read the Han Solo part opposite the actors trying out for the roles of Luke Skywalker and Princess Leia. Ford did this as a favor for Lucas, even though he knew the director wasn't planning to cast him. But he did feel a bit peeved about it, so he read the part with a sarcastic, edgy manner. His reading ultimately impressed Lucas so much that he gave Ford the role that would make him famous.

The Star Wars movies were created by George Lucas. He envisioned a nine-part epic and then went on to make three of the films: *Star Wars* (1977), *The Empire Strikes Back* (1980), and *The Return of the Jedi* (1983). The Star Wars films are basically old-fashioned adventure stories mixed with mythology, fairy tales, and up-to-the-minute special effects. This trilogy, which is really parts four, five, and six of Lucas's original nine-part epic, tells the story of a struggle between the forces of good and evil, played out in a science fiction fantasy. An evil empire is bent on domination of all creatures in the universe. To fight this power, the forces of good form a rebel force to vanquish their foe. The three films, which star Ford as Han Solo, Carrie Fisher as Princess Leia, and Mark Hamill as Luke Skywalker, chart the history of the conflict.

Han Solo, as played by Ford, is the brash, cocky, and cynical pilot of an inter-galactic pirate ship, the Millennium Falcon. Playing the part with understated wit, Ford gave a seemingly effortless performance as a swash-buckling sol-dier-of-fortune with a heart of gold. He won the hearts of moviegoers everywhere, as viewers of all ages loved the films. *Time* magazine called it "A grand and glorious film, the best movie of the year," while *Newsday* called it "An escapist masterpiece, one of the greatest adventure movies ever made."

Audiences of a new generation had their chance to enjoy all three Star Wars films when they were re-released in movie theaters in 1997. And George Lucas is reportedly working on a new Star Wars movie, a "prequel," that would be the first part of the original nine-part epic, detailing the events that take place years before those in *Star Wars*. Ford is not expected to appear in that film.

From Indiana Jones and the Temple of Doom

The Indiana Jones Movies

After appearing in *Star Wars*, Ford had minor parts in several less successful films, including *Heroes* (1977), *Force 10 from Navarone* (1978), *Hanover Street* (1979), and *Frisco Kid* (1979). He also had a small role as Colonel Lucas in Francis Ford Coppola's critically acclaimed film, *Apocalypse Now* (1979). But his first big role, after Han Solo, came as Indiana Jones. Again, Ford originally wasn't considered for the part, as *Newsweek* explains here: "Lucas hadn't considered using his Han Solo for another heroic role, and he was the last actor interviewed for the lead, at which point the unthinkable became the inevitable." Ford played Indiana Jones in three films: *Raiders of the Lost Ark* (1981), *Indiana Jones and the Temple of Doom* (1984), and *Indiana Jones and the Last Crusade* (1989).

These three movies tell the adventures of an archeologist named Indiana Jones, played by Ford with droll and self-deprecating wit. Through his search for valuable and ancient artifacts, he has a series of astonishing and death-defying exploits, surviving various traps, ambushes, and double-crosses in numerous exotic locales. He faces such threats as tarantulas, boulders, spears, runaway trucks, snakes, rats, and armored tanks. The films are exhilarating and wildly imaginative, a thrill-a-minute ride. The Indiana Jones movies were wildly successful, largely because of their hero. "It was Harrison's charisma and ability that carried the movie," director Steven Spielberg pointed out. And David Ansen wrote in *Newsweek* magazine, "The spirit of the piece is beautifully captured in Harrison Ford's performance. . . . He's a wry hero, but he's a real one — exuding just that quiet, sardonic masculinity that made stars like [Humphrey] Bogart and [Clark] Gable at once larger than life and down to earth." Although Ford had experienced success with the Star Wars movies, it was his performance as Indiana Jones that truly made him a star.

Recently, Ford has said that he will appear in a fourth Indiana Jones movie when the script is finished and when he and director Steven Spielberg are available at the same time.

Later Films

Interspersed with his appearances as Han Solo and Indiana Jones, Ford made several other unrelated films. Back in 1982, he appeared in *Blade Runner*, a futuristic science fiction story in which he played a Los Angeles police officer in about 2020 who hunts down and destroys rebellious replicants, dangerous androids that look exactly like humans. By the mid-1980s, after appearing in all three Stars Wars movies and two of the Indiana Jones movies, Ford was looking for something new. He was ready for something completely different from his roles as an action hero in an adventure story filled with special effects. So Ford appeared in the romantic thriller *Witness* (1985). He played a Philadelphia police officer, John Book, who protects a young Amish boy, Samuel, who has witnessed a murder. In Samuel's Amish community, which eschews violence, Book falls in love with the boy's mother. For Ford it was a breakthrough role, his opportunity to prove that he was more than a cartoon-character style action hero. He earned praises from viewers and critics alike, as well as his first Academy Award nomination for Best Actor.

Since that time Ford has appeared in over ten different films, including some hits and some misses, in an ongoing effort to try new and different types of work. In *Mosquito Coast* (1986), he plays Allie Fox, an inventor and idealist who moves his family to the jungles of Central America. In *Frantic* (1988), a thriller set in Paris, Ford plays a heart surgeon whose wife is kidnaped. The light comedy *Working Girl* (1988) tells the story of a Wall Street secretary who tries to get ahead — and to take over her boss's job — with the help of an executive, played by Ford, who just happens to be the boss's lover. His next film was *Presumed Innocent* (1990), based on the novel by Scott Turow. In this courtroom drama, Ford's character, a district attorney, is accused of murdering one of his coworkers, with whom he had been having an affair.

Ford continued to widen his range with his next film, *Regarding Henry* (1991). He plays a high-powered, unscrupulous New York attorney who suffers a serious brain injury that leaves him amnesiac. He is forced to recreate his life, gradually discovering that he doesn't like the person he used to be. Next came *Patriot Games* (1992), a screen adaptation of the novel by Tom Clancy featuring Dr. Jack Ryan (a character that had previously been played by the actor Alec Baldwin in *The Hunt for Red October,* an earlier Clancy adaptation). In *Patriot Games,* Ford plays Ryan, an analyst for the CIA (Central Intelligence Agency), whose family's security is threatened by Irish terrorists. That was followed by *The Fugitive* (1993), based on the 1960s television series, a tense thriller that features a chase between a man who has been unjustly convicted of killing his wife and the law enforcement officer who is hunting him. Next came *Clear and Present Danger* (1994), another adaptation of a Tom Clancy novel. Ford again plays Dr. Jack Ryan, now serving as advisor to the president. Navigating political intrigues in Washington, Ryan is pulled into the drug war in Columbia and is forced to make some tough choices about how to do the right thing.

Ford next went on to *Sabrina* (1995), a remake of the 1954 romantic comedy starring William Holden as the playboy younger son of a wealthy family, Audrey Hepburn as the daughter of the family chauffeur who is infatuated by him, and Humphrey Bogart as the serious, workaholic older brother who gradually falls in love with her; in this remake, Ford had the Bogart role. After that came the thriller *The Devil's Own* (1997), in which Ford plays an Irish-American New York City police officer who offers his friendship and his home to an Irish immigrant, played by Brad Pitt, who turns out to be with the Irish Republican Army (IRA) who has come to the United States to buy guns.

Air Force One

Ford's latest film is the action thriller *Air Force One* (1997), in which he plays James Marshall, the president of the United States. President Marshall strongly opposes political tyranny and terrorism. But then he and his family are on board the presidential plane, Air Force One, when it is hijacked by foreign terrorists. When the First Family becomes hostages, the president must decide how to balance two opposing priorities: his strong convictions against bargaining with terrorists and his determination to protect the safety of his family. Defeating the terrorists becomes the only way. The movie opened to rave reviews from all quarters, including the current First Family. *Air Force One* took in almost $38 million in its opening weekend alone, guaranteeing another blockbuster for Harrison Ford.

Ford's outstanding success comes, according to critic Josh Young, because he is the great American hero. "Ford has played the role of America's savior for 20 years," Young wrote in *George* magazine. "With remarkable consistency, in each of his films, he accepts the call to adventure, goes deep into enemy territory, and saves his family, his country's honor, or other priceless intangibles, using a mix of brains and brawn. . . . He is the most successful actor in film history, having starred in seven of the 30 top-grossing films of all time. His work . . . has become so ingrained in American culture that it is hard to

From Air Force One

fathom. Yet Ford has no desire to be personally loved. He simply wants to be respected for doing his job and then be left alone. In his ideal vision of himself, the 55-year old is not a hero, but the highest-paid blue-collar worker in the world."

MARRIAGE AND FAMILY

Ford has been married twice. His first wife, Mary Marquardt, was an honors student at Ripon College, where they first met. They married in 1964 while still living in Wisconsin. They had two sons, Benjamin and Willard, who are both now grown. They were married for about 15 years before they divorced in 1979. Ford has said that the breakup of his first marriage was the saddest thing that ever happened to him.

Ford's second wife is Melissa Mathison, an accomplished writer who created the screenplays for *E.T.: The Extraterrestrial, The Black Stallion,* and *The Indian in the Cupboard,* among other notable films. They met in 1978 in the Phillippines. At the time, both were working on the film *Apocalypse Now*: Ford had a small part as Colonel Lucas, and Mathison worked as assistant to the director. Ford and Mathison were married in 1983, and they have two young children, Malcolm and Georgia. They have homes in Los Angeles, New York

City, and Jackson Hole, Wyoming, an 800-acre ranch filled with woods, a trout stream, and wild animals, including antelope, deer, herons, bald eagles, otters, beavers, moose, and a herd of several hundred elk. In this private refuge, Ford enjoys hiking in the woods, fishing, and spending time with his family. Although the Jackson Hole retreat is Ford's favorite, the family has been staying in New York City since he moved there to film *The Devil's Own*; Ford says they're staying there now to provide continuity for the kids.

HOBBIES AND OTHER INTERESTS

Ford most enjoys his time at his western ranch, working on maintenance projects and spending time with his family. Lately he has also learned how to fly, and he bought his own small plane. He also enjoys collecting and riding motorcycles.

SELECTED CREDITS

Dead Heat on a Merry-Go-Round, 1966
American Graffiti, 1973
The Conversation, 1974
Judgement: The Court-Martial of Lt. William Calley, 1975 (TV movie)
James A. Michener's Dynasty, 1976 (TV movie)
Star Wars, 1977
Heroes, 1977
Force 10 from Navarone, 1978
Hanover Street, 1979
Frisco Kid, 1979
Apocalypse Now, 1979
The Empire Strikes Back, 1980
Raiders of the Lost Ark, 1981
Blade Runner, 1982
Return of the Jedi, 1983
Indiana Jones and the Temple of Doom, 1984
Witness, 1985
Mosquito Coast, 1986
Frantic, 1988
Working Girl, 1988
Indiana Jones and the Last Crusade, 1989
Presumed Innocent, 1990
Regarding Henry, 1991
Patriot Games, 1992
The Fugitive, 1993
Clear and Present Danger, 1994

Sabrina, 1995
The Devil's Own, 1997
Air Force One, 1997

HONORS AND AWARDS

Box Office Star of the Century (National Association of Theater Owners): 1994
Hasty Pudding Man of the Year Award (Hasty Pudding Theatricals, Harvard University): 1996

FURTHER READING

Books

Clinch, Minty. *Harrison Ford: A Biography*, 1987
Pfeiffer, Lee, and Michael Lewis. *The Films of Harrison Ford*, 1996
Thomson, David. *A Biographical Dictionary of Film*, 3rd ed., 1994
Who's Who in America, 1997

Periodicals

Cosmopolitan, June 1988, p.178
Current Biography Yearbook 1984
Esquire, Oct. 198, p.112
George, Aug. 1997, p.64
GQ (Gentleman's Quarterly), June 1994, p.160
Ladies' Home Journal, Jan. 1996, p.88
Mademoiselle, Feb. 1988, p.182
Movieline, July 1997, p.40
New York Times Biographical Service, July 1977, p.942
Newsweek, July 21, 1997, p.66
People, Aug. 4, 1997, p.90
Seventeen, July 1983, p.114
Us, Aug. 20, 1990, p.16; June 1997, p.77
Vanity Fair, July 1993, p.66
Vogue, Mar. 1997, p.442

ADDRESS

10279 Century Woods Drive
Los Angeles, CA 90067

Bryant Gumbel   1948-
Television Sportscaster and News Anchor
Co-Host of the NBC "Today" Show for 15 Years

BIRTH

Bryant Charles Gumbel was born in New Orleans, Louisiana, on September 29, 1948, the second child of Richard Dunbar Gumbel and Rhea Alice (LeCesne) Gumbel. Bryant was barely in grade school when the family moved to Chicago. His father, who was the son of a New Orleans gambler, worked his way through Georgetown University Law School. He went on to become a probate judge in Cook County under Chicago's famous mayor, Richard Daley. Bryant had one older brother, Greg, and two younger sisters, Rhonda and Renee.

YOUTH

The Hyde Park section of Chicago was a racially mixed, middle-class neighborhood where many African-American physicians and other professionals lived. The Gumbel children grew up in an atmosphere of achievement and support, relatively sheltered from the racial prejudice common in the United States at that time. "People in Hyde Park were very proud that they were black," he recalls.

When Bryant was a child, playing sports and having a good time were his main interests in life. His father introduced him and his brother to baseball as soon as they were old enough to catch. They would stand in front of a full-length mirror and practice their pitching, taking turns announcing plays from imaginary games. Bryant rarely missed a Cubs game at nearby Wrigley Field, and he could recite the name of every .300 hitter in the Cubs' history.

EDUCATION

Bryant attended St. Thomas the Apostle Grammar School in Hyde Park and served as an altar boy every Sunday at the local Catholic church. Both he and his brother graduated from De La Salle High School, a private Catholic school. But while Greg was handsome and popular, Bryant lacked self-confidence and hated high school. He didn't date much, didn't drink, and was in every way the opposite of his older brother. The only place he felt confident was on the playing field. "I was a real jock," Bryant recalls. Even though he grew up to be a gifted speaker, he never participated in his high school's speech club, theatrical productions, or debating team. "I was one of the kids who beat up the kids on the debating team," he says.

Bryant attended Bates College, a small, liberal arts college in Lewiston, Maine, where he was one of only three African-Americans in a student body of 900. He continued to play baseball and football there. "Women loved him," a former Bates classmate recalls, because he could "turn on the charm with his good manners and soft voice." Although Gumbel attended college during the late 1960s, a turbulent period when students across the country were demonstrating for civil rights and protesting the Vietnam War, he never became an activist. He majored in Russian history, let his hair grow long, and took a fairly casual attitude toward his studies. Even though his grade average slipped to a C, he acquired the self-confidence that would serve him so well later on in his career. Gumbel graduated from Bates College in 1970.

FIRST JOBS

Gumbel graduated from college during the Vietnam War, when many young men were being drafted to serve in the armed services. But a sports-related wrist injury prevented him from being drafted and sent overseas. Instead, he went to New York City and worked as a sales representative for Westvaco Corp., a company that made paper bags and folding cartons. He didn't like the job and wasn't very good at it, so he quit after six months. His family hoped that he would take up a career in law like his father, but Gumbel was convinced that he was destined to become a sports writer. He submitted an article about Harvard's first black athletic director to *Black Sports* magazine and was offered a job there. Nine months later, he became the magazine's editor.

CHOOSING A CAREER

It was while he was working at *Black Sports* that Bryant received a phone call from a family friend on April 10, 1972, informing him that his father had just collapsed in the courtroom with a heart attack and died. The loss was very sudden, and Bryant never really got over it. But a week after the funeral, his career began to take off. An acquaintance at KNBC-TV in Los Angeles suggested that he audition for the weekend sports anchor job. Although he was only 23, he was hired on the spot. Fearing that his inexperience would lead to mistakes on the air and earn him a nickname like "Stumble Gumbel," his new employer tried to persuade him to change his name. Refusing to do so, Bryant quickly earned a reputation for flawless sports reporting, with or without a script.

He stayed at KNBC-TV for eight years. In 1976, after only four years, he became the station's sports director — an unusually rapid climb for an African-American in television at that time. Some observers have conjectured that his rapid rise at KNBC was aided by affirmative action, the deliberate effort to hire, promote, and create opportunities for members of disadvantaged groups. Gumbel himself has admitted that this may be true. But it was soon obvious that it was talent — not skin color — that enabled him to succeed. Someone who worked with him at the time described him as a "television animal." Gumbel knew that he would do his best work in front of a TV camera.

CAREER HIGHLIGHTS

It soon became obvious that Gumbel had a flair for sports commentary as well as straight news. While still working in Los Angeles, he was invited to serve as co-host of a new NFL pre-game show in New York called "Grandstand" that combined live events, features, and sports news. So he started commuting to New York on weekends to anchor NFL football, major league baseball, and NCAA basketball for NBC Sports. It wasn't long before he was covering the Super Bowl, the World Series, and major golf tournaments.

In June 1980 Gumbel signed a three-year, $1.5 million contract with NBC that included doing three sports features a week on the "Today" show, television's oldest morning news program. First broadcast in 1952 with Dave Garroway as

Gumbel on "Today" set with co-host Katie Couric

its host, the "Today" show was America's favorite morning news program until 1975, when "Good Morning America" debuted on ABC. The two shows quickly became intense rivals, competing with each other for viewers and advertising dollars. In August 1976 Tom Brokaw became the "Today" show news anchor, and in October of that year he was joined by Jane Pauley.

Becoming a News Anchor

Gumbel joined the "Today" show as a sports commentator in 1980. In August 1981 he was asked to sit in for Pauley when she was absent, and he appeared so relaxed and confident on camera that he was later asked to substitute for Tom Brokaw. Soon, he began doing news reports as well as sports commentary. When Brokaw left in December 1981 to become an anchor for the "NBC Nightly News," there was little question whom the new co-host would be. Gumbel made his debut on January 4, 1982, with Pauley, news anchor Chris Wallace, and Willard Scott, the show's popular weatherman.

Bryant Gumbel was not the first African-American to anchor a network news show. ABC had hired Max Robinson in 1978, and Ed Bradley started on "60 Minutes" in 1981. But Gumbel was the first to host a network morning news program. NBC soon discovered, however, that his race didn't matter to

Americans. His warm, relaxed manner, radiant smile, and ability to speak off-the-cuff on almost any subject impressed people far more than the color of his skin. With the increasing competition from "Good Morning America" and the newly expanded "CBS Morning News," though, Gumbel had to build up his credibility as an interviewer. He started reading more newspapers and writing out his interview questions on index cards the night before. He soon proved that he could interview politicians, diplomats, and economists as skillfully as he handled sports figures. His colleagues marveled at his ability to put his subjects at ease and, at the same time, to get them to respond to tough, often personal, questions.

On the Road with "Today"

Eventually surpassing Pauley as the show's main host, Gumbel stayed at "Today" for 15 years, longer than any other host in the show's history. He was responsible for taking "Today" to Moscow for a week in 1984, where he interviewed everyone from the members of an ordinary Soviet family to a first deputy foreign minister. The Moscow broadcasts not only marked a turning point for the "Today" show—which pulled ahead of "Good Morning America" in the ratings—but also enhanced his reputation as a full-fledged journalist. The Overseas Press Club recognized his achievement by giving him the Edward R. Murrow Award, named after one of America's most famous news broadcasters.

The trip to Moscow was such a success that Gumbel pushed for more foreign broadcasts, eventually taking the show to Cuba and Vietnam. He even managed to arrange an audience with the Pope in Rome. But the trip that meant more to Gumbel than any other was the week that "Today" spent in Africa in 1992. Hoping to counter the image that most Americans had of Africa as a jungle filled with wild animals, Gumbel went to Zimbabwe. He did stories on economics and government, the tourist industry, and threats to African wildlife. Contrary to popular assumptions, however, the Zimbabwe broadcasts had little to do with Gumbel's sense of his African-American heritage. "I have hosted the program from North and South America, from Europe, from Asia, and from Australia," he said at the time. "There's only one continent [Antarctica] that we haven't been to." He did, however, take his then 13-year-old son with him.

In addition to his travel assignments for "Today," Gumbel also covered the 1988 Winter Olympics in Seoul, South Korea.

Behind the Scenes

Although Gumbel and Pauley generally worked well together, the producers of the "Today" show were constantly on the lookout for ways to improve the show's ratings. In 1989 they replaced Jane Pauley with a younger, more glamorous female co-host named Deborah Norville. The decision prompted outrage from devoted viewers, who thought the network's move was a sexist attempt to boost ratings by putting a younger woman's face on the screen. Instead, the show's ratings plummeted. When Norville went on maternity leave in 1991, the producers did not invite her back, instead replacing her with Katie Couric from NBC's Washington bureau. Couric was immediately popular with viewers, who saw her cheerful, down-to-earth personality as the perfect complement to what has been described as Gumbel's intense, aggressive, "attack-dog" approach to interviewing.

The "Today" show encountered other setbacks as well. One of the most serious was the 1989 memo that Gumbel sent to the show's producers. He had been invited by the producers to critique the program (but not to discuss Jane Pauley), with the assurance that his response would be kept strictly confidential. But no one was prepared for how Gumbel would lash out at his fellow "Today" staffers. Willard Scott, the folksy weatherman who had been with the show for years, bore the brunt of Gumbel's criticism. "Each and every day [Scott] holds the show hostage to his assortment of whims, wishes, birthdays, and bad taste," Gumbel wrote. "This guy is killing us and no one's even trying to rein him in." He was referring to Scott's hundredth-birthday wishes to people across the country, which Gumbel found too sentimental. Somehow the memo was leaked to the press, and soon it was making headlines across the country. It caused a great deal of embarrassment for Scott, Gumbel, and the rest of the cast.

Gumbel also locked horns with Andrew Lack, president of the NBC News division. Lack refused to let him participate in the network's planned interview of O. J. Simpson following the criminal trial verdict because Simpson and Gumbel had often played golf together. Gumbel was "out sick" for an entire week following the network's decision to let Tom Brokaw and Katie Couric handle the interview. At the last minute, though, Simpson ended up canceling the interview.

Gumbel has faced other controversies as well. He has been criticized by some members of his own race for not being "black" enough in his speech, appearance, and attitudes. Indeed, white television viewers are rarely conscious of the fact that he is African-American—race is simply not an issue in many white viewers' opinions of him. Gumbel has also come under criticism by the press for being too self-confident and egocentric, and for not showing enough respect to women on and off the set of the "Today" show. In fact, Jane Pauley described his attitude toward women as "Neanderthal." Gumbel says that he is a "man's man" who loves Cuban cigars, all male clubs, and Arnold Schwarzenegger movies. But his behavior off the set of the "Today" show has been described as insensitive and, at times, downright childish. For example,

President Clinton and Gumbel

he loved to scare female staffers by waving a dead mouse in their faces and to show his affection by massaging their shoulders.

Despite such criticisms, no one disputes the fact that Gumbel possesses a near-perfect memory for facts and figures about sports and world events, or that he radiates self-confidence and self-control. He is known for being a perfectionist who sets extremely high standards for himself and who has little patience for those who don't do the same.

Farewell Appearance

Gumbel decided it was time to leave "Today" in 1996, appearing on the show for the last time on January 3, 1997. It had just completed its 52nd consecutive week as the highest rated network morning news program, and Gumbel felt that it was better to leave while the show was on top. "I've had the pleasure of going around the world, of meeting everyone I could ever want to meet," he said in one interview, referring to the fact that he had conducted more than 12,000 interviews, with everyone from former President Richard Nixon to Miss Piggy. "Fifteen years is a long time in one place, and the world's too exciting to enjoy from just one vantage point."

Matt Lauer, a "Today" contributor since 1993 and one of Gumbel's close friends, took over as co-host with Katie Couric.

FUTURE PLANS

On March 13, 1997, Gumbel announced that he would be going to the CBS network. He signed a five-year deal with the network for a reported $5 to $7 million per year. In his new job, Gumbel will be hosting his own weekly prime time news magazine show. The show is slated to appear in September 1997. In addition, he will produce three prime-time specials for the network each year and also develop shows for syndication.

The weekly prime time news magazine show will emphasize interviews and live TV segments, two of his acknowledged strengths. Gumbel stated that part of his package with CBS included a new internship program to help minorities in TV careers. He also said that he would continue his "Real Sports" program, which he produces for HBO.

Gumbel would also like to spend more time organizing his annual charity golf tournament, "The Bryant Gumbel Walt Disney World Celebrity Golf Tournament," which raised more than $600,000 for the United Negro College Fund last year.

MARRIAGE AND FAMILY

Bryant Gumbel met June Baranco, a student at Louisiana State University who would later become a Delta flight attendant, while she was in Chicago visiting a friend in 1968. They were married on December 1, 1973, and now have two children: Bradley, 17, and Jillian, 13. The Gumbels have an apartment in New York City and a 17-room Victorian house in Westchester, just an hour outside the city. June, who is an artist, maintains a studio there. The house also has a private screening room where the family watches movies.

Bryant's older brother Greg is also a successful TV sportscaster. He covered the 1992 Winter Olympics in Albertville, France, the 1994 Winter Games in

Lillehammer, Norway, and the 1996 Summer Games in Atlanta. He lives in nearby Connecticut with his wife and daughter.

MAJOR INFLUENCES

Gumbel's father, Richard, had an enormous impact on his son's life. Richard Gumbel worked his way through Xavier University in New Orleans while holding down a full-time job to support his young family. Then he put himself through Georgetown Law School, graduating second in his class. One of Bryant's favorite stories about his father is that when he was serving in the Philippines during World War II, he continued marching even though he was very ill. A medic finally pulled him aside, sat him down on a nearby rock, and took out his tonsils. A few minutes later, he was back on his feet.

His father's opinion always mattered a great deal to Bryant. In fact, it was his father's approval of June Baranco that gave Gumbel the courage to marry her. Richard Gumbel's sudden death when Bryant was only 23 merely served to increase his respect for the man who had first introduced him to sports and who had in many ways prepared him for the career path he would eventually follow. "He was always there for me, stressing how important was my ability to write, to read, to listen, to speak," Gumbel recalls. Friends and business associates have often attributed Gumbel's perfectionism to his father's high standards.

FAVORITE BOOKS

Gumbel says that *The Autobiography of Malcolm X* influenced him more than any other book he has ever read. Malcolm X preached self-esteem and self-responsibility. He conveyed the message that it was important to stand up for who you are, without apologies. These were the same lessons that Gumbel's father tried to teach him as he was growing up.

HOBBIES AND OTHER INTERESTS

Bryant Gumbel is a passionate golfer; he even listens to golf matches on the radio. Playing golf with close friends has always been his favorite escape from the pressures of his career. One of the things he likes best about it is that he doesn't have to talk while he's playing. "I consider it to be like no other sport," he says, "except maybe chess. Who talks during chess?" Gumbel's golf partners say that he is every bit as intense and competitive on the golf course as he is in the television studio.

A lesser known fact is that Gumbel also enjoys writing and has at least started a dozen books, mostly thrillers and historical fiction. When he left the "Today" show, he said that he would love to be a successful novelist some day.

HONORS AND AWARDS

Emmy Award: 1976, 1977

Golden Mike Award (Los Angeles Press Club): 1978, 1979

Edward R. Murrow Award (Overseas Press Club): 1984, for outstanding foreign affairs reporting from Moscow

Best Morning Television News Interviewer (*Washington Journalism Review*): 1986

Best National Morning TV Anchor Team (*Washington Journalism Review*): 1990, with Jane Pauley

FURTHER READING

Periodicals

American Visions, Oct./Nov. 1992, p.22

Black Enterprise, Apr. 1992, p.32

Current Biography Yearbook 1986

Detroit Free Press, Dec. 27, 1996, p.F1

Los Angeles Times, Mar. 14, 1997, p.F1

New York, Aug. 4, 1986, p.30

New York Times, Dec. 18, 1996, p.C15

New York Times Magazine, June 10, 1990, p.26

Newsday, Jan. 19, 1997, p.C8

Sports Illustrated, Sep. 26, 1988, p.72

TV Guide, June 17, 1995, p.26

USA Today, Jan. 2, 1997, p.A1

Washington Post, Mar. 14, 1997, p.G4

ADDRESS

CBS Inc.
51 West 52nd Street
New York, NY 10019

John Johnson   1918-
American Magazine Publisher and Entrepreneur
Founder, Chairman, and CEO of Johnson Publishing
Company
Creator of the Successful Magazines *Ebony, Jet,*
and *EM*

BIRTH

John Harold Johnson, as the magazine publisher is known
today, was born on January 19, 1918, in Arkansas City,
Arkansas. His given name was Johnny Johnson, which he
changed to its current form while in high school after a teacher
suggested that he might want a more formal name as an adult.

His mother was Gertrude (Jenkins) Johnson (later Gertrude Williams), who had a daughter, Beulah, young Johnny's stepsister, from an earlier marriage. His father was Leroy Johnson, a sawmill worker who died in an industrial accident when Johnny was about eight.

YOUTH

In his early years, Johnson and his family lived in a shack with a tin roof in a small town in rural Arkansas. They were cold in winter and hot in summer, and there was no indoor plumbing. In many ways, it was a tough life. The rural South in the early 20th century was openly hostile to African-Americans. Jim Crow laws mandated completely segregated facilities for whites and blacks. Theaters, schools, railroad stations, restaurants, drinking fountains—all were segregated by race, and the facilities for blacks were consistently second rate. And black people themselves were continually treated as inferior to whites, and they were expected to act subservient.

Johnson's parents worked very hard to provide for the family. After his father's death, his mother married James Williams, a bakery delivery man who was a good father to his stepson. Gertrude Williams worked as a domestic, cleaning and cooking in white people's homes. She often brought used clothes and left-over food home for her family. Even young Johnny helped out, taking odd jobs from an early age. "I can't say I had a very happy childhood," Johnson recalls. "But it wasn't an unhappy childhood. . . . I had no contact with the world outside, and when you have nothing to compare with you aren't aware that you should be unhappy."

In fact, there is a lot of good that he remembers from his upbringing. Race relations were certainly strained and African-Americans were treated very poorly. But there was rarely outright violence against blacks as there was across the river in Mississippi and in other parts of the South, where beatings and even lynchings were more common. Arkansas City had a strong black community, and people looked out for one another. All the adults watched over all the kids, and his mother was sure to get a report—and he was sure to get a whipping—if he was caught misbehaving anywhere in town.

Johnson's mother was a powerful force in his young life. Although Gertrude Williams had little schooling, "She was one of the most educated people I've ever known," he recalls. "She was aware of the world. She wanted to see black people succeed. She was active in the church. She was a leader. Whatever group she ended up joining, she always became president. She was looked up to by people in the community. . . . There was something about her that made her believe in herself and made her have great faith in education and, I guess, great faith in me."

EDUCATION

Johnson attended the local segregated elementary school. The Arkansas City Colored School was run by C.S. Johnson, a graduate of what is today Morehouse College, one of the country's best black schools. It was an excellent grade school with high standards for the children's behavior and academic achievement. Johnny's older stepsister Beulah had finished school there, and she had gone on to a teaching job in a nearby town. But the school only ran through eighth grade, and there was no high school for African-Americans in Arkansas City. Many local people would send their children to board with black families in other towns so the kids could finish school, but Gertrude Williams couldn't afford that for her son. Yet she was convinced that education was essential to future success and determined that he would continue his schooling.

She decided to start saving up for the family to move to Chicago, Illinois. She had a close friend who had moved there and who had offered the family a place to stay until they got on their feet. His mother took on extra jobs, doing cooking and cleaning and laundry, to save up enough money for the train fare north. But even with young Johnny's help, they hadn't saved up enough money by the time he finished eighth grade. So his mother made him repeat the grade, because she didn't want him to hang around with nothing to do, or to get used to working in menial jobs for little pay. By the end of that year, she had saved up enough for the move. Her husband was skeptical about her plan, afraid that they wouldn't find work up north. He refused to go. Gertrude Williams loved him, but she was determined that her son would get an education. She decided to go ahead without her husband.

Attending High School in Chicago

In 1933, Johnson and his mother joined a wave of millions of blacks who migrated to northern cities in search of a better life. Johnson was 15 when they arrived in Chicago. Things started out well for them. Gertrude got a decent-paying job as a housekeeper and Johnny started school. Soon they were joined by Johnny's stepfather, James Williams. But shortly afterward, things fell apart. Gertrude lost her job, and James couldn't find work. It was the depths of the Great Depression, and millions of Americans, white and black, were out of work. For two years, the family was "on relief," receiving welfare from the federal government. But at that time, families didn't receive a check in the mail. Instead, a government truck would drive through the neighborhood and deliver food to all the families on relief. It was a source of great embarrassment and shame to Johnson's proud family. After two years on relief, though, Johnson's stepfather got a job through the Works Project Administration (WPA), a government agency that created public service jobs during the Depression. Johnny Johnson also got a job through a similar agency for youth, and the family was back in business.

Johnson enrolled at Wendell Phillips High School; later, after a fire, he and the other kids were transferred to Jean Baptiste Pointe du Sable High School. At first, things at school were tough for the new kid with the home-made clothes and thick southern accent. But the kids' teasing only made him more determined to succeed. After school he would read self-help books about positive thinking, like Dale Carnegie's *How to Win Friends and Influence People,* and he would stand in front of the mirror and practice public speaking. It worked. During his junior year, when it was time for class elections, he was the only student who had the courage and ability to get up and speak in front of the whole class. He was elected president of his class. As a senior the following year, he was also president of his class, as well as an honors student, president of the student council, business manager of the yearbook, and editor of the school newspaper. He even gave the commencement speech at his high school graduation in June 1936.

Starting College and a Career

At about that time, Johnson had what proved to be a pivotal experience. He attended a luncheon given by the Urban League in honor of outstanding black honors graduates from all of Chicago. The speaker at that luncheon was Harry Pace, a respected leader in the black community. Pace was the president of the Supreme Liberty Life Insurance Company, then the largest black-owned business in Chicago. Pace asked Johnson what he planned to do after high school. Johnson explained that he had received a partial scholarship to study at the University of Chicago. But the scholarship wasn't enough to cover the cost of school, he said, and so he wouldn't be able to attend. Pace ended up giving Johnson a part-time job as an office boy so he could go to college. He attended the University of Chicago from 1936 to 1938, when he became an assistant to Pace. He switched to night classes at Northwestern University then, from 1938 to 1940, when he dropped out of school to devote himself to work.

CHOOSING A CAREER

It was during his years at Supreme Liberty Life Insurance that Johnson decided on a career in publishing. He has said that his experiences at Supreme Life were pivotal in shaping his career, in part because of the excellent role models he met there. "It was a turning point because I had an opportunity there to observe black people *running* a business. For the first time I believed that success was possible for *me* in business. Up to that point, I had seen lawyers, ministers, and doctors, but I had never seen black businessmen. And here I was working for a company, which was the largest black business in the North at that time, and I saw black men making big decisions. I saw them moving around with dignity and security, and it inspired me. It made me know that my career could be in business, and that success was possible."

Johnson started out as a lowly office boy and worked his way up through the ranks. He began working on the company magazine, eventually becoming the editor. As assistant to Pace, he was asked to compile a digest of articles related to black life—at that time, there was limited coverage of the black community in the white press. Based on this work, Johnson soon hit on the idea of creating a new monthly magazine, like *Reader's Digest*, that would condense and reprint articles about black life, offering a broad picture of the state of the black community around the country.

It was a great idea, but there were many obstacles to overcome. The first was financing. At that time, most banks wouldn't loan money to African-Americans. So Johnson took out a $500 loan using his mother's new furniture as collateral, meaning that if he was unable to pay back the loan they could come take her furniture as repayment. Fortunately, that never happened. With the $500, Johnson mailed letters to 20,000 policy holders at Supreme Life, offering them a yearly subscription to the new magazine for just $2. About 3,000 readers were interested enough to send in the money, and by November 1942 Johnson was able to print the first issue of *Negro Digest*.

The next obstacle was distribution. He had a good start on a subscriber list, but he would need many more buyers. And in order to get his publication on the newsstands, where it would be available to the public, he would have to convince the white magazine distributors that there was a market for a black-oriented magazine. Johnson hit on a creative solution to his problem. He recruited many of his friends from Supreme Life to go to different newsstands around Chicago and ask for the magazine. Soon, the newsstand owners were clamoring for this new magazine that everyone wanted to read. Then, he sent his friends out to buy up copies of the magazine so the newsstand owners would think that it was wildly popular. His trick worked. The newsstand owners ordered even more copies and started advertising them to their patrons. Soon the magazine was selling in other cities as well. Within eight months, *Negro Digest* had a circulation of 50,000. When Johnson succeeded in persuading Eleanor Roosevelt, then the nation's First Lady, to write an article for the popular feature "If I Were a Negro," the circulation doubled overnight. Johnson Publishing Company was on its way.

CAREER HIGHLIGHTS

John Johnson has successfully climbed from a tin-roofed shack in Arkansas and welfare in Chicago to become the founder and chief executive officer (CEO) of a multi-media corporation. He had to overcome both poverty and racism along the way. As his approach to *Negro Digest* suggests, his story is one of ambition, hard work, dedication, vision, resourcefulness, and creative problem solving.

John Johnson with his daughter Linda Johnson Rice, now president and chief operating officer of Johnson Publishing Company

Ebony

With the success of his first venture, *Negro Digest* (later renamed *Black World*), Johnson was soon ready for something new. He wanted to publish a general interest monthly magazine about blacks that would be similar to *Life*, a glossy magazine filled with photographs. Johnson's wife, Eunice, came up with the perfect name for the new magazine: "Ebony," a fine, dark, African wood known for its lustrous and beautiful appearance. *Ebony* would include stories and photos, with regular features on blacks in politics, sports, and entertainment, as well as black society events. Above all, it would highlight the achievements of successful African-Americans at a time when such stories were routinely ignored in the white mainstream press. In the first issue, in November 1945, Johnson's first editorial offered the magazine's mission statement: "*Ebony* will try to mirror the happier side of Negro life — the positive everyday achievements from Harlem to Hollywood. But when we talk about race as the No. 1 problem of America, we'll talk turkey."

Ebony was an immediate success, selling out its first print run of 25,000 copies in a matter of hours and continuing to do well in succeeding months. But there was one ongoing problem. Magazine publishing is an expensive business. Most magazines can not support themselves with subscriber and newsstand income alone, which usually covers only about 30% of the expenses; they need advertising to survive. In the mid-1940s, there was a color barrier in advertising. Most American businesses were run by whites, and they did not see any need to advertise in a publication for blacks. They simply didn't view black readers as important consumers who would be likely to purchase their products if enticed by ads designed just for them.

With a lot of ingenuity and personal attention, Johnson soon proved this view wrong. He knew many blacks owned Zenith radios, so he decided that Zenith should advertise in *Ebony*. He got an appointment with the company president, Eugene McDonald, but first Johnson did his homework. He learned that McDonald had taken part in an expedition to the North Pole with Matthew Henson, a black explorer. Johnson arrived at his meeting with McDonald with an *Ebony* article on Henson as well as a signed copy of the black explorer's autobiography. This personal contact seemed to make all the difference, because by the end of the meeting McDonald had decided that Zenith would advertise in *Ebony*, and he offered to urge his business contacts at other large companies to do the same. With Johnson's creative approach, *Ebony* became the first magazine to break that color barrier and to attract advertising from white-owned businesses.

Confronting Racism

But it wasn't always that easy. There was a constant struggle to overcome the racism that was so pervasive at the time. The magazine's black salespeople couldn't invite their clients out to a nice club for a meal, the way other salespeople would; with segregation still in existence, the *Ebony* staff wouldn't even be allowed in the club. So they created a fine dining room at the company headquarters and brought their clients there. They had similar problems when they were traveling on business. Johnson recalls that because he was black he couldn't rent a room in a hotel, so he hired a light-skinned man to travel with him. This man would go up to the hotel desk and rent a suite of rooms, and then the group from *Ebony* would pose as hotel employees and ride the freight elevator up to their floor. Johnson also tells a story about one salesman who traveled from Chicago to Detroit every week for over ten years before he persuaded one of the big auto companies to advertise in *Ebony*.

Johnson has been publishing *Ebony* magazine for over 50 years, since 1945. In 1951, six years after he launched *Ebony*, he started *Jet* magazine, a pocket-sized weekly news magazine that covers current issues for blacks. Throughout that time, both magazines have reflected the monumental changes that have taken place in the lives of African-Americans and in American society. In the earliest days, *Ebony* and *Jet* were a record of black achievement and an inspiration to the readers, although some accused them of emphasizing glamour rather than substantive issues. Johnson himself described it this way: "We're not really a celebrity book. When I was a kid my mom would give me castor oil in orange juice so I'd swallow it. We may put celebrities on our cover, but it's orange juice; when readers get inside, there's still plenty of castor oil." Over time, though, they began to take a more aggressive editorial approach, which was particularly true of their approach to the Civil Rights Movement. They covered the murder of Emmett Till, the Montgomery bus boycott, the career of Martin Luther King, Jr., the 1963 March on Washington, and the assassinations of King and Malcolm X. Despite earlier criticism of the magazines' focus, all praised this compelling coverage of the Civil Rights Movement and the constant encouragement of black pride.

Other Business Ventures

In addition to *Ebony* and *Jet*, Johnson has gone on to other business ventures. The company later started several new magazines, although only one, *EM* (*Ebony Man*), first launched in 1985, has become a success. But the company has diversified beyond magazine publishing over the years. Johnson Publishing company owns three radio stations and a small book publishing company. Back in 1958 they started the *Ebony* Fashion Fair, the world's largest traveling fashion show, which raises money for charity. Out of that grew Fashion Fair cosmetics, which they created in 1973 to address the black fashion models' need for cosmetics that matched their skin tones. And overall, the company has been a tremendous financial success. In 1995, Johnson Publishing Co. was listed as the second largest black-owned company in the country, with over $316 million in sales that year.

All this success has not come without a price, though. Johnson is known as a very tough boss—in fact, he was selected as one of the top 10 toughest bosses in America by *Fortune* magazine. Workers often use the word "plantation" to describe the environment at company headquarters in Chicago. Johnson reputedly has an autocratic and even hostile management style. "He has wild temper tantrums. He threatens to fire his top people every other week," one former staffer said. Another employee said, "It's like a crescendo with Johnson. First he puts you down with words. Then when you're down, he flattens you out. Then he walks on your face." Johnson responds to such criticism as follows: "Yes," he says, "I am tough. I make no apologies. People from all over the world have come here to see . . . the miracle of Johnson Publishing. It is something of a shrine. In the days of Alexander the Great and Napoleon . . . I am trying to be that kind of leader, riding ahead of the other horses. I am considered a legend in my time."

In recent years, Johnson's daughter, Linda Johnson Rice, has become more involved in the family business. She joined the company after completing college and business school. After several years of training with her father, she is now president and chief operating officer of the company. Yet at age

79 John Johnson has no plans to retire, saying that he will continue to work as long as he is able. "I've been to the White House under eight presidents, can go anywhere in the world whenever I want, and I don't have to worry about checks bouncing," he said. "I've been blessed with a company where people keep writing saying they're proud of what we're doing and we've been No. 1 for 50 years. I think that's a pretty good run. I'm satisfied. I can't think of anything I want to still do."

MARRIAGE AND FAMILY

In 1940, when Johnson was still a young man working at Supreme Liberty Life Insurance Company, he attended a dance where he met Eunice Walker, his future wife. Then a student at Talladega College in Alabama, Walker was in Chicago at the time on vacation. John and Eunice had each arrived at the dance with a date, but once they were introduced they spent all their time with each other. Soon afterward, though, Eunice had to return to school in Alabama.

Fortunately, after Eunice graduated from college, she chose Loyola University in Chicago for her master's degree in social work. She and John now had time to spend together, and their feelings for one another grew. They were married on June 21, 1941, in Selma, Alabama, and then returned to Chicago to make their home. They have been married for over 50 years.

In the mid-1960s, John and Eunice adopted two children: a son, John Harold Jr., and a daughter, Linda. When John Jr. was only two, he became ill with sickle-cell anemia. This is a hereditary and often fatal blood disease that affects people of African descent. Many of its victims die in their teen years. John Jr. suffered through alternating periods of illness and health, and he died in 1981, when he was only 25 years old. Though his death was not unexpected, it was a crushing blow for the whole family, one that Johnson was unable to discuss for the next ten years.

HOBBIES AND OTHER INTERESTS

Johnson doesn't have many hobbies. He enjoys reading autobiographies of successful people and watching inspirational movies, but that's about all. He has never taken up any recreational pursuits like golf or tennis. Johnson once made clear the reason for his lack of hobbies. "When I was young enough to develop hobbies, I never really had the time. I've always been interested in getting ahead, in watching for new opportunities, in reading books on how to improve myself, books on how to be a public speaker and on how not to be afraid of the things that I'm afraid of. I never learned to play golf, for example, because at the time I would have learned to play golf, Black people were not permitted to play on courses in major cities."

Although the family owns a vacation home in Palm Springs, Johnson finds it difficult to relax there. According to his wife, Eunice Johnson, "I suggested [buying the Palm Springs home] because I thought he might want to take a vacation. And he said, 'Vacation? Now why do you want to start a fight?'" And Johnson adds, "People always ask me what is the most exciting thing I do in Palm Springs. I make my calls to my office in Chicago." In fact, he is well known for his devotion to his work. He is often the first person to arrive at the office, he works Saturdays and Sundays too, and he often takes work home to read at night. But as he explains here, Johnson works so hard and avoids long vacation because that's what he truly likes to do. "Someone asked me once why I didn't take long vacations, and I asked them, 'What do you do when you're on vacation?' And they said 'Anything you want to do.' And I said, 'I do that every day.'"

In addition to the demands of running Johnson Publishing, he also contributes time and money to many charities, particularly those benefitting African-Americans. He also serves as a director on the boards of many charitable groups and corporations.

WRITINGS

Succeeding against the Odds: The Inspiring Autobiography of One of America's Wealthiest Entrepreneurs, 1989 (with Lerone Bennett, Jr.)

HONORS AND AWARDS

Ten Outstanding Young Men (U.S. Jaycees): 1951
Spingarn Medal (NAACP): 1966
Horatio Alger Award: 1966
John Russwurm Award (National Newspaper Publishers Association): 1966
Henry Johnson Fisher Award (Magazine Publishers Association): 1972
Columbia Journalism Award (Columbia University): 1974
The Most Outstanding Black Publisher in History (National Newspaper Publishers Association): 1977
United Negro College Fund Award: 1983
Robie Award (Jackie Robinson Foundation): 1985
Distinguished Contribution to Journalism Award (National Press Foundation): 1986
Inducted into Black Press Hall of Fame: 1987
Entrepreneur of the Decade (*Black Enterprise* magazine): 1987
Lifetime Achievement Award (National Association of Black Journalists): 1987
Salute to Greatness Award (Martin Luther King Center for Nonviolent Social Change): 1988

Harold H. Hines Benefactors' Award (United Negro College Fund): 1988
Equal Opportunity Award (National Urban League): 1988
EXCEL Award (International Association of Business Communicators): 1989
Founders Award (National Council of Christians and Jews): 1989
Distinguished Service Award (Harvard University Graduate School of Business Administration): 1991
Africa's Future Award (UNICEF): 1992
Booker T. Washington Speaker's Award (Booker T. Washington Business Association): 1992
Heritage Award (Executive Leadership Council): 1992
Dow Jones Entrepreneurial Excellence Award (Dow Jones and the *Wall Street Journal*): 1993
Presidential Medal of Freedom: 1996

FURTHER READING

Books

Contemporary Authors, Vol. 135
Encyclopedia Britannica, 1995
Falkof, Lucille. *John H. Johnson: The Man from "Ebony,"* 1992 (juvenile)
Greenberg, Keith. *John Johnson: Media Magnate,* 1993 (juvenile)
Hawkins, Walter L. *African-American Biographies: Profiles of 558 Current Men and Women,* 1992
Johnson, John H., and Lerone Bennett, Jr. *Succeeding against the Odds: The Inspiring Autobiography of One of America's Wealthiest Entrepreneurs,* 1989
Kranz, Rachel C. *Biographical Dictionary of Black Americans,* 1992
Pile, Robert B. *Top Entrepreneurs and Their Businesses,* 1993
Sobel, Robert, and David B. Sicilia. *The Entrepreneurs: An American Adventure,* 1986
Who's Who in America, 1996
World Book Encyclopedia, 1996

Periodicals

Black Enterprise, June 1987, p.150
Chicago, Oct. 1992, p.57
Chicago Tribune Sunday Magazine, Mar. 19, 1995, p.18
Current Biography 1968
Ebony, Nov. 1985, p.44; Nov. 1992 (Special Anniversary Issue: 50 Years of Johnson Publishing Company)
Forbes, Dec. 20, 1982, p.104

Fortune, Aug. 6, 1984, p.18
Time, Dec. 9, 1985, p.68

ADDRESS

Johnson Publishing Company, Inc.
820 S. Michigan Avenue
Chicago, IL 60605

Michael Johnson   1967-

American Track Star
Winner of Two Gold Medals at the 1996 Olympics;
World-Record Holder in the 200- and 400-Meter
Sprints

BIRTH

Michael Johnson was born on September 13, 1967, in Dallas,
Texas. He was the youngest child of Paul Johnson, a truck driver, and Ruby Johnson, an elementary schoolteacher. He had
one brother and three sisters.

YOUTH

Johnson grew up in the Oak Cliff section of Dallas, a quiet neighborhood of middle-class homes. Both of his parents stressed values that would be important to him for his whole life. From his mother he learned the importance of education, and from his father he learned to be prepared and work hard.

Though Johnson and all of his siblings enjoyed sports, education always came first. Their mother would tutor them in the summer, telling them, "You can go out and play and go swimming in the afternoon, but the mornings are mine." Thanks to his mother's efforts, Johnson always excelled in school. He was often placed in classes for gifted children during elementary school and junior high. Ruby Johnson would have it no other way: "I never entertained the thought that my children wouldn't do as well as they could," she said. "It was expected of them."

Their father felt the same way. After growing up as an only child on a Texas farm, Paul Johnson always had a strong work ethic, and he passed that trait on to his children. "I didn't want them driving a truck like me," he once said. Young Michael would listen closely while his father read stories out of the newspaper, stories about people making mistakes or failing in business because they had not been prepared. From an early age, planning, neatness, and organization were very important to him. He shared a room with his brother, Paul Jr., and always kept his half of the room spotless. He would even clean up the cosmetics and brushes that his sisters left in the bathroom, until they finally got the message and began to clean them up themselves.

Johnson began running when he was 11 years old, first in summer track meets and then for his junior high school team. He was always the fastest child in his neighborhood, but running was important for only one reason — to make it easier for him to get a good education. "Track didn't matter one way or the other with us," his parents explained. "Education was everything. He just happened to run well, according to time." Johnson felt the same way about his athletic abilities. "I loved track," he stated, "but at the time it was a way to get to a better college. I wasn't as concerned with track as I was with education."

Johnson also played football in junior high, but he gave up the sport when he realized that it was not for him. "I'm not a person who likes someone screaming and hollering at me. The football environment is too much aggression," he recalled. "You have to have some aggression on the track, but it's not the same." As running became Johnson's only sport, his efforts on the track and in the classroom were rewarded. His combination of strong academics and athletic ability helped him gain entrance to Skyline High School, a career magnet school that had a reputation as the best in Dallas. It was at Skyline that his abilities really began to shine through.

EDUCATION

Johnson traveled 15 miles each way to attend Skyline, where he studied architecture. He had been interested in architecture since childhood, and hoped to one day become an architect. During his freshman year at Skyline, he concentrated solely on academics and did not participate on the track team. Though he joined the team his sophomore year, he concentrated on the long-jump event rather than on sprinting. Finally, in his junior year, Johnson returned to his first love: running the 200-meter sprint.

At first, Skyline track coach Joel Ezar did not think that Johnson was anything special. "He didn't look like an athlete—he looked like an Oxford scholar," says Ezar. For school each day, Johnson wore black horn-rimmed glasses, crisply pressed clothes, and a tie, which gave him a very studious appearance. Ezar even remembered one race in which Johnson "caught a crosswind and his glasses blew off. It looked as if he might stop to pick them up." Looks were deceiving, however. Johnson had very high expectations for himself and pushed to become the best. "I always expected I should be the best," he admitted. "On my high school team, I wasn't at the beginning. I felt like: 'I'm not working hard enough. I should be the best.' Not because I wanted to be. I felt that was the way it was supposed to be."

Only the fact that Johnson attended school in one of the best track-and-field areas in the United States kept him from becoming the best in the 200 meters. As a junior, he finished third in his district. The winner of the district that year was Roy Martin, who still holds the national schoolboy record of 20.13 seconds. As a senior, Johnson won his district and then finished second in the state finals, losing to Derek Florence, who went on to win the world junior championships. With such great competition, even a second-place finish was enough to attract the attention of college coaches. Upon graduation from Skyline in 1985, Johnson earned an athletic scholarship to attend Baylor University in Waco, Texas.

At Baylor, Coach Clyde Hart recruited Johnson to become a member of the school's powerful 4 x 400-meter relay team. "I'd be lying if I said I thought Michael was going to be a world-class sprinter. I don't think anybody did," Hart admitted. However, Johnson had a growth spurt that brought him to his present size of six feet, one inch, and he also began training year-round, which he had never done before. The results were immediate and impressive. In his first 200-meter outdoor meet, Johnson clocked a time of 20.69 seconds. In his second, he improved to 20.49 and finished second to Floyd Heard, who was then ranked number one in the world. Additionally, Johnson ran in his first 400-meter race and finished with a more-than-respectable time of 46.29 seconds. "You're supposed to improve [on the college level], but I think I improved more than my coach or I had anticipated," Johnson recalled.

It was at Baylor that Johnson first gained notice for his unusual running style. Most sprinters try to take as long a stride as they can to reduce the total number of steps they take, but not Johnson. Instead, he runs almost straight up, with his torso and head held very erect and his elbows tight to his body. Instead of raising his knees up high on every step, Johnson keeps his knees low, which causes his strides to be three to six inches shorter than those of his competitors. At full speed, it sometimes seems as if Johnson's feet don't even leave the track. What he lacks in stride length, however, he makes up for in repetition—his smaller steps mean that he takes much faster steps that seem to propel him down the track. In fact, his running style has been compared to that of Olympic legend Jesse Owens.

Tommie Smith, the 1968 Olympic champion in the 200 meters, marveled at Johnson's style. "I applaud Michael's every stride, but with his technique, I don't see how it's possible to run that fast," Smith stated. "He looks like he's drafting tires behind him, hooked to his neck. But he has the tenacity to train, to create a threshold of pain and like it."

In college, Johnson concentrated almost exclusively on the 200 meters until his senior year. Only a series of ill-timed injuries kept him from becoming a force on the international track scene. Each year something seemed to go wrong. During his freshman year, he pulled a hamstring muscle and missed the National Collegiate Athletic Association (NCAA) finals. In his sophomore year, he was leading in the finals of the 200 meters at the NCAA championship when he broke his fibula, an injury which also took him out of the running for the 1988 Olympics in Seoul, South Korea. The disasters continued in his junior year, when he strained a hamstring at the Southwestern Conference finals and again missed the NCAA meet. "Michael got the label of being injury-prone, which he really isn't," Coach Hart noted. "It was just the dramatic timing of those two injuries."

To help avoid injuries and to break up the monotony of training only for the 200, Johnson also began training seriously for the 400-meter race his senior season at Baylor. The dual training surprised many track fans, since the 200 and 400 are considered very different races with very different training requirements—the 200 is an all-out sprint, while the 400 requires strength and strategy. Johnson was surprised by the attention his choice gained. "People are really into that 200-400 thing," he said at the time. "I think there's always been a stereotype: If you ran the 200, you also ran the 100. If you ran the 400, that was all you did."

His decision to run both races proved to be a smart one. Running the 200-meters in 1990, Johnson won 14 of his 15 races (losing only to Leroy Burrell in the Southwest Conference championships) and finished undefeated in the 400 meters. He became the first man to finish a season ranked number one in the world in both the 200 and the 400. He was also named the Male Athlete of the Year by *Track and Field News,* and he became the only man to appear among the top 10 all-time performers in both events. As Johnson himself put it, "I was the hottest thing in the track world." To cap off the great year, Johnson closed out his collegiate career by graduating from Baylor in December 1990 with a degree in marketing.

CAREER HIGHLIGHTS

After leaving Baylor, Johnson turned professional and began competing in track events for money and other rewards. In 1991, he picked up right where he left off at the end of 1990, finishing the year undefeated in the 400 meters and winning his first world championship in the 200 meters in Tokyo, Japan, with a time of 20.01 seconds. At the International Amateur Athletic Federation meet later that year, he turned in the fastest 200 time of the year by any runner, finishing in 19.88 seconds. He again ended the year ranked first in the world in both the 200 and the 400.

Unfortunately, 1992 proved to be one of the most disappointing years of Johnson's life. Early that year, he and Coach Hart had decided to drop the 400 meters and concentrate only on the 200 to prepare for the Barcelona Olympic Games. The 200 was Johnson's best event, and both he and Hart wanted to make sure that he had the best shot possible to win the Olympic gold medal. Two weeks before the Games, however, Johnson was struck by a bout of food poisoning after eating at a restaurant in Salamanca, Spain. The illness caused Johnson to lose several pounds and become quite weak. Though he won his first-round race and managed to finish second in the second round, those two races took everything out of him. Wiped out by the illness, Johnson failed to even qualify for the 200-meter finals and missed out on any shot at a medal. He did manage to salvage one gold medal by running one leg on the world-record-setting American 4 x 400-meter relay team, but it was little consolation. Johnson was philosophical about his bad fortune. "It was good that I lost, because I was starting to believe people when they were calling me Superman," he said. "Everything happens for a reason."

After the disappointment at Barcelona, Johnson rededicated himself to his sport in 1993 to show that what happened at the Olympics was a fluke. He decided at that time to prove that a man could successfully run both the 200 meters and the 400 meters at the highest level, but a slight hamstring pull made him change his mind. He concentrated just on the 400 for the first time in his career, with great results. He won the U.S. national championships by running the fastest time ever on American soil (43.74) and then shocked the track world when he easily won at the world championship in Stuttgart, Germany, in a meet-record time of 43.65. It was his second individual world

championship gold medal. He also won a gold medal as a part of the U.S. 4 x 400-meter relay team, running 42.94 in the second leg. It was the first time he ever broke 43.00 in the relay. For his efforts, Johnson was named Athlete of the Year by the U.S. Olympic Committee, and also became the American Track and Field Athlete of the Year.

More success followed in 1994 and 1995, as Johnson's legend continued to grow. The man known as "Magic" in Europe and Japan (where track and field is very popular) continued to win race after race. In 1994, he won all of his 400-meter races and earned the gold medal in that event at the Goodwill Games in St. Petersburg, Russia. He also won the prestigious Jesse Owens Award for the first time. His hamstring injury fully healed, Johnson began running the 200 meters in competition again and, for the third time in history, finished the season ranked number one in both that race and the 400 meters.

Johnson used 1995 to set the stage for the 1996 Olympic Games in Atlanta, Georgia. In March, he set the world indoor record for the 400 meters with a time of 44.63 seconds (breaking his own record, which he had set just weeks earlier). In June, at the national championships in Sacramento, California,

Johnson broke through another barrier, becoming the first American to win both the 200 and the 400 in the same championship meet since Maxie Long accomplished the feat in 1899. Two months later in Goteborg, Switzerland, Johnson proved that he was one of the greatest runners ever when he pulled off the same double victory there—winning the 200 with a time of 19.79 and the 400 with a time of 43.99 (the second-fastest time in history). With those dramatic victories, the stage was set for the Atlanta Games. Johnson's friends knew what to expect from him in 1996. "He carries that burn from 1992," said former Baylor teammate Tony Miller. "The only thing that will cool him off is winning the double in Atlanta. He started a job, and he hasn't finished it. Michael Johnson has a job to finish." As the track world soon learned, finishing the job was exactly what Johnson intended to do.

The 1996 Olympic Games

Before he could attempt to become the first man to pull off the double victory at the Olympics, Johnson had to receive some help from the International Amateur Athletic Federation, which was in charge of scheduling at the Games. Originally, the two events were scheduled too close together—Johnson would have had to choose one race and drop the other. Recognizing that Johnson was easily the biggest track star in the world, and that his quest to win both races would be one of the biggest stories of the Games, the IAAF finally gave in to the pressure and changed the schedule so that there was more time between the events. Johnson recognized how important the schedule change was to his place in history. "There are two household names in the history of track and field—Jesse Owens and Carl Lewis," he stated. "I'm in position to be the third."

With the world watching and tens of millions of dollars in endorsement money on the line, Johnson finally had things go his way. No injuries, no food poisoning—just success. Wearing gold shoes prepared especially for him by Nike, Johnson won his first-ever individual Olympic gold medal on day 11 of the Olympiad, when he won the 400-meter race in a time of 43.39 seconds. The time was an Olympic record and just 0.2 seconds off the world-record (outdoor) time. Three days later, Johnson completed the double by running what is possibly the greatest race ever run by a sprinter, winning the 200 in a time of 19.32 seconds. That time was a stunning .34 seconds better than the world-record 19.66 that Johnson had set during the Olympic trials earlier in the year. It can often take decades for a track record to be lowered by three-tenths of a second, and Johnson had done it in one race. Even Johnson was amazed by his accomplishment. "I thought I could do 19.5," he said. "But not this, not 19.3. I'd have lost a lot of money betting that I wouldn't get 19.3." Third-place finisher Ato Boldon bowed to Johnson after the runners crossed the finish line and marveled at his rival's record. "Nineteen-point-thirty-two," said Boldon. "That's not a time. It sounds like my dad's birthdate."

For Johnson, the dual Olympic gold medals were the reward for years of hard work. "I know a lot of people say when they succeed, suddenly it's like throwing off a huge weight," he said, "but I enjoy it so much. . . . Well, it's not like it's exactly fun, not birthday-party fun, but I love it so, I do."

HOME AND FAMILY

Johnson is unmarried and continues to work and train in Waco, Texas. "Running is what I do. I don't want to do anything else right now. I just run," he explained. "If I don't do well, it's bad. I'm not going to act like it's not a big deal. It is." In Waco, Johnson can get away from things and concentrate on his running. He does not have to worry about being recognized as much as he does in Europe, where he is a superstar. In Waco, there are "no distractions," he noted. "Most nights I'm in bed by nine."

Johnson also spends time in Dallas, as his parents and siblings continue to be a driving force in his life. "If I'm not exciting to everyone else, so be it. I excite myself," he stated. "That's all that matters to me. There are no secrets to hide, no skeletons in the closet. It's just the way I am. I don't trust easily. Because I've always been so close to my family, I knew I could rely upon them. So I don't really go out and trust other people. It may have caused me to miss out on some opportunities. But it's much safer for me. I'd rather be safe than to trust someone and they end up turning on me."

MAJOR INFLUENCES

Because of his upright running style, Johnson has often been compared to Jesse Owens. A legendary African-American sprinter, Owens foiled Adolph Hitler's plans for using the 1936 Olympics in Berlin, Germany, to showcase white domination by winning four gold medals. Johnson is happy about the comparison because he has always idolized Owens. He carries with him a letter from Ruth Owens, Jesse's widow, in which she tells Johnson that she sees her late husband in him. "Greatest compliment I've ever been paid," Johnson said. "A lot of things he suffered through as an athlete, we can't even understand, with all the freedoms we have."

HOBBIES AND OTHER INTERESTS

Not too surprisingly, Johnson has a love for all things fast, especially automobiles. One of his favorite memories of winning the world championships in Goteborg, Sweden, was visiting the Volvo factory and being allowed to test-drive cars and trucks. He also enjoys tennis and horseback riding and recently became the owner of a 2 percent share of the Dallas Mavericks basketball team.

All the hobbies do not compare to Johnson's first love, however. "The fun part of my life is running," he admitted. "I think I have the best job in the world. I get to do something I love and I get paid for doing it. I feel like I am getting away with something. When you cross the line first, you did it all alone. You set goals for yourself, and when you achieve those goals, it's a great feeling."

WRITINGS

Chasing the Dragon: From Small Steps to Great Strides, How to Achieve Your Own Personal Best, 1996 (with Jess Walter)

HONORS AND AWARDS

Goodwill Games, 200 meters: 1990, gold medal; 1994, gold medal
Male Athlete of the Year (*Track and Field News*): 1990
U.S. National Track Championships, 200 meters: 1990, first place; 1991, first place; 1992, first place; 1995, first place; 1996, first place
World Track Championships, 200 meters: 1991, first place; 1995, first place
Olympic Track, 4 x 400 meter relay: 1992, gold medal
American Track and Field Athlete of the Year: 1993, 1994, 1995
Athlete of the Year (U.S. Olympic Committee): 1993
U.S. National Track Championships, 400 meters: 1993, first place; 1995, first place; 1996, first place
World Track Championships, 400 meters: 1993, first place; 1995, first place
Jesse Owens Award: 1994, 1995
Jesse Owens International Trophy Award: 1995, 1996
Olympic Track, 200 meters: 1996, gold medal
Olympic Track, 400 meters: 1996, gold medal

FURTHER READING

Books

Johnson, Michael, and Jess Walter. *Chasing the Dragon: From Small Steps to Great Strides, How to Achieve Your Own Personal Best*, 1996

Periodicals

Boy's Life, July 1996, p.14
Current Biography Yearbook 1996
Essence, Apr. 1996, p.66
GQ-Gentleman's Quarterly, June 1996, p.158

Jet, Mar. 27, 1995, p.46; Aug. 26, 1996, p.52
New York Times, June 13, 1996, p.B13; June 24, 1996, p.C1; July 30, 1996,
    p.A1; Aug. 2, 1996, p.A1; Aug. 4, 1996, p.S9
Newsweek, July 22, 1996, p.36; July 31, 1996, p.58
Runner's World, July 1995, p.38; Nov. 1995, p.57; Sep. 1996, p.54
Southern Living, May 1996, p.28
Sports Illustrated, May 20, 1991, p.46; June 28, 1993, p.36; Aug. 21, 1995, p.40;
    July 22, 1996, p.72; Aug. 12, 1996, pp.26, 44
Time, Summer 1996, p.54; Aug. 12, 1996, p.44
Wall Street Journal, July 19, 1996, p.R12

ADDRESS

Gold Medal Management
1350 Pine Street
Suite 3
Boulder, CO 80302

WORLD WIDE WEB SITE

http://www.usatf.org

Maya Lin 1959-

American Artist

Acclaimed Architect and Sculptor Who Created the
Vietnam Veterans Memorial, the Civil Rights
Memorial, and Other Notable Works

BIRTH

Maya Ying Lin was born on October 5, 1959, in Athens, Ohio.
Her name has many meanings: Maya is a Hindu goddess; Ying
means "precious stone"; and Lin means forest. Both of her parents, Henry Huan Lin and Julia Chang Lin, were professors at
Ohio University. Her father was also a ceramic artist and the
dean of fine arts, while her mother was a poet who taught

Oriental and English literature. Maya has one brother, Tan, who is also a poet and a professor.

Maya's parents were born in China and grew up during a turbulent time in that country's history. Both of their families were part of an elite class of professionals, including doctors, lawyers, and scholars. They belonged to the Nationalist political party of Sun Yat-sen, who overthrew China's last dynasty and became its first president in 1911. A period of political turmoil followed. For the next 30 years, an ongoing civil war between the Nationalists and the Communists tore China apart. Ultimately the Communists, led by Mao Zedong, took power in 1949. Many Nationalists, led by Chiang Kai-shek, fled to the island of Taiwan. But some, including Maya Lin's parents, chose to leave the country. Her father left Beijing for the United States in 1948. Her mother was smuggled out of the country with a $100 bill pinned to her coat lining in 1949, as the Communists were bombing her city of Shanghai. They met and were married in the United States.

YOUTH

The Lins settled at Ohio University to teach. They lived in a glass-walled house filled with books and art in the woods around Athens, Ohio, a small Midwestern college town. Lin has called it a perfect place to grow up: "You could leave your keys in your car, leave your door unlocked." Yet she has also said that she didn't really feel at home there, reflecting the background of her immigrant parents. Isolated by feeling like outsiders, the Lin family was very close.

Lin's childhood wasn't very typical for an American kid, as she explains here. "Growing up I didn't play with dolls, didn't do a lot of traditional girl stuff—not that I was doing a lot of traditional boy stuff, either. I was doing nerd stuff. . . . I was very, very serious. Even as a kid, I worried about environmental issues. When I was eight I found out about extinction, and I remember being horrified that one species was causing the massive extinction of all these other species." This interest in the environment showed up years later in her efforts to make her architecture harmonious with the natural site.

Maya's parents treated both children equally. At a time when sexism was common throughout society and expectations were very different for girls and boys, she never felt that being female limited her in any way. She thrived in the creative atmosphere her parents created. Maya enjoyed a lot of solitary activities, but she never describes herself as lonely or bored. She played chess with her brother, Tan, and read fantasy books by C.S. Lewis and J.R.R. Tolkien. She loved working with clay in her father's studio and often begged to use his potter's wheel and other equipment. She spent hours in her room constructing little towns from paper and other materials. Later, she added silversmithing and sculpture to her art interests. She took long walks in the woods around their home, watching the birds.

EARLY MEMORIES

"My parents very much brought us up to decide what we wanted to do, what we wanted to study," Lin recalls. "There was very little discipline, and yet I don't think we ever did anything that was irresponsible. Maybe that is an Eastern philosophy—that you don't force an opinion on a child. You allow them to draw their own conclusions."

EDUCATION

Lin attended school in Athens, Ohio. For grade school she attended Rufus Putnam Elementary School. This laboratory school was a training center for new teachers from the School of Education at Ohio University. "The student teachers were extremely dedicated and eager, and very new to teaching methods," Lin explains. With only 15 students in each class, excellent teachers, a flexible curriculum that allowed students to work at their own speed, and no grades, Maya thrived in elementary school.

After junior high, Lin went on to Athens High School. An excellent student with top grades, she took college courses while in high school for the challenge. She was especially interested in math, biology, and the environment. But outside of class she felt different from other kids her age, as she tells here. "I never socialized in high school. I didn't go to the prom. And I didn't wear makeup. It wasn't about androgyny; I was just pursuing other things. I remember people being incredibly preoccupied about dating and how they looked, and I was just not interested."As Lin recalls, "everyone was worried about getting A's, B's, and C's. I really thought it was kind of stupid. High school was really miserable. I disliked talking to people. Socially, I kind of ignored the whole scene. Boys and girls all taking themselves so seriously. It was just not my idea of a life, of anything interesting." Lin graduated from Athens High School in 1977 as co-valedictorian, one of the top students in her class.

College Years

Lin was accepted by her first-choice school, Yale University in New Haven, Connecticut. It proved to be an excellent experience for her. She has said that it was "the first place where I felt comfortable," accepted for her academic achievement, creativity, and love of art. She started out studying liberal arts, taking classes in literature, philosophy, science, and art. After two years, she began to concentrate on architecture, which combined her interest in mathematics and art.

During her junior year at Yale, she participated in an overseas study program through the School of Architecture, spending one semester in Denmark. She attended Copenhagen University and took classes in city planning and landscape design. She was also able to visit other European cities while she was there, to study the architecture and the use of public land. She learned that many cities in Europe are densely packed with buildings, so the cemeteries there are designed like public parks — gardens where people come to walk or sit. This appreciation for the living element of memorials to the dead would later serve her well.

"The Wall"

Lin also had a more disturbing experience in Europe. One day in Copenhagen she got on a bus and sat down. Everybody nearby got up and moved away from her. It was Lin's first experience with racial prejudice, and it upset her deeply.

After her semester in Europe, Lin returned to finish her studies in the United States. She graduated from Yale University with a bachelor of arts degree in 1981. After that, she took a year off before returning to graduate school. In 1982 she enrolled in the Graduate School of Design at Harvard University. But she was unhappy there, so she left Harvard and returned to Yale to complete her graduate studies. She earned her master's degree in architecture from Yale in 1986.

CAREER HIGHLIGHTS

Designing the Vietnam Veterans Memorial

It was while Lin was an undergraduate student at Yale that she designed her first major piece, which is still her best-known work to date — the Vietnam Veterans Memorial, more commonly known as the Wall.

At Yale, Lin and some of her fellow students had suggested a course in memorial architecture for their senior seminar. During the course, they learned about an upcoming design competition. It was sponsored by the Vietnam Veterans' Memorial Fund, a non-profit group of Vietnam vets who had banded together to create a memorial that would honor those who had served in the U.S. armed forces during the Vietnam War. A panel of distinguished architects, sculptors, and design specialists would judge the blind competition; the judges would not know who had submitted each design. Lin's professor assigned each student to create a design for their final class project, and she got to work. Although she didn't read up on the Vietnam War itself, she spent several months doing research on memorials and their meanings. She thought about the design requirements: the memorial should list all the names of those killed or missing in action, it should be apolitical, and it should be in harmony with its site. In November 1980 she traveled to the site in Washington, D.C. The proposed memorial would be in Constitution Gardens located on the National Mall, a grassy park that extends from the U.S. Capitol building to the Washington Monument. It was a beautiful fall day when Lin visited, sunny and crisp, and people were playing frisbee. She knew that she wanted to preserve that feeling of a quiet, peaceful park.

While Lin was standing in Washington photographing the site, the design started to take shape in her mind. She "thought about what death is and what a loss is — a sharp pain that lessens with time but can never quite heal over. A scar. The idea occurred to me there on the site." She envisioned a rift in the earth, "with the memorial going into the ground, then emerging from it, symbolizing death and calling for remembrance." As Lin later explained it, "I had an impulse to cut open the earth . . . an initial violence that in time would heal. The grass would grow back, but the cut would remain, a pure, flat surface, like a geode when you cut into it and polish the edge. . . . [It] was as if the black-brown earth were polished and made into an interface between the sunny world and the quiet, dark world beyond, that we can't enter."

After returning to Yale, she sketched the idea, then used her professor's and her fellow students' critiques to help her perfect it. Ultimately her design included two walls, each over 245 feet long, made of highly polished black granite. The walls form a wide angled V, with one end pointing directly to the Washington Monument and the other end pointing directly to the Lincoln Memorial. The ground rises up to meet the top of the walls in the back, then dips down in front before rising up again, creating a shallow amphitheater in front. At the center, the walls rise up to 10 feet high, and gradually taper off to just eight inches high at the two ends. Carved in gold on the walls in chronological order are the names of over 58,000 Vietnam veterans — those who were killed in the war and those who were MIA (Missing in Action). Descending along the path into the memorial was meant to feel like entering an enclosed space, what Lin described as "a quiet place meant for personal reflection and private reckoning." Following the path out again feels like returning to the world after a meditative experience.

Lin submitted her design to the competition and continued with her final year at Yale. The design earned her a B in the senior seminar class. Ultimately, she was the only student in her class to submit a design. Just over a month later, she got a phone call from the committee asking if they could come up to Yale to discuss her design. She was certain that she hadn't won; perhaps she would receive a smaller prize, like an honorable mention. Lin was astounded to learn that she'd won first prize, by unanimous vote of the judges.

What Lin didn't know at that point was that she had beaten out 1,420 entries by nationally famous professionals in the field to win the contest and the $20,000 first prize. There were so many submissions that they had been set up in an airplane hangar. The jury spent one week reviewing them, gradually narrowing down the field of entries. But one design, the jurors would later report, kept haunting them. In their final report, the judges said that this "memorial, with its wall of names, becomes a place of quiet reflection, and a tribute to those who served their nation in difficult times. All who come here can find it a place of healing. This will be a quiet memorial. . . . The designer has created an eloquent place where the simple meeting of earth, sky, and remembered names contain messages for all who will know this place." At first, when the winning design was announced in May 1981, many were surprised at the designer's youth and inexperience. Yet all praised the quality of her work.

That positive attitude about her design soon changed, though. Shortly after the winner was announced, a firestorm of criticism about both the design and the designer broke out. The criticism about Lin's memorial dates back to the controversy about the Vietnam War itself.

Understanding the Vietnam War

The Vietnam War was a long-running conflict in Southeast Asia. After enduring occupation by China from the fifth to the 15th century, Vietnam was colonized by France during the mid-19th century. In the 20th century, a Vietnamese nationalist movement rose up seeking independence from French control. This led to the bloody conflict known as the French Indochina War (1946-1954). In 1954, with the defeat of the French, Vietnam was divided into two countries, North and South Vietnam, with the intent that they would soon be reunited under one government. But South Vietnam refused to participate in elections for the government of this new, unified nation, sure that the country would become communist. What was essentially a civil war soon broke out between the two parts of the country, with the south supported by the United States and the communist north supported by China and the Soviet Union.

At first, the U.S. sent in forces to act merely as military advisors to the South Vietnamese troops. Soon, however, U.S. forces were involved in the fighting. The first American soldier died there in 1959. By 1963, there were 16,000

"The Wall"

American troops in Vietnam, by 1969, at the height of the war, there were almost 550,000 Americans serving there. Repeated efforts to craft a peace agreement between the opposing sides culminated with the Paris Accords in 1973, when American involvement in the war officially ended. The final U.S. troops were withdrawn two years later, in 1975, when North Vietnam overran South Vietnam. The two parts were reunited in 1976 under a communist government as the Socialist Republic of Vietnam. By the end of the U.S. involvement in Vietnam, over 58,000 Americans were killed or missing in action and 300,000 were wounded; over 3.6 million Vietnamese were killed, and many more suffered serious injuries. Both sides were left with the long-term devastating effects of exposure to deadly chemicals that were sprayed throughout the countryside during the war.

According to all accounts, it was an ugly war for American soldiers to fight. Although most of the war was fought in the countryside of South Vietnam, there were many Communist sympathizers there (known as Viet Cong) who supported the North Vietnamese cause. Both sides used tactics of guerrilla warfare, including deception and ambush rather than direct confrontation. The Viet Cong looked and dressed just like all the other Vietnamese people, and they were often shielded by South Vietnamese sympathetic to their side. That meant that U.S. troops could never tell who was a friend and who was an enemy just waiting to kill them. Farmers, old people, even children could be Viet Cong. Many innocent people were killed. And most of the American soldiers were young—often, just out of high school. Survivors of that experience have testified to the horror and despair they felt, both during the war and later, after they came home. For many, the experiences in Vietnam left great emotional wounds.

Their experiences when they got home were painful, also. In the past, after previous wars, returning soldiers were greeted as heroes. Not so for Vietnam veterans. The country was deeply divided over the war, and the opposing viewpoints profoundly split American society. At that point it was the height of the cold war and the buildup of the nuclear arms race, and many Americans had grave fears about the power and influence of the Soviet Union and China. Those who supported the war felt that it was imperative to stop the spread of communism. Those who opposed the war felt that the United States had no business getting involved in another country's civil war and forcing our political views on them. They also considered the South Vietnamese government corrupt and dictatorial. For many Americans, their opposition was fueled by television news coverage of the war, which showed American soldiers coming home in body bags. There were huge demonstrations around the country, on college campuses and on the streets of Washington, D.C., as protesters called on the U.S. government to bring our boys home.

Many veterans, returning to the U.S. at the end of their tour of duty, felt that the country had turned against them. For some Americans who protested against the war, their opposition to U.S. policy turned into opposition to the veterans themselves. Many people seemed to blame the soldiers, rather than the military or the lawmakers in Washington who had sent them overseas. The veterans didn't receive the traditional heroes' welcome when they returned from the war; they were never honored for their service to their country. Instead, they were treated miserably. They were booed or called ugly names. Sometimes, people even spit on them. The veterans deserved better—which was the whole point of the group behind the Vietnam Veterans' Memorial Fund, when they decided to build a memorial to honor the veterans for their service.

Controversy over the Wall

But it wouldn't be that easy—nothing involving Vietnam was ever easy. Soon after the design for the memorial was announced, a huge public controversy ensued. It was only six years after the final pullout of American troops from Vietnam, and Lin's abstract design, which was open to different interpretations, seemed to bring back all the feelings of anger, shame, bitterness, divisiveness, and rage engendered by the war.

Objections to Lin's design took all forms. Some veterans had hoped for a more traditional, realistic statue of soldiers to symbolize their service to the nation. They strongly objected to the lack of an American flag. These opponents began a very public campaign against the design. They believed that it sent a message that was unheroic, unpatriotic, and dishonorable, a negative political statement about veterans and the war. They called it "a degrading ditch" and a "black gash of shame and sorrow." One critic called it "a black scar — black, the universal color of sorrow and shame and degradation in all races and all societies worldwide." The color black came in for such criticism until retired Brig. Gen. George Price, one of the army's highest ranking African-American officers, very publicly and angrily decried such negative comments. Some even objected to Lin's heritage. People called her a "gook," an ugly racial slur used against Vietnamese people. Repeated public hearings were held, and the government withheld the permit to build on the National Mall until the design was changed. Ultimately, a compromise was reached. A realistic sculpture showing three servicemen would be placed near the memorial. Many called it a desecration to take an accepted design and tamper with it against the artist's wishes — Lin herself said it was "like putting mustaches on other people's portraits." But the compromise was accepted, and construction on the memorial finally began. Lin spent about a year working at an architectural firm that was doing the construction-related detail work on her design, enduring daily battles over the proposed changes.

For Lin, the misunderstandings about her work were very difficult. "It always baffled and haunted Maya Lin," Peter Tauber wrote in the *New York Times Magazine*, "that critics of her work termed it austere, attacking the abstract aspects of her designs as though they were antihuman, the minimalist as if that meant cold-blooded. In her installations, humans are the necessary missing element, unique emotional engagement her specific aim."

As soon as the Vietnam Veterans Memorial was dedicated on Veterans' Day in November 1982, all doubts about it subsided. Thousands of vets poured into Washington, D.C., creating the homecoming parade that they were denied. The Wall was immediately and universally greeted with acclaim. The atmosphere it created was quiet, poignant, and contemplative. The Wall was cathartic. It evoked in all who saw it a deep emotional response, drawing out powerful feelings of grief and anger. Everyone cried — the vets, their families, the journalists standing nearby. The black color and the reflective, mirror-like quality of the stone drew the viewer into an interaction, a direct involvement with the Wall. The ability to touch the names had the same effect. Many were moved to make rubbings of the names. People began bringing objects to leave at the memorial — a beloved teddy bear from a soldier's mother, a pair of army boots from a comrade, a love letter from a wife, a picture of grown children who would never know their father. Reconciliation and remembrance — the Wall had the power to heal. Lin's critics were silenced.

Since it was created in 1982, the Vietnam Veterans Memorial has become the most popular memorial in the country, a place of pilgrimage for over 30 million visitors so far. Many of these visitors have left personal mementoes, which have been carefully collected and stored in warehouses. Recently, the Smithsonian's National Museum of American History has set up special exhibitions of these pieces. The Wall has spawned many similar Vietnam memorials in cities and towns around the country, as well as two smaller traveling versions. It even inspired the creation of the AIDS Quilt. In the words of John Wheeler, the former chair of the Vietnam Veterans Memorial Fund, "The Wall has become an emblem of America—and its meaning continues to unfold, to grow, and to surprise."

The Civil Rights Memorial

The period that Lin spent working on the Wall during 1981 and 1982 was very difficult for her. Shortly before the Wall was completed she returned to school. It was then that she started at Harvard University, then decided to take some time off before returning to Yale to complete her master's degree. Although she was enrolled in Yale's architecture program, she studied sculpture there as well. She dropped out of the public eye, studying and creating art on her own terms.

After several years, Lin returned to the public arena with another moving memorial, commissioned by the Southern Poverty Law Center (SPLC). This nonprofit group, based in Montgomery, Alabama, was founded to protect the rights of poor people and minorities; it also fights racist and discriminatory activities through legal means. It has been especially active in fighting the Ku Klux Klan, a white supremacist hate group. The SPLC decided that they wanted to build a memorial to the civil rights movement at their headquarters in Montgomery, which was the site of many major events during the movement. It seemed fitting that a civil rights memorial should go there: Montgomery was the home of the Dexter Avenue Baptist Church, where Martin Luther King, Jr. used to preach, the site of the 1955 bus boycott started by Rosa Parks, and the endpoint for the famous 1965 march from Selma.

When the SPLC started thinking about who should design the memorial, they immediately thought of Maya Lin. They didn't know how to locate her, though, so they called every Lin in the New York City phone book until they reached her. After her experiences designing the Vietnam Veterans Memorial, Lin had said that she would never design another memorial. But she reconsidered when she heard that there had never been a memorial for the many people who had fought for civil rights.

Lin decided to accept the challenge. She started doing research into the civil rights movement, and in 1988 she flew down to Montgomery to view the site. On the airplane, she was reading some of the words of Dr. Martin Luther

The Civil Rights Memorial

King, Jr. One passage, a paraphrase from the book of Amos in the Old Testament, kept coming back to her. "We will not be satisfied until justice rolls down like waters, and righteousness like a mighty stream." As Lin recalls, "The minute I hit that quote I knew the whole piece had to be about water. I learned that King had used the phrase not only in his famous 'I have a dream' speech at the Washington civil rights march in 1963 but at the start of the bus boycott in Montgomery eight years earlier, so it had been a rallying cry for the entire movement. Suddenly the whole form took shape, and half an hour later I was in a restaurant in Montgomery with the people from the Center, sketching it on a paper napkin. I realized that I wanted to create a time line: a chronological listing of the movement's major events and its individual deaths, which together would show how people's lives influence history and how their deaths made things better." She also started thinking about water—its cooling effects in a hot climate and its quiet, peaceful sound. Returning later to New York, she set to work.

Lin envisioned the Civil Rights Memorial as consisting of two parts made of black granite, surrounded by a plaza of white granite. In the back is a highly polished black wall inscribed with gold lettering as follows:

> . . . until justice rolls down like waters
> and righteousness like a mighty stream
> Martin Luther King, Jr.

171

She left off the first part of the quote, starting with the word "until," to show that the struggle for civil rights still continues. A steady stream of water spills down over the words on the wall. In the foreground is an oddly shaped disk or table, also made of black granite. The top of the table, which is almost 12 feet in diameter, sits on a base that narrows down to only 20 inches across, giving the impression that the table top is floating in space. Water seeps out from the center of the table and flows over the words, to encourage people to touch the names. The table is only 31 inches high, to allow children to come and read about our nation's past.

Here is how Lin describes some of her considerations in designing the memorial. "The water is as slow as I could get it. It remains very still until you touch it. Your hand causes ripples, which transform and alter the piece, just as reading the words completes the piece." In the Civil Rights Memorial, as in the Vietnam Veterans Memorial, the use of touch creates an important interaction between the individual and the memorial, as Lin explains here: "Psychologically, I wanted people to be able to feel like they really were a part of making this piece come alive."

To memorialize those who fought for civil rights, the names of those who were killed and the names of important events are inscribed on the table top, forming a time line of the struggle. The events start with "17 May 1954, the Supreme Court ruling outlawing school segregation," and end with "4 April 1968, Martin Luther King, Jr. assassinated." Here are just a few of the people who are memorialized there: Vernon Dahmer, a businessman from Mississippi who offered to pay the voting tax for anyone who couldn't afford it and was killed when his house was firebombed; Viola Luizzo, a mother from Detroit who was shot by the Ku Klux Klan for driving freedom marchers from Montgomery to Selma; Virgil Ware, a 13-year old boy who was shot while riding on his brother's bicycle handlebars by white teenagers who had just left a segregationist rally; Jimmie Lee Jackson, who was shot by Alabama state troopers for trying to protect his mother and grandmother from a state trooper who was attacking a voting rights march; and Emmett Till, a 14-year-old boy who was shot for speaking to a white woman in Mississippi.

The Civil Rights Memorial was dedicated in November 1989. It was a resounding success. On opening day, 600 family members of the people named on the memorial joined a crowd of 5,000 visitors in an emotional and inspiring ceremony. One of the most touching moments came when Rosa Parks reached through the water to touch her name on the memorial. For Lin, another powerful moment came when Mamie Till Mobley, the mother of Emmett Till, stepped up to the memorial. As Lin later said, "I was surprised and moved when people started to cry. Emmett Till's mother was touching his name beneath the water and crying, and I realized her tears were becoming part of the memorial."

Lin's Other Works

Lin has completed other major works besides her two well-known memorials. One of the earliest was the Peace Chapel, which she created for Juniata College in Huntingdon, Pennsylvania, in about 1990. For this open-air gathering place, Lin devised a circle of stones that form a center for contemplation and non-denominational services, in harmony with the natural environment. Lin went on to *Topo*, a whimsical piece created in 1991 with landscape architect Henry Arnold for the Charlotte Coliseum. The site, a wide grassy median strip on the auto entrance to the Coliseum, is about 600 feet long and 60 feet wide, with a drop of about 60 feet. This commission came soon after the Civil Rights Memorial, and Lin wanted to do something fun. For *Topo* (which comes from topography and topiary), she and Arnold invented a game of balls rolling down a hill — and used huge holly bushes, trimmed into rounded shapes, as the balls. "I was trying to create a sense of place out of the landscape," Lin explains, "because you can walk onto the median strip, and all of a sudden you're part of the game. It's sort of *Alice in Wonderland*."

Lin went on to work on the *Women's Table*, commissioned by Yale University to honor the presence of women at Yale, which had once been an all-male school. She created a dark-green stone table in an oval shape, again with water bubbling out of the center. The top is set on a black stone base that doubles as a bench and serves as a gathering place for students. The table top tilts at a 69 degree angle, in a subtle reference to 1869, when the graduate school of fine arts first admitted women, and 1969, when all of Yale went coed. A spiral time line starts at the center and lists the dates of important events at Yale, from its founding in 1701 through 1993, with a lengthy series of zeros for the many years in which women weren't admitted there. Also in 1993, Lin completed a renovation of the interior space for the Museum for African Art in New York City, using subtle shades of color, African fabric, and a "forest" of copper pipes and copper mesh screens. Lin's *Groundswell,* an installation at the Wexner Center at Ohio State University, also dates to 1993. This piece includes three unusual outdoor gardens, all made of crushed blue-green safety glass. Lin shaped 43 tons of glass, provided by a recycling company and an auto manufacturer, into mounds that are reminiscent both of Japanese Zen gardens and of the Native American burial mounds on the nearby Ohio landscape. The sculpture has been vandalized twice since its installation — once when indelible red paint pigment was poured into the glass, and a second time when three men climbed into the exhibit and started kicking the glass mounds — but each time *Groundswell* was reassembled.

Lin's next major piece was *Eclipsed Time*, which involved almost five years of work before it was unveiled in 1994. This sculpture is set into the ceiling of Penn Station, an underground railroad station in New York City. A 14-foot illuminated glass disk is embedded in the ceiling, with the numbers of the clock etched onto the disk. A parallel aluminum disk glides back and forth over the glass, casting a shadow, or eclipse, over the numbers, which tell the time of day. *Eclipsed Time* was called "technologically sophisticated, yet visually simple." Lin tried something completely different in the 1995 *Wave Field* at the aerodynamics complex at the University of Michigan. While thinking about the piece, Lin was reading up on aerodynamics when she came across a picture of a regular pattern of ocean waves. Lin decided to recreate this regular but fluid pattern in a sculpture of mounded earth covered with green grass. Like all of her works, *Wave Field* was acclaimed for its integration into the physical site.

In addition to these pieces, Lin has designed several houses and many smaller sculptures, which often include lead, broken glass, and beeswax. She has adamantly refused to limit herself, defining herself as both an artist and an architect. "For me, art is like poetry, architecture like prose. When you write a novel, there's an overlying general idea, and then you have to make sure it all works sentence to sentence. Just like in a house: there's an overlying idea, but you have to worry about the doorknobs, the finishes, everything down to the last detail. But in a poem, it's an initial gut thing — you have to have that immediate touch to the soul. To me, that is the difference between art and architecture. I wouldn't say one is easier than the other. They're just different. A lot of people have said, 'why doesn't your art look like your architecture, or your architecture look like your art?' But I like the separation. I like art and architecture for their differences."

Future Plans

Recently Lin has been designing a water sculpture for the Cleveland Public Library, a recycling plant for the South Bronx section of New York City, and a house in Connecticut. But she has also talked about some long-term plans. When asked whether she would ever do another memorial, Lin talked about doing one more on the subject of extinction and the environment. As she explains here, "I really care about the environment. It has been my love since I was a child. This work will probably take my lifetime to do, and it won't be a monument in a traditional sense. We are the one species that has rapidly caused he extinction of so many other species, and that is unique. We have to stop. We have to begin to understand that we cannot continue to overuse. Again, for me it is about teaching. I don't know how it will manifest itself, but this is my dream."

MARRIAGE AND FAMILY

Lin, who is unmarried, lives in New York City with her long-time boyfriend, the sculptor Peter Boynton, and their cats. She also has a little farmhouse in Vermont where she likes to do some of her work. Despite many offers, Lin has never gone to work for an architectural firm; instead, she works out of her home studio. "I'm very lucky," she says. "I get to do whatever my imagination wants me to do, and people want to support that. I'm just following my muse."

HONORS AND AWARDS

Presidential Design Award: 1988, for the Vietnam Veterans Memorial

FURTHER READING

Books

Ashabranner, Brent. *Always to Remember: The Story of the Vietnam Veterans Memorial*, 1988 (juvenile)
Donnelly, Judy. *A Wall of Names: The Story of the Vietnam Veterans Memorial*, 1991 (juvenile)
Ling, Bettina. *Maya Lin*, 1997 (juvenile)
Malone, Mary. *Maya Lin: Architect and Artist*, 1995 (juvenile)
Who's Who in America, 1997
Who's Who among Asian Americans, 1994-95

Periodicals

Current Biography Yearbook 1993
McCall's, June 1988, p.42
Ms., Sep./Oct. 1990, p.20
National Geographic, May 1985, pp.552, 556, and several other articles
New York Times, May 7, 1981, p.A20; June 29, 1981, p.B5; Oct. 29, 1995, Section 2, p.17
New York Times Magazine, Feb. 24, 1991, p.49
Newsweek, Oct. 25, 1982, p.30
Ohio Magazine, Nov. 1993, p.43
People, Mar. 8, 1982, p.38; Nov. 20, 1989, p.78
Smithsonian, Sep. 1991, p.32
Time, Nov. 9, 1981, p.103; Nov. 6, 1989, p.90
USA Weekend, Nov. 1-3, 1996, p.4
Vogue, Apr. 1995, p.346
Washington Post, July 7, 1992, p.A1; Sep. 13, 1992, p.C3

Other

Maya Lin: A Strong, Clear Vision, 1994 (Video; Winner of the 1995 Academy Award for Best Achievement in Feature Documentary)

ADDRESS

Vietnam Veterans Memorial Fund
1012 14th Street NW, Suite 201
Washington, DC 20005

George Lucas   1944-

American Filmmaker
Creator of *Star Wars* and the *Indiana Jones* Movies

BIRTH

George Walton Lucas, Jr., was born on May 14, 1944, in
Modesto, California. His father, George Walton Lucas, Sr.,
owned an office-supply store. His mother, Dorothy Bomberger
Lucas, was a homemaker who also helped out with bookkeeping
for the business. He has two older sisters, Ann and Katherine,
and one younger sister, Wendy.

YOUTH

When George was young his mom was sick a lot. Dorothy Lucas's health was poor for years, and she was frequently hospitalized. Doctors were uncertain about the cause, but they suspected pancreatitis. When he was eight months old, the family hired a housekeeper to care for George and, later, his younger sister Wendy. Lucas was especially close to Wendy and to a couple of friends in the neighborhood. They used to set up makeshift carnival rides and funhouses, and they even made a zoo using the pets in the neighborhood. Lucas and his friends also liked to build elaborate miniature cities and farms. They also spent time watching a lot of cartoons. George liked to watch Westerns, "Perry Mason," and "Adventure Theater," which featured such action-adventure movies from the 1930s and 1940s as Flash Gordon and the Masked Marvel. Lucas developed his taste for fast-moving action stories from the movies he saw on "Adventure Theater." He also loved reading comic books, like Scrooge McDuck, Batman, Superman, and *Amazing Stories*. He had so many comic books that his father built a shed to hold them all.

Lucas did the usual things growing up in middle-class suburban America. He was involved in Cub Scouts and Little League, but he didn't play very well. When he was 11, Disneyland opened in Anaheim, California, and he and his family visited often. "I loved Disneyland. I wandered around, I'd go on the rides and the bumper cars, the steamboats, the shooting galleries, the jungle rides. I was in heaven."

EDUCATION

Lucas attended Roosevelt Junior High School and Thomas Downey High in Modesto. His grades were just average. "I was never very good in school, so I was never very enthusiastic about it. One of the big problems I had, more than anything else, was that I always wanted to learn something other than what I was being taught. I was *bored*. I wanted to *enjoy* school in the worst way and I never could." He didn't like reading, spelling, or math, but he did well in art and music.. He paid the most attention when the teacher showed a film.

When Lucas was 14 or 15, the family moved to another house in Modesto set on 13 acres of walnut trees. But the move was hard on him. "I was very upset to leave Ramona [street]," he recalls about the street they had lived on. "I was very attached to that house." He became depressed and withdrawn and missed his old friends, who now lived too far away to bicycle over. He spent most of his time in his room, reading comic books, listening to his records, and eating candy bars. Eventually, he became interested in photography. He enjoyed devising trick shots and especially liked to take pictures of low-flying planes and his nieces and nephews.

Lucas also developed a passion for car racing. When he was 15, he got his first car, a two-cylinder Fiat. He spent hours giving it more power and fitting it with special equipment for racing, like roll bars and heavy-duty seat belts. He wanted to be a race car driver and he competed in small races whenever he could. He became acquainted with racing champion Alan Grant, whom he admired tremendously. Lucas spent so much of his time on his racing interests that he almost didn't graduate from high school. When he wasn't racing, he was cruising the streets of Modesto, along with many other kids his age. He would be out in his car from 3:00 in the afternoon until 1:00 in the morning, and even longer on the weekends. His parents started to worry that he wouldn't amount to anything. While he never got involved in drinking or drugs, he did accumulate speeding tickets—enough to have to go to court. By this time, he also looked like a kid headed for trouble. He wore old blue jeans and slicked-back hair, and he hung out with a gang, although he didn't officially become a member. When his first hit movie, *American Graffiti,* drew on those teenage memories, Lucas would joke that his time spent cruising was not wasted.

In June 1962, when Lucas was 17, he was involved in a car crash that nearly killed him. It was two days before graduation, and he was just finishing up his last term paper at the library. Driving home, he was turning into his driveway when he was hit by another car. Lucas's car flipped over several times, his special racing seat belt broke, and he was thrown clear from the car, which then smashed into a tree. He was in a coma for 48 hours and spent weeks in the hospital. Later, he said, "You can't have that kind of experience and not feel that there must be a reason why you're here. I realized I should be spending my time trying to figure out what that reason is and trying to fulfill it. The fact is, there is no way I could have survived that accident if I'd been wrapped around that tree. Actually, that seat belt never should have broken, under any circumstances. All that affected me seriously." Lucas continues, "The accident made me more aware of myself and my feelings. I began to trust my instincts. I had the feeling that I should go to college, and I did. I had the same feeling later that I should go into film school, even though everybody thought I was nuts. I had the same feeling when I decided to make *Star Wars,* when even my friends told me I was crazy. These are just things that have to be done, and I feel as if I have to do them."

College and Film School

After recovering from the crash, Lucas entered Modesto Junior College, where he finally had a chance to study subjects that fascinated him—sociology, anthropology, and literature. "These were the things I was really interested in, and that sparked me. It was very hard, and I didn't have the background I needed—I couldn't even spell." He also read adventure fantasies by

Jules Verne, *1984* by George Orwell, and *Brave New World* by Aldous Huxley. And his grades now sometimes crept into the A and B range. He graduated from junior college in 1964.

While in college, Lucas still frequented race tracks, but now as a photographer instead of a driver. There, he met a man who was to point him toward his eventual career. Hanging out at the track he met Haskell Wexler, who enjoyed racing but was also an accomplished cinematographer in Hollywood. He and Lucas became friends, and Wexler encouraged him to go to film school. Yet Lucas's decision to attend film school was challenged by just about everyone else. His friends in college thought it was a terrible idea; they said that nobody from film school every gets into the film industry, and that Lucas would end up as a ticket taker for Disney. And his father deeply opposed the idea. He wanted his son to take over the family business, or at least to study something useful. The tension between them became so acute that Lucas stood up to his father and vowed to be a millionaire by the time he was 30. "It was one of those things that at the time I was shocked I had said," Lucas recalls. "It sort of came out of left field. But it actually came true." His father agreed to help him attend film school, but made it clear that Lucas would have to work hard. Lucas pays tribute to his father as he reflects that "the way my father brought me up gave me a lot of the common sense I use to get me through the business world."

In 1964, Lucas entered the University of Southern California (USC) bachelor's program in film. The USC film school trained its students in every skill it takes to make a movie, with separate classes in script writing, directing, working cameras, working with sound, and editing film. In addition, the curriculum also included film history and theory. The emphasis at USC was on making educational films and documentaries, not feature films for Hollywood. And at the end of the program, students would have the chance to make a 15-minute movie, using equipment and film provided by the university and a crew made up of fellow students.

Lucas calls his time in film school "a time when I really blossomed. When I went in there, I didn't know anything. . . . They helped me become what I am today." Lucas remembers being awed by it all. "When I finally got there, everything seemed way over my head." At first, he had a lot of catching up to do, because he hadn't taken any film classes during his years at junior college. He worked so hard his first year that his health suffered. He ate a lot junk food, pulled many all-nighters, and came down with mononucleosis.

After a year at USC, Lucas was already well-known. His first formal student film, *Look at Life* (1965), was a montage of violent and peaceful photographs related to the Vietnam War, shown at a very fast pace. These visual images were overlaid with a soundtrack that combined jazzy calypso music with bits from news broadcasts. *Look at Life* won several awards at student film festivals, drew the attention of fellow students and instructors, and convinced them of his talent.

The USC film program had many rules and limited resources, which proved to be challenging for many of the students. Yet Lucas always found a way to work around those restrictions. "If I got 16 feet of film, I made a 16-foot-long movie," he recalls. Other students had trouble completing one or two films; Lucas made six. He usually made abstract films, often using impressionistic montage techniques. From the beginning, he had trouble writing scripts and creating characters, so he compensated with other elements, including structure, visual elements, dialogue, action, and pacing. The more he learned about film, the more Lucas began to see a focus for his studies. Editing became his favorite part of filmmaking because the editor really has the final control: he or she arranges all the scenes that have been shot on film and determines what the audience will see. In 1966, Lucas graduated from USC with a bachelor of arts in cinema. He later returned to USC for just one semester of graduate school, but he never completed the program.

FIRST JOBS

When Lucas finished his undergraduate degree in 1966, he thought that he would be drafted—at that time the U.S. was drafting all eligible young men to serve in the Vietnam War. He tried to enlist in the Air Force so that he could become an officer in the photography unit, but he was rejected because of his long record of speeding tickets. Then he got drafted and was rejected on a 4-F medical classification. During the routine physical, the doctor found that Lucas had diabetes. Diabetes is a lifelong disorder in which the body doesn't produce enough of the hormone insulin to function well. There is no cure, and if left untreated, diabetes can cause death. Lucas has been able to control the disease by taking medication, maintaining a healthy diet, and avoiding sweets.

In 1967, Lucas returned to USC for graduate school. At about the same time he got a job making films for the United States Information Agency (USIA), an agency that created educational and propaganda materials for the government. He worked on USIA films during the day and as a teaching assistant at night. He was making a film of President Lyndon Johnson's trip to South Korea, and his bosses "objected to it on political grounds. They said I made the South Koreans look a little too fascist." He continues, "I realized that I didn't want other people telling me how to cut a film. *I* wanted to decide. I really wanted to be responsible for what was being said in a movie." At the same time, Lucas was making his first version of *THX 1138:4EB*, which he remade into his first full-length feature film in 1970. This short student film about an individual trying to escape from a futuristic, totalitarian society was considered powerful but simplistic.

In 1967, Lucas started to work in the commercial film industry. He won a Columbia Pictures scholarship that enabled him to watch the making of a movie called *McKenna's Gold* and to direct a ten-minute film based on it. Next he won a Warner Brothers scholarship that allowed him to work on the set of *Finian's Rainbow*, a musical directed by Francis Ford Coppola, who would later become famous as the director of such films as *The Godfather* and *Apocalypse Now*. Lucas was Coppola's assistant, and they became friends. In 1968, Lucas worked on the production of Coppola's next film, *The Rain People*. On the set, Lucas made an acclaimed documentary about the process called *Filmmaker*. Eventually, he went to work for Coppola's film company, American Zoetrope. There he made his first feature film, *THX 1138* (1970), an expanded, reworked version of his student film. In this grim futuristic tale of a dehumanized, drugged world, humans have created underground societies after destroying the earth. The movie tells the story of one man's attempt to escape from society's control. *THX 1138* didn't have much of an impact among the general public when it was released. But it did earn Lucas a cult following among film buffs and a reputation in the industry for making cold, arty, science fiction films—a reputation he would immediately dispel with his next movie, *American Graffiti*.

CAREER HIGHLIGHTS

In over 25 years of filmmaking, Lucas has created some of the most popular and most successful movies of all time, including the Star Wars trilogy and the Indiana Jones series. He has worked in many different capacities on these projects. On some, he's been the director, the person in charge of all the creative and technical aspects, including the actors, sets, costumes, and special effects. On others he's been the producer, the person responsible for all the business aspects of filmmaking, particularly the financial decisions. But no matter what his title on the project, Lucas always makes sure he is the last one to edit, to ensure that his vision reaches the screen.

American Graffiti

Lucas's first big hit was *American Graffiti*, although he had a tough time getting it made. For over a year and a half, he tried to get financing from a studio, but he was unsuccessful until Francis Ford Coppola agreed to be the executive producer. The movie was shot in 28 days on a budget of just $780,000—tiny by Hollywood standards. The film depicts one summer night in 1962, when a group of four friends cruise around the streets of their small town in hot rods. The movie is based on Lucas's teen years—he has said that the main characters are composites that reflect some part of his own experiences. *American Graffiti* launched the careers of many actors who went on to become big stars, including Richard Dreyfuss, Harrison Ford, Ron Howard, Suzanne Somers,

From Star Wars

and Cindy Williams. Released in 1973, *American Graffiti* touched off a wave of nostalgia for an earlier, more innocent era. It also became one of the most profitable movies ever made: the movie cost less than $1 million to make, but it has grossed over $120 million. When Lucas received his share of the profits from the movie, he began a tradition of sharing the wealth by giving bonuses to everyone who had contributed to the project. Several years later Lucas made a sequel called *More American Graffiti,* which did not do well.

Star Wars

Lucas came up with the idea that eventually became the Star Wars trilogy even before he started filming *American Graffiti.* After finishing that film, he went to work on *Star Wars.* It took him three years, working eight hours a day, to write just the first film in the trilogy. From the beginning, he envisioned an epic of mythic proportions. He studied social psychology and mythology, especially the work of mythologist Joseph Campbell. "I was trying to get fairy tales, myths, and religion down to a distilled state, studying the pure form to see how and why it worked." He also read science fiction and fantasy by Isaac Asimov, Alex Raymond, Edgar Rice Burroughs, and J.R.R.

Tolkein, and studied earlier movies, including Flash Gordon, Buck Rogers, and *2001: A Space Odyssey*. By the time Lucas was done, he had the plans for a nine-part epic. What became the three movies that exist today—*Star Wars* (1977), *The Empire Strikes Back* (1980), and *Return of the Jedi* (1983)—are really the middle section of his planned nine-part epic. The other six stories that Lucas envisions tell what happened before and after the existing trilogy.

The Star Wars trilogy tells the story of a struggle between the forces of good and evil, played out in a science fiction fantasy. An evil empire is bent on domination of all creatures in the universe. To fight this power, the forces of good form a rebel force to vanquish their foe. The three films, which star Harrison Ford as Han Solo, Carrie Fisher as Princess Leia, and Mark Hamill as Luke Skywalker, chart the history of the conflict. Lucas was the creator of the Star Wars movies and wrote the stories for all of them; he was the director of only the first one, and the executive producer of the next two. But in all three films, he was involved in everything from reviewing the setups of shots to visiting the special effects labs to laboriously editing the films.

"The onscreen world of *Star Wars* is a sliver of Lucas's imaginary universe," Denise Worrell wrote in *Icons: Intimate Portraits*. "Lucas constructed back stories not only for his main characters but for his creatures as well." She cites as an example the Wookie Chewbacca, for whom Lucas has constructed an entire cultural history. The Wookie race, in Lucas's fertile imagination, comes from a damp jungle planet, where they live in wood and bamboo tree houses 100 feet off the ground. They are mammals who eat meat and vegetables and who live to be 350 years old. The Wookies were rounded up by imperial forces and sold as slaves. But Han Solo freed a group that included Chewbacca, and the two became friends.

Lucas's crowning achievement came in the area of special effects. There were over 300 special effects in the original *Star Wars*, and many more in the later movies. And the effects took all forms. The famous cantina scene in *Star Wars*, where creatures from all over the galaxy are gathered in a bar, showed several types of effects. Lucas created elaborate makeup, masks, and costumes, as well as the sounds of the intergalactic languages, in which odd bits of speech from various human languages were distorted through a synthesizer. There were several versions of the robots, R2D2 and C3PO, depending on the requirements of the scene: some that couldn't move, some that moved with remote control, and some that could be inhabited by an actor. But the best special effects in the movie were those used to create the scenes in space. No one had ever created space scenes, space ships, and space battles that looked like those in *Star Wars*. To create these realistic looking scenes, Lucas and his team studied news footage of World War II planes in battle. They devised a special camera that could move in all directions and at all angles. Because this motorized camera was computerized, it could replicate its movements exactly. Then they filmed miniature planes with the moving cameras, which gave the effect that the planes were moving. They made repeated passes of the same action, each time adding different elements. They did this with both the planes and the miniature Death Star, which was only a couple of feet in diameter. And then they layered as many as 38 pieces of film over each other, creating the compelling scenes.

"The movies changed forever with *Star Wars*," according to director Lawrence Kasdan, who was the co-writer with Lucas on *The Empire Strikes Back* and *Return of the Jedi*. "The film was cut like an action movie. In the past, they'd show you one great special effect and let you stare in awe for 30 seconds. But George believed in action—he didn't want to slow the movie down. He piled all the special effects on top of each other, layer on layer. It changed the way you experienced movies, because if you wanted to see everything, you had to go back three or four times."

Response to the film was tremendous. *Star Wars* was something entirely new for American moviegoers. Everybody loved it—kids and their parents, as well as film critics. It quickly became a cultural phenomenon as well as a movie. *Star Wars* won Oscars for film editing, art direction, costume design, original musical score, visual effects, and sound, as well as a special Oscar for sound creation. Ironically, though, Lucas did not win an Oscar for Best Screenplay, Best Picture, or Best Director.

"[What] really made the film such a seminal experience for moviegoers was its crackling aura of youthful adventure," Patrick Goldstein wrote in the *Los Angeles Times Magazine*. "*Star Wars* is a fairy tale filmed like a fantasy ride— mythology at 24 thrills per second. During filming, Carrie Fisher says Lucas had only one direction for his cast: 'OK, let's do this take faster and more intense.' The film shifts gears like a race car, each narrative scene accelerating into a full throttle blast of quick-cut action." *Star Wars* changed the way the film industry made movies. Many have charged that *Star Wars*, along with Steven Spielberg's *Jaws*, ushered in the era of the Hollywood blockbuster, because they showed movie studios the incredible amounts of money that movies could make.

Lucas re-released the Star Wars trilogy in 1997, citing several reasons. He wanted parents to be able to take their kids to see it on the big screen—in fact, his own young son had never seen any of the films, and Lucas looked forward to taking him to the theater. He also wanted people to be able to see all three of the films as episodes coming out every few weeks. Finally, he wanted to change things that he was unhappy with the first time around, when he didn't have the money or technology to accomplish his vision. As of mid-March 1997, the original and new versions of *Star Wars* together have grossed more than $450 million in the U.S. alone, making it the top-grossing movie of all time. Worldwide box-office receipts for all three films now total over $1.5 billion. As the box-office bonanza shows, the Star Wars films have lost none of their magic.

Lucas on the set of Willow

The Indiana Jones Movies

After the Star Wars trilogy, Lucas's next big project was the Indiana Jones movies: *Raiders of the Lost Ark* (1981), *Indiana Jones and the Temple of Doom* (1984), and *Indiana Jones and the Last Crusade* (1989). Years earlier, Lucas had dreamed of creating a movie like the old Saturday serials that were shown in movie theaters during the 1930s and 1940s. In those serials, each week's episode would end with a cliffhanger, leaving the audience wondering what would happen next. To capture the excitement of those old serials, Lucas dreamed up the stories in the Indiana Jones movies. Lucas served as the producer of the films, while his friend Steven Spielberg directed them. These three movies tell of the adventures of an archeologist named Indiana Jones, played with droll wit by Harrison Ford. Through his search for valuable and ancient artifacts, he has a series of astonishing and death-defying exploits, surviving various traps, ambushes, and double-crosses. He faces such threats as tarantulas, boulders, spears, runaway trucks, snakes, rats, and armored tanks. It is exhilarating and wildly imaginative, a thrill-a-minute ride. Audiences loved it, and the Indiana Jones movies were wildly successful.

In 1992, Lucas created a TV show based on the movies, "The Young Indiana Jones Chronicles," which followed Indy's adventures as a young man. Lucas saw the young Indiana Jones character as a means to introduce young viewers to some of the events and people that helped shape the 20th century, people like Teddy Roosevelt, Sigmund Freud, Pablo Picasso, and Albert Schweitzer. Lucas wanted to create a fun educational series, but the show was not a big hit.

Other Projects

Not all of Lucas's films have been as successful as the Star Wars and Indiana Jones movies. He also worked as the producer on *Howard the Duck* (1986), a film about a duck that comes to earth from another dimension; *Labyrinth* (1986), a fairy tale about a teenage girl who has to search through a labyrinth to find her brother, who was kidnaped by an evil king; *Willow* (1988), an adventure fantasy about a little person who rescues a baby and tries to find the family, only to meet up with a vicious sorceress and a fire-breathing dragon; *Tucker: The Man and His Dream* (1988), the story of Preston Tucker, a businessman and visionary from the 1940s who tried, and failed, to build "the car of the future"; and, finally, *Radioland Murders* (1994), a farce about murder at a radio network in 1939. Each of these films was a financial disappointment.

In addition to his work as a filmmaker, Lucas is also the owner and chief executive officer (CEO) of several related businesses. In 1971, he created his own production company, Lucasfilm Ltd. Today, this company includes film and TV production departments as well as the THX sound division, which created the digital sound system used in movie theaters. During the making of *Star Wars*, Lucas set up several companies to create the new kinds of special effects that he wanted for his movie: Industrial Light & Magic (ILM) for visual special effects, and Skywalker Sound for sound special effects. These companies, later combined into Lucas Digital Ltd., are widely considered the premier special effects shops in the industry. They have won numerous awards for the effects in the Star Wars movies as well as *ET, Jurassic Park, Terminator 2, Forrest Gump, Twister,* and many others. There is also a computer games company, LucasArts Entertainment, which has developed such games software as "Rebel Assault," "Dark Forces," "X-Wing," "Monkey Island," and "Maniac Mansion." In the mid-1980s, Lucas created a new company, Lucasfilm Learning, to develop such educational technology as interactive software and video games. The goal of this company has been to take the technological expertise gained in making movies and use it to create innovative learning materials. His empire also oversees all the Star Wars toys and other items that are sold. "I took control of the merchandising not because I thought it was going to make me rich, but because I wanted to control it. I wanted to make a stand for social, safety, and quality reasons. I didn't want someone using the name *Star Wars* on a piece of junk."

In 1991, Lucas founded the George Lucas Educational Foundation, driven by memories of his dissatisfaction with his own educational experience. In addition, he serves as a director on the boards of the National Geographic Society Education Foundation, the Artists Rights Foundation (he was a founding member), the Joseph Campbell Foundation, the Film Foundation, and the University of Southern California School of Cinema-Television Board of Councilors.

Lucas also created an artistic retreat called Skywalker Ranch, which occupies 3,000 acres in a beautiful area of rolling hills and forests in northern California. It was Lucas's longtime dream to create a place where young filmmakers can develop their skills and where experienced filmmakers can use top-notch production equipment in idyllic surroundings. "George Lucas has the best toys of anybody I have ever known, which is why it's so much fun playing over at George's house," Steven Spielberg once said. For Lucas, Skywalker Ranch guarantees his ability to exercise complete independence and control of the process of filmmaking, without any interference from a studio.

Current Plans

Lucas is currently working on the first movie of a new Star Wars trilogy. This "prequel," set 40 years before *Star Wars,* covers how the Empire rose to power. Scheduled to be released by 1999, this new film will be the first film Lucas has directed since the original *Star Wars.*

MAJOR INFLUENCES

Lucas's greatest influences are the directors François Truffaut, Jean-Luc Godard, and Akira Kurosawa. He also cites certain films, including Stanley Kubrick's *Dr. Strangelove,* Orson Welles's *Citizen Kane,* and Richard Lester's Beatles movies, *Help!* and *A Hard Day's Night.*

MARRIAGE AND FAMILY

While working at the USIA in the late 1960s, Lucas met Marcia Griffin, a fellow film editor. They were married in February 1969. In 1981, they adopted a daughter, Amanda. While George was becoming immersed in his film projects Marcia was building her career as an award-winning film editor, and the demands of their work often kept them apart. The couple divorced in 1983. As a single parent, Lucas later adopted a daughter, Katie, now 8, and a son, Jett, now 4. They live in California just a few miles from Skywalker Ranch.

WRITINGS

Star Wars, 1976 (the novel)
Shadow Moon, 1995 (co-written with Chris Claremont)

FILM AND TELEVISION CREDITS

THX 1138, 1970 (writer and director)
American Graffiti, 1973 (co-writer and director)
Star Wars, 1977 (writer and director)
More American Graffiti, 1979 (executive producer)
The Empire Strikes Back, 1980 (writer and executive producer)
Raiders of the Lost Ark, 1981 (executive producer)
Return of the Jedi, 1983 (writer and executive producer)
Indiana Jones and the Temple of Doom, 1984 (creator and co-executive producer)
Howard the Duck, 1986 (executive producer)
Labyrinth, 1986 (executive producer)
Willow, 1988 (writer and executive producer)
Tucker: The Man and His Dream, 1988 (executive producer)
Indiana Jones and the Last Crusade, 1989 (executive producer)
"The Young Indiana Jones Chronicles," 1992-93 (TV show; creator and
    executive producer)
Radioland Murders, 1994 (creator and executive producer)

HONORS AND AWARDS

Best Dramatic Film (National Student Film Festival): 1967, for *THX
    1138:4EB*
Irving G. Thalberg Award (Board of Governors of the Academy of Motion
    Picture Arts and Sciences): 1992

FURTHER READING

Books

Champlin, Charles. *George Lucas: The Creative Impulse,* 1992
Ebert, Roger, and Gene Siskel. *The Future of the Movies: Interviews with
    Martin Scorsese, Steven Spielberg, and George Lucas,* 1991
Encyclopedia Britannica, 1995
Mabery, D. L. *George Lucas,* 1987
Pollack, Dale. *Skywalking: The Life and Times of George Lucas,* 1983
Pye, Michael, and Lynda Myles. *The Movie Brats: How the Film Generation
    Took Over Hollywood,* 1979
Smith, Dian G. *American Filmmakers Today,* 1983 (juvenile)
Wakeman, John, ed. *World Film Directors, 1945-1985,* Vol. 2, 1988
Who's Who in America, 1997
World Book Encyclopedia, 1997
Worrell, Denise. *Icons: Intimate Portraits,* 1989

Periodicals

Current Biography Yearbook 1978
Film Comment, July-Aug. 1981, p.49
Film Quarterly, Spring 1974, p.2
Life, June 1983, p.84
Los Angeles Times, Feb. 4, 1997, p.F1
Los Angeles Times Magazine, Feb. 2, 1997, p.6
New York Times, May 21, 1987, p.C25; May 21, 1989, p.1
New York Times Biographical Service, July 1981, p.966
New Yorker, Jan. 6, 1997, p.40
Newsweek, Jan. 20, 1997, p.52
Philadelphia Inquirer Magazine, May 29, 1983, p.10
San Francisco Chronicle, May 21, 1989, Sunday Datebook section, p.20
San Francisco Examiner, Mar. 21, 1993, p.I8; Oct. 19, 1994, p.C3
Time, May 23, 1983, pp.62 and 66; Feb. 10, 1997, p.68
Wired, Feb. 1997, p.160

Videos

Star Wars — From Star Wars to Jedi: The Making of a Saga, 1983

ADDRESS

Lucasfilm Ltd.
P.O. Box 2009
San Rafael, CA 94912-2009

WORLD WIDE WEB SITE

http://www.starwars.com

John Madden 1936-

American Color Commentator for National Football
League Television Broadcasts
Former Head Coach of the Oakland Raiders

BIRTH

John Madden was born in Austin, Minnesota, on April 10,
1936. His father, Earl Madden, was an auto mechanic, while his
mother, Mary (O'Flaherty) Madden, was a homemaker. He
also had two younger sisters, Dolores and Judy. When John
was six years old, his family moved to Daly City, California,
near San Francisco on the Pacific Coast.

YOUTH

Madden enjoyed a happy and carefree childhood in Daly City. Behind his family's house was an empty lot where all the neighborhood children would gather to play football and baseball. He also spent a great deal of time hanging around at nearby Marchbank Park, a minor-league baseball facility, picking up broken bats and used balls. Madden's closest friend growing up was John Robinson, who went on to become a successful football coach with the University of Southern California Trojans and the Los Angeles Rams. As young boys, the two future coaches enjoyed playing sports, sneaking into movies, and hitching rides on freight trains heading toward San Francisco. "We had fun with no money," Madden recalled. "No kid ever had a better time growing up than I did."

EDUCATION

Madden attended a Catholic elementary school, Our Lady of Perpetual Help, where the nuns who were his teachers smacked his hands with a wooden pointer when he misbehaved. "The most scared I've ever been was the day Sister Superior . . . wanted to talk to my parents about me one night," Madden remembered. "When my dad got home from work, he never liked to go out, much less get dressed up to go out to see Sister Superior about me. When he and my mom got home, he was even more annoyed. 'John,' he said, 'that nun told us you talk in class too much.' I'm sure I did talk too much. And now [television] pays me to talk."

At Jefferson Union High School, Madden was an average student but an exceptional athlete. He played football and basketball and was a star catcher on the school's baseball team. Upon graduating from high school in 1954, Madden was offered contracts to play minor-league baseball for the New York Yankees and the Boston Red Sox, but he turned them down in favor of a college education. This decision was influenced by his experiences working as a golf caddy at local country clubs during the summers: "Walking along with the members under those beautiful oak and eucalyptus trees, I realized that the reason they all had money was because they were college graduates," Madden explained. "That's when I put it in my head never to quit school."

Along with his friend Robinson, Madden accepted a football scholarship to the University of Oregon in 1954. When a knee injury ended his freshman season, he returned to California and attended the College of San Mateo for a year. He then transferred to California Polytechnic State University (Cal Poly) at San Luis Obispo, where he played both football (as a tackle) and baseball (as a catcher) in 1957 and 1958. After receiving his bachelor of science degree in education from Cal Poly in 1959, Madden was selected in the 21st round of the National Football League draft by the Philadelphia Eagles. Unfortunately,

Madden's NFL playing career was cut short by another knee injury, which occurred during one of the first scrimmages at the Eagles' training camp. He spent part of the football season undergoing treatment for his knee in Philadelphia, then returned to Cal Poly to continue his studies. After receiving his master's degree in education in 1961, he continued to take courses over the next few years until he was close to earning his doctorate.

CHOOSING A CAREER

Madden first began to consider coaching football as a career when he was rehabilitating his knee in Philadelphia in 1959. Though he never actually played in a pro game, he did have an opportunity to watch game films with the Eagles' future Hall of Fame quarterback, Norm Van Brocklin. "I just watched and listened," Madden recalled. "Until then, I didn't know much about football except for what I did as a lineman on offense and defense. But sitting in that little room, I learned how to attack and how to defend. I learned the basic philosophy of being a coach. It's a good thing I did. I never played another game."

Later that year, while he was completing his practice teaching requirements at San Luis Obispo High School, Madden ended up coaching the school's football team for three weeks of summer practice. He soon discovered that the skills needed in coaching were closely related to those he had gained as a teacher. "Coaching is teaching. Some coaches try to make what they do sound mysterious and complicated when it's not. It's just football. But to be a good coach, you have to be a good teacher," he noted. "I learned how to get up in front of a group, present something, and get it done. In preparing for class, a teacher has to be organized. Once in the classroom, a teacher has to get the students to settle down, to pay attention, to understand. After you teach, you discuss and then you test. Coaching football is basically the same thing. You teach in meetings. You discuss on the practice field. You test in the game."

After deciding to become a football coach, Madden found that he still had a lot to learn when he attended a clinic taught by Vince Lombardi, the legendary coach of the Green Bay Packers. According to the program, Lombardi was going to provide a detailed explanation of one of his team's famous plays, the Green Bay Sweep. "As we filed into the lecture hall that day, I didn't expect to be there long. After all, how long could even Vince Lombardi talk about one play? Eight hours, that's how long!" Madden recalled. "Going into the lecture, I thought I knew everything there was to know about football. But suddenly I realized I didn't have any depth to my knowledge. In those years, I might have been able to talk for half an hour on one play. But not eight hours. Nowhere near eight hours. After that I went to all the clinics I could."

CAREER HIGHLIGHTS

In 1960, Madden was offered a job as a line coach in the football program at Allan Hancock Junior College in Santa Monica. He held this position for two years, and then acted as the team's head coach until 1964. That year he became the defensive coordinator at California State University, which was then the top-ranked small college team in the nation. Madden also taught health, recreation, and physical education at these schools during his college coaching career. In 1967, Madden accepted a position as linebacker coach with the NFL's Oakland Raiders. "I knew I wanted to be a head coach in the NFL, not in college," he explained. "In college a head coach has to be involved with recruiting, with alumni, with booster clubs. But in the NFL a head coach just has to coach. That's all I wanted to do — coach."

The Oakland Raiders

During Madden's first full season with the Raiders (1967), under head coach John Rauch, the team posted a 13-1 record but was defeated in Super Bowl II by the Packers, 33-14. The following year, Rauch left the team suddenly as a result of disagreements with the Raiders' opinionated owner, Al Davis. Davis named Madden as the new head coach on February 4, 1969. Since he had limited prior head-coaching experience, Madden admitted that he was "learning as I went along, learning from other people's advice, learning from what I remembered" during the 1969 season. Nevertheless, the Raiders posted an impressive 12-1-1 record, and Madden was named coach of the year. He also developed a positive working relationship with Davis. "Most head coaches have to make their reports to people who aren't football men, guys who don't understand," he once told a reporter. "Would you rather talk to Al Davis or to a guy who owns an oil company?"

Over the next ten years, Madden gradually grew into one of the best NFL coaches of all time. Under his guidance, the Raiders never had a losing season, even when they struggled with injuries at key positions. After making the playoffs in 1970 with an 8-4-1 record, Madden's team lost to the Baltimore Colts, and then they failed to reach the playoffs the following year. But they rebounded in 1972 to post a 10-3-1 record and fought their way to the conference championship game, where they lost to the Pittsburgh Steelers. The Raiders lost in the conference championship again in 1973, this time to the Miami Dolphins, after posting a 9-4-1 season record. In 1974 they topped the NFL at 12-2, only to lose another conference championship to the Steelers. History repeated itself the following year, as the Raiders went 11-3 but were again denied a chance to play in the Super Bowl by the Steelers.

By the start of the 1976 season, Madden had become the first NFL coach to win 70 games in his first seven years in the league. Even though the Raiders

were weakened by injuries, which forced Madden to change his defensive for-mation in mid-season, they posted a 13-1 record and finally earned a long-awaited trip to the Super Bowl in January 1977. There they faced the Minnesota Vikings, who had appeared in the big game in three of the previous four years. Still, the Raiders dominated Super Bowl XI from the opening kickoff and ended up winning by a score of 32-14. "After the gun went off ending the game," Madden recalled, "my three tallest players—John Matusak, Ted Hendricks, and Charles Philyaw—were carrying me off the field on their shoulders when one of them tripped over a photographer in front of us. One by one, Tooz, Ted, and Charles went down in a heap and I went down on top of them. That's the picture the *New York Times* used on its front page the next day." Adding to the sweetness of victory was the fact that the game had been played at the Rose Bowl in Pasadena, California—near Madden's childhood home—where just a few days earlier his old friend Robinson had coached the USC Trojans to victory in one of college football's premier post-season games.

During his coaching days, Madden became known for his ability to turn around the careers of "problem players" who had been dropped from other NFL teams because of their bad attitudes or work habits. "Yes, the Raiders took a few players that other teams had given up on—not that Al [Davis] and

I thought we had a magic formula to reform them. Our reasoning was, when a player's back is against the wall, when he realizes that no other team wants him, when he knows that the Raiders will be his last stop, that's when he should realize that if he doesn't shape up, his career will be over. We also never gave up much, if anything, to get that type of player," Madden noted. "For us, it was always a no-lose situation. If the guy didn't work out, we hadn't lost any important players or draft choices. But some of our renegades really worked out, like Matusak, who became the left defensive end on our Super Bowl XI team."

The Raiders always played with discipline and intensity on the field, but Madden was not particularly strict as a coach. In fact, he became known for the genuine concern he showed toward his players. Madden established a few basic rules, but other than that he gave the players a great deal of freedom. For example, he did not require his team to get dressed up to go to games. "Maybe it was because I didn't particularly like a coat and tie, but I preferred my players to be comfortable when they traveled. I never agreed with coaches who thought that a coat and tie develop discipline, or with coaches who thought that rules against long hair, beards, or sideburns developed discipline. To me, discipline in football occurs on the field, not off it. Discipline is knowing what you're supposed to do and doing it as best you can," he stated. "I had only three rules on the Raiders — be on time, pay attention, and play like hell when I tell you to."

Another thing Madden was known for during his coaching career was his theatrical outbursts on the sidelines. He could often be seen yelling at the referees, jumping around, or gesturing wildly with his arms during games. Early in his career, many officials seemed almost frightened of him, but later they seemed to understand that their best strategy was to ignore him. "That's how the officials were reacting to me my last few seasons as a coach. Humoring me. Almost laughing at me. If one of them was near me after a close call, I would yell at him but he would hardly acknowledge it. 'You're something today,' the official might mutter. They stopped fighting with me, which is the best way to avoid a fight. They had taken me seriously my first few seasons as the Raider coach. But after that, the officials acted like they were just putting up with me, that I was noisy but harmless. In a way they were correct," Madden recalled.

Retirement from Coaching

Despite the thrill of winning the Super Bowl, Madden soon found that he had grown tired of coaching. He also learned that he had developed an ulcer — a painful condition where excess digestive acid eats away the lining of the stomach—and his doctors put him on medication and recommended that he avoid stress. "By itself, the ulcer didn't persuade me to stop coaching. Lots of people work with ulcers. I could've kept coaching with it, but I just didn't *want* to keep coaching," he explained. "It seemed like I never had a chance to recharge my batteries, especially after we won Super Bowl XI—I never had time to enjoy it. As soon as we got back from that Super Bowl, we started thinking about the college draft and our minicamp and then training camp and, boom, the season was starting. It seemed like we went from the Super Bowl to training camp without any break. Without any time off for myself or my family."

Still, Madden continued coaching the Raiders through the 1977 and 1978 seasons, partly because he hoped to become the first coach to win 100 games in ten years with the same NFL team. But during a Raiders exhibition game in August 1978, something happened that clinched his decision to quit. Darryl Stingley, a wide receiver for the visiting New England Patriots, broke his neck in a collision with Raiders free safety Jack Tatum. Stingley was carried from the field on a stretcher and remained in an Oakland hospital for several weeks. His injury caused him to be permanently paralyzed from the neck down. Madden felt terrible about Stingley's injury and visited him frequently in the hospital. "In my decision to stop coaching, Darryl's situation was a factor. Not the only factor, but *a* factor," Madden noted. "During the weeks he was in Eden Hospital, not many people seemed to care enough. That's when I started wondering if football people really care about a player, or if football people just care about what a player does. And when a player suddenly can't do what he does, if football people don't care about him then, they probably never really cared about him to begin with."

Madden announced his retirement as head coach of the Oakland Raiders on January 4, 1979, after surpassing his personal goal by posting 103 career regular-season wins. As he told the audience at his emotional press conference, "I'm not resigning, quitting for doing anything else. I'm retiring. I'll never coach another game of football. I gave it everything I had for ten years, and I don't have any more." When asked about his plans for the future, Madden replied, "I'm not the type of guy who's ever going to have a TV show or a radio show. I'm not the type of guy who's ever going to do a book." But within the next five years, he had done all that and more.

TV Broadcaster

Shortly after his retirement, Madden signed a contract with CBS to provide analysis during televised NFL games. This job required him to sit in a broadcast booth with a play-by-play announcer, who would describe the action on the field. Madden, meanwhile, was responsible for providing the viewing audience with extra insight into what was taking place. At first, Madden found many aspects of his new job confusing and difficult. For example, he had to get used to seeing the action from far above the playing field, rather than along the sidelines. He also had to adjust to wearing a headset and hearing his producer's instructions in his ear while he was talking. During one game, when a picture of the coach of one of the teams appeared on the TV screen, Madden's producer prompted him by saying, "Coach, coach." The producer wanted Madden to give the viewers some inside information about the man they saw on their screens. Instead, Madden replied, "Yeah, what do you want?" He was so used to having people call him "Coach" that he assumed the producer was talking to him.

But Madden adapted quickly to his new role and within three years had become the main color commentator for CBS. Many people praised him for breaking down the technical aspects of football and making the game more understandable for TV audiences. "For me, TV is really an extension of coaching. My knowledge of football has come from coaching. And on TV, all I'm trying to do is pass on some of that knowledge to the viewers," he explained. "One of my tests for a good telecast is if I didn't miss anything. If the coaches or players later mention something significant about the game that I didn't mention, I'm not happy. Another test is whether I feel the viewer has learned something about football or football people." Madden was the first football analyst to use a telestrator, or "chalkboard," to help him teach TV audiences about the game. This device allowed him to draw lines on the screen showing where various players would move during a particular play.

Madden soon came to enjoy his new job. As he became more comfortable behind the microphone, he became known as an animated, entertaining presence during NFL broadcasts. "In the TV booth, I'm the same guy I was as a coach on the sideline," he stated. "Most announcers sit down, but I prefer to stand up, to swing my arms, to move around as much as possible. I once knocked [fellow broadcaster] Gary Bender's glasses off. Just before the game and at halftime, you see me with my tie on straight and wearing a blue blazer. CBS rules. But when I'm not on camera, my tie is loose and I'm in shirtsleeves, just like I was on the sideline. For me to do it any other way wouldn't be natural. And on TV, you have to be natural or you come across as a phoney."

Almost from the beginning of his broadcast career, Madden has been paired with play-by-play announcer Pat Summerall. The two men developed a close friendship as well as a productive working relationship. "Pat Summerall is as easy to work with as he is to be with. He's easy to hang out with, to tell stories with, and I think that comes across to the viewer. He's just a good guy," Madden explained. "I like to bluster about a play, but Pat will sum it up in a few words. One time I was raving about a great catch a wide receiver had made, about how he had juggled the ball like an acrobat before finally hanging onto it. 'That guy,' Pat commented, 'should've been a waiter.' As simple as that. As quick as that. As good as that." In 1994, Fox Television outbid CBS for the right to broadcast NFL games, but both Madden and Summerall were hired by the new network. In fact, Madden's four-year, $32 million contract meant that he earned a higher salary than any NFL player.

Over the years, as Madden traveled extensively in his careers as NFL coach and broadcaster, he gradually developed an acute fear of flying. He never did enjoy stuffing his burly frame into cramped airplane seats, but his discomfort intensified after the Cal Poly tragedy of 1960. Just two years after Madden's playing career there had ended, a plane carrying the Cal Poly football team crashed, killing 22 of the 44 people on board, including 16 players. Madden experienced more and more anxiety each time he had to fly in a plane, until one day he felt he could not take it anymore. He then began taking the train back and forth across the country, and he soon found that he enjoyed it. "Like the Amtrak ads say, you really do see America—the mountains, the desert, the prairies, the farmland, the little towns, the big cities. What's even more fun, you see the people," he noted. More recently, he began traveling in a specially equipped Greyhound bus, known as the "Maddencruiser," which can be seen outside of football stadiums across the United States. The bus allows Madden to set his own schedule and enjoy his time on the road. "I'm lucky. I'm a football guy. My life revolves around the football season," he stated. "From the time I was a little kid, I've always had a football season. As a player. As a coach. And now as a broadcaster. I'm doing what I love and I love what I'm doing."

Actor in Popular Commercials

In addition to his broadcasting career, Madden has written several books, including a best-selling 1984 autobiography, *Hey, Wait a Minute (I Wrote a Book!).* He has also hosted two syndicated radio talk shows out of Jumbo Studios, a production facility he built in 1993 near his home in California. But Madden is probably best known for his appearances in a series of popular TV commercials for Miller Lite beer during their "Tastes Great, Less Filling" advertising campaign. The amusing commercials featured a number of well-known former professional athletes and coaches—including Billy Martin, Red Auerbach, Dick Butkus, Deacon Jones, Bubba Smith, and Tom Heinsohn—arguing about whether they drank Miller Lite for its taste or because it was low in calories. In one spot, Madden is shown in a bar, calmly explaining, "I'm not the same crazy coach you've seen on TV." But he becomes more and more animated as he continues talking, until he is ranting and raving like he used to do on the sidelines. At the end of the commercial, he bursts through a paper wall and says, "And another thing. . . ." Madden later claimed that "breaking through that paper for Miller Lite made me more famous than I ever was as a coach." He appeared in a number of subsequent commercials, including ones that took place in a bowling alley, on a baseball field, and in a corporate boardroom. Madden particularly enjoyed working with the other coaches and athletes, as they all became close friends and played relentless practical jokes on one another.

MARRIAGE AND FAMILY

John Madden met his wife, Virginia Fields Madden, in a bar while they were both students at Cal Poly. They got engaged before he went to Philadelphia for the Eagles training camp, and they were married shortly after his return. They have two sons, Mike and Joe, who both ended up playing football in college. Madden enjoyed attending his sons' sporting events while they were growing up, and he claimed that he managed to avoid the temptation to coach them: "Watching my kids play, I hardly said a word. I didn't even yell at the umpires or the officials. One reason was that I didn't want to let people know I was there. But the main reason was I didn't want to act like some of the other parents. It's one thing to yell *for* your kid's team, but it's another to yell *at* your kid." Today, Madden lives with his wife near Pleasanton, California, and also keeps an apartment in Manhattan, New York.

HOBBIES AND OTHER INTERESTS

Despite his wealth and fame, Madden lives a relatively simple life. "I don't like fancy clothes. I don't like fancy food. Just let me wear a sweat suit and sneakers to a real Mexican restaurant for nachos and a chile colorado. That's my idea of a big night," he stated. "I love poker games. I love to just hang out. I never go to the movies or the theater. I'm not even big on music, unless it's Willie Nelson."

SELECTED WRITINGS

Hey, Wait a Minute (I Wrote a Book!), 1984 (with Dave Anderson)
One Knee Equals Two Feet (And Everything Else You Need to Know about Football), 1986 (with Dave Anderson)
One Size Doesn't Fit All (And Other Thoughts from the Road), 1988 (with Dave Anderson)
All Madden: Hey, I'm Talking Pro Football, 1996 (with Dave Anderson)

HONORS AND AWARDS

Coach of the Year (Washington Touchdown Club): 1977
Vince Lombardi Dedication Award: 1979
Emmy Award for Sports Broadcasting (Academy of Television Arts and Sciences): 1981-83, 1985-88
Golden Mike Award (Touchdown Club of America): 1982
Sports Personality of the Year (American Sportscasters' Association): 1985, 1992

FURTHER READING

Books

Information Please Sports Almanac, 1995

Madden, John. *Hey, Wait a Minute (I Wrote a Book!),* 1984 (with Dave Anderson)

———. *One Knee Equals Two Feet (And Everything Else You Need to Know about Football)* 1986 (with Dave Anderson)

———. *One Size Doesn't Fit All (And Other Thoughts from the Road),* 1988 (with Dave Anderson)

Who's Who in America 1997

Periodicals

Buffalo News, Jan. 26, 1997, p. TV24

Chicago Tribune, Mar 20, 1994, Section: Travel, p.1; Sep. 2, 1994, Section: Football, p.16; Sep. 1, 1995, Section: Football, p.18

Columbus Dispatch, Oct. 9, 1995, Section: Business Today, p.1

Current Biography Yearbook 1985

Forbes, Dec. 20, 1993, p.21

Los Angeles Times, Jan. 23, 1982, p.B1; Dec. 19, 1982, p.C3; Dec. 23, 1983, p.C1

New York Times, Jan. 6, 1977, p.E3

Newsweek, Jan. 8, 1984, p.66

People, Jan. 25, 1982, p.99

San Francisco Chronicle, Aug. 10, 1994, p.D1; Jan. 23, 1995, p.A13; May 23, 1997, p.E2

Sport, Nov. 1976, p.45; Aug. 1983, p.59

Sporting News, Jan. 20, 1979, p.31

Sports Illustrated, Nov. 17, 1980, p.77; Sep.1, 1983, p.38

TV Guide, Jan. 8, 1983, p.20; Feb. 5, 1994, p.36; Sep. 3, 1994, p.5

Washington Post, Jan. 8, 1984, p.C3; Sep. 10, 1996, p.D2

ADDRESS

Fox Sports
1211 Avenue of the Americas
Second Floor
New York, NY 10036

WORLD WIDE WEB SITE

http://www.foxsports.com

Bill Monroe   1911-1996

American Singer and Songwriter
Father of Bluegrass Music

BIRTH

William Smith Monroe was born September 13, 1911, in Rosine, Kentucky, to James and Melissa Monroe. James was a farmer and lumberman and Melissa was a homemaker. Bill was the youngest of eight children in the family, including brothers James, Buchanan, Charlie, Birch, and Speed, and sisters Melissa and Bertha.

EARLY MEMORIES

Bill grew up on the family farm in Rosine in a large family that loved music. One of his earliest memories is of his mother playing the fiddle while she made dinner. "She'd be cookin' dinner, and she would have a fiddle laying on the bed, and she'd go by the bed and pick it up and play, maybe one number, then go on in the kitchen and do some more cookin'. And she could play the accordion some. But she could also play the fiddle, and she could sing. She had a good voice." Bill's father, James, didn't play an instrument, but was a great dancer.

Each of the children played an instrument, so when Bill came along the guitar and violin, his first two choices, were taken. So he had to settle for the mandolin, a small, stringed instrument which Bill Monroe would one day master and play like nobody else.

Music was a family activity, played in the afternoons and evenings as the family sat on the porch. Mostly they played the traditional Scottish fiddle tunes that the Monroes had all grown up with. They also played and sang gospel tunes, influenced by the singing they did in church. "The first singing that I tried to do, we'd go to church there in Rosine, Kentucky, at the Methodist, or Baptist, then there was a Holiness church that moved in later on," Monroe recalled. "They sang some fine songs there at Rosine, Kentucky. That played a part in the kind of a sound and the kind of feeling that I wanted in my music, too. Taken right from the gospel song."

In rural Rosine, as in much of the rural South at the time Monroe was growing up, barn dances took place very weekend. The Monroes would ride the wagon to the barn dance, sing, play, and dance, and ride back home.

YOUTH

Monroe was terribly shy as a young child, mostly because he was born with crossed eyes He had an operation to have them straightened, but the experience left him self-conscious. When company would come, he'd "get under the floor if I could, just anything to get away from 'em, so I could see them and they couldn't see me. I was the most bashful kid in the world."

When Bill was just seven or eight, his older brothers went off to fight in World War I (1914-1918). He remembered being lonely at the time, and working the fields behind a plow pulled by a single mule. Sometimes he would sing to himself as he worked. Later, he thought this was the source of what became his signature "high lonesome" sound, the tenor, or high pitched, male voice, singing a lonely tune.

One day, while he was working in the fields, he heard a sound he couldn't believe. It was his brothers returning home from the war, singing a gospel tune. The loneliness was over for awhile, but that high lonesome sound would be around for years to come.

Bill Monroe's young life was marked by early loss. His mother died when he was 10, and his father when he was 16. After that, he moved in with his uncle, Pendleton Vandiver, whom he would immortalize years later in his famous song "Uncle Pen." He and Uncle Pen "batched it" for several years, going to barn dances on the weekends and playing music whenever they could. "Uncle Pen and me used to play the square dances; I tried to back him up on guitar. We'd play for the parties and the dances. Sometimes we'd ride the same horse back on the little country roads." Another major influence on Monroe's music was a friend of Uncle Pen's, a black blues musician named Arnold Schultz. Schultz was a guitar and fiddle player whose bluesy sound came to influence Monroe's bluegrass sound years later.

EDUCATION

Monroe went to the local public schools in Rosine. Life revolved around the farm work that had to be done, though. "We'd go to school through the end of school. Then we'd stay home and work and help out all we could," Monroe recalled. He went to school though the sixth grade, then quit to help out on the farm.

Moving North

When Monroe was in his late teens, he moved north to the Chicago area to join his brothers, who had moved years before in search of work. He found a job moving oil barrels and lived with his siblings in Chicago. "I went to work up there in 19 and 30—up in East Chicago, Indiana," he recalled. "I worked at the Sinclair Refinery Co. I worked for them about four or five years and we were playing music on the side. We were playing a lot of different places and singing and it was giving us some practice."

At one point, Bill was the only one working. It was the Great Depression, a time of severe economic hardship throughout the United States, when millions of Americans were out of work. "Well, there was a time when my brothers couldn't find any work. And my two sisters were there, and they wasn't workin' either. But I worked every day. The people out at the Sinclair refineries, some of 'em was from Kentucky, and they knew that I needed the money to take care of everything—pay our rent and buy groceries. And they let me work thirty days in the month, 'cause they knew that I needed the work. And I took care of everything."

Soon all the brothers were back to work, and the Monroes were playing music again. They became regulars on the WLS National Barn Dance tours, where they would dance for the audience, then get up and play.

BIOGRAPHY TODAY • 1997 Annual Cumulation

After several years, Birch decided to take a full-time job in the refineries. Bill and Charlie wanted to pursue music full time, so they formed a group, the Monroe Brothers, that played together for several years. Their schedule was incredible, Monroe remembered. "We had two programs a day on radio, one in Greenville, South Carolina, and one on WBT-Charlotte really early in the morning. We drove 100 miles from one place to another and then we played schools at night. They kept after us to make these records, but we threw away the first several letters they wrote to us. We finally went up to their studio in Charlotte, but we told 'em we didn't have much time, that we had to get back in time to play a school that night."

The brothers had a notoriously stormy relationship. They argued all the time, and finally, in 1938, they split up. Bill went on to form his own group, "The Kentuckians," who later became "The Blue Grass Boys."

THE BIRTH OF BLUEGRASS

Monroe's Blue Grass Boys played a kind of music that had never been heard before. Monroe had developed it himself, blending the influences of Scottish and Irish fiddle tunes, gospel, blues, and jazz, played by an old-time traditional string band ensemble that included fiddle, guitar, mandolin, banjo, and bass. Monroe described it this way: "It's got a hard drive to it. It's Scotch bagpipes and old-time fiddlin'. It's Methodist and Holiness and Baptist. It's blues and jazz, and it has a high lonesome sound. It's plain music that tells a good story. It's played from my heart to your heart, and it will touch you."

And touch people it did. Monroe and the Blue Grass Boys auditioned for the Grand Old Opry in 1939. They played "Mule Skinner Blues" and "Boil Them Cabbage Down." The judges were impressed. They were invited to join, beginning a relationship that lasted six decades, ending in the 1990s with Monroe's death.

CAREER HIGHLIGHTS

In the 1940s bluegrass music took the country by storm. People loved the rapid-fire delivery of the tunes and the sweet, sentimental lyrics about love, home, and religion. They loved the instrumental drive and the sound of Monroe's "high lonesome" tenor, a sound he worked on for years. "I knew what I wanted to do," he said. "I could hear it. Back in the early days of the Monroe Brothers, I sung a lot of high baritone, you see. Charlie didn't carry the lead so high. So I would mix the high baritone with tenor. And then when I started the bluegrass group, why, I went up in tenor, you know, up high. We pitched our music up higher."

By the late 1940s Bill Monroe was recognized as an artist who had invented a new type of music, "bluegrass," named for his home state and his own band.

Some of the most important names in bluegrass and country music passed through Monroe's band over the years. Included among them are the legendary Lester Flatt and Earl Scruggs, Mac Wiseman, Jimmy Martin, Bill Keith, Chubby Wise, Howard Watts, Kenny Baker, Peter Rowan, Clyde Moody, Don Reno, Sonny Osborne, Richard Greene, Roland White, Bobby Thompson, Norman Black, and modern country giant Ricky Skaggs. "All of them have played a part in the music," said Monroe. "Everybody that's worked for me has played a part when they were working for me, when they were coming along with some good ideas. Some of the fiddle players, some of the banjo players, some of the guitar players had different ideas that they would come along with that I would use and put in the music."

Monroe said this about the musicians who played with him over the years: "Well, I'm glad that they got their start from bluegrass, and I hope that they'll take care of it, and make a future for theirself, and make plenty of money with it, make a good livin'. If you take care of bluegrass music right, and play it right, it will tell you down through a lot of it what you should do, and how you should treat people."

Flatt and Scruggs

One of the most famous bands Monroe ever put together was the Flatt and Scruggs band of the 1940s. Scruggs is credited with virtually inventing the style of banjo playing that is one of the hallmarks of bluegrass, a three-finger plucking style that is immediately recognizable. Monroe's innovations to music include trading off the melody during a song, so that a banjo solo can be featured, followed by a vocal solo, then another instrumental solo, showcasing and highlighting all the talent in a band.

In the late 1940s Flatt and Scruggs left Monroe and founded their own band. Monroe was hurt by what he considered their "defection" from his group, and he refused to speak to them for 23 years. As Flatt and Scruggs became a well-known group in their own right, they became more mainstream country in their sound, and they drew away some of Monroe's old audience. But Monroe kept performing and composing some of bluegrass's greatest hits, including "Footsteps in the Snow," "Kentucky Waltz, "My Little Georgia Rose," "The Old Mountaineer," "Blue Moon of Kentucky," and "Remember the Cross."

Monroe also continued to record throughout the 40s and 50s, signing for the Decca label and producing such great hit albums as *Knee Deep in Blue Grass, The High Lonesome Sound of Bill Monroe,* and *Bill Monroe and His Blue Grass Boys.* He was also a prodigious composer, turning out new songs throughout his long life. "I don't know how I do it, but I can write a number in two or three minutes," Monroe remembered. He composed with ease: "I never

wrote a tune in my life," he claimed. "All that music's in the air around you all the time. I was just the first one to reach up and pull it out." Monroe always talked of the importance of bluegrass as dance music, how understanding the rhythms of the tunes was so important. "I learned how to keep time on mighty near every kind of music when I was a boy, real young," said Monroe. "The schottische, waltzes, two-steps, and all that, marches, polkas, the old-time square dance music. It doesn't matter what kind of music you're playing, it doesn't hurt to know the time of all the music."

Frequently touring throughout the 1940s and 1950s, Monroe offered a unique entertainment for his audiences. The band traveled with a baseball team as part of a traveling tent show. When they reached a site, they would pitch the tent, and for 25 cents the audience could enjoy a concert, then a baseball game, starring the bluegrass musicians themselves! "We would seat around 3,000 people in the tent. And then I had the baseball club, the team that traveled with us, and we would play a ball game in the evening and then the show would start." Asked if one of the requirements for a being a Blue Grass Boy was being able to pitch, hit, or field, Monroe said, "Well, it helped out if you could play baseball."

Monroe was a tough boss. He made his musicians work hard, and the band toured constantly, roaming the country in a tour bus. He set high standards of playing and conduct. "They got to do what I say," Monroe said of his musicians. "I don't want nobody comin' around workin' drunk. And a filthy mouth, I wouldn't put up with that. Bluegrass music is respectable." Monroe was known as a man who was famously taciturn. Music writer Charles Wolf remembers that Monroe "was moody, he was introspective. He did not tolerate fools very well. He had a tremendous respect for good musicians, but he didn't have a lot of patience. You know, if somebody asked him a perfectly stupid question, he would just simply stare at you with that wonderful radar stare that would just wither a normal person."

One of the famous stories about Monroe concerns his beloved Gibson mandolin. He had sent the instrument back to the manufacturer for repairs. "I needed some work done on it," remembered Monroe. "I needed a new finger board. I had wore the finger board out, the frets, and it needed some new keys. Well, I sent it back, and they kept it four months, you see. And it shouldn't take that long to fix a mandolin. So it just hurt me so bad, then I thought, well, I'd just take the name of Gibson off it, they treated me that way." So he scratched the Gibson logo off the mandolin. He and Gibson made peace years later. When vandals broke into his log cabin home in Tennessee in the 1980s, they smashed his priceless mandolin. The Gibson people took three months reconstructing the instrument, which had been broken into 200 pieces.

By the mid-1950s, the sound of American popular music was changing. Elvis Presley, Jerry Lee Lewis, and other singers were trying out the new sound of rock and roll, which would also affect Monroe's audience over the years. Ironically, one of Monroe's most famous tunes, "Blue Moon of Kentucky" became, in a rockabilly version, the first hit of a Southern singer named Elvis Presley. Later, Monroe remembered this about Presley. "Elvis had a good voice. I thought he had a beautiful voice. And he come up to the Grand Ole Opry one time and come in the dressin' room. And he apologized for the way that he changed 'Blue Moon of Kentucky.' I told him 'Well, if it give you your start, it's all right with me.'"Monroe had very little use for rock, or for its affects on country music as it yielded to the influence of rock. He refused to use electric instruments and remained true to the original sound of bluegrass.

The folk music movement of the 1960s brought a new audience to Monroe's music. College students on campuses throughout the country were thrilled by bluegrass and Monroe's playing. He played folk festivals and saw the birth of bluegrass festivals around the nation. In 1968, he founded his own bluegrass festival, Bean Blossom, on property he had bought in Indiana. Bean Blossom still hosts one of the largest bluegrass festivals in North America.

In 1970, Monroe was inducted into the Country Music Hall of Fame. Later in the 1970s, Monroe took his first tour of the Holy Land. He had always been a religious man, and he was baptized in the Jordan River during his trip to Israel. He also played three bluegrass concerts in Israel, giving that country its very first taste of live bluegrass music. They loved it. "The people didn't know nothin' about bluegrass music. But they were *crazy* about it when they heard it," remembered Monroe.

During the 1980s, Monroe, in his 70s, began to have health problems. He had heart problems and fought stomach cancer. One of his most haunting songs dates from this time, "My Last Day on Earth." "It could have been my last days," says Monroe of that time. "But I had willpower and hope. I don't want to give up. I never give up." In 1984 Monroe founded the Blue Grass Hall of Fame and Museum in Nashville as a showcase for the music he had brought into being. Also in 1984, country music great Ricky Skaggs made a recording of Monroe's "Uncle Pen," the tribute to his musical uncle, and made it the first bluegrass song to top the country charts. Skaggs had first played for Monroe when he was just 11, and bluegrass has always influenced his music. Skaggs said this about Monroe: "I think Bill's music will go down in history as being one of the most pure, traditional, forms of American music. In fact, I think it really does epitomize American music."

In the 1990s Monroe continued to perform up to 150 shows a year. In his signature white cowboy hat, suit, and tie, he continued to bring new fans to the musical form he had created. Briefly sidelined by a broken hip in 1994, he was back on the concert stage as soon as he could. He was also honored by his home state when "Blue Moon of Kentucky" was chosen to replace "My Old Kentucky Home" in 1991 as the official state song.

In April 1996, Monroe suffered a stroke that left him unable to walk or talk. He died in a hospice in Tennessee on September 9, 1996, just four days before his 85th birthday.

Tributes to Monroe poured in from all over the world. His influence on music was enormous: musicians as diverse as the late Grateful Dead's guitarist Jerry Garcia and modern day bluegrass star Alison Krauss called him one of the greatest influences on their music. Ricky Skaggs said, "There's probably nobody really on the face of the Earth that ever influenced more music than Bill Monroe. In all of history, he's the biggest single influence in country music. And he didn't just influence country music, he influenced music in general." Monroe was celebrated in a concert given in his honor at Ryman Auditorium in Nashville, the old home of the Grand Ole Opry. Playing in tribute to Monroe were Skaggs, Emmylou Harris, Vince Gill, Ralph Stanley, and former Blue Grass Boys Earl Scruggs, Mac Wiseman, and Sonny Osborne.

MARRIAGE AND FAMILY

Monroe was married twice. With his first wife, the former Carolyn Brown, he had two children, James and Melissa. That marriage ended in divorce. Monroe and his second wife, Della, were married in 1985, but the marriage ended in divorce within a few years.

Monroe had a 288-acre farm outside of Nashville, Tennessee, where he still enjoyed plowing his fields behind a mule. He had to sell the farm in 1994 when debts piled up. But the property was purchased by the owners of the Grand Old Opry, and Monroe was allowed to use the 140-year old cabin on the property, plus the surrounding acres, until the end of his life. He enjoyed vigorous farm labor up until the time of his stroke.

Monroe is buried in his hometown of Rosine, and his grave has become something of a national shrine to his music. Fans come to pay tribute to the father of bluegrass, and they leave mementos, like mandolin and guitar picks.

MONROE'S LEGACY

This is how Monroe himself wished to be remembered: "Father of Bluegrass Music. That's a good line there. I appreciate that. I'm really glad and proud that I've done somethin' good for America. And I'm glad that the music was called "bluegrass," comin' from the state of Kentucky, since I was born and raised there. It's spread all over the world, and I'm really proud of that. I don't think bluegrass music will ever die now. So I would just like for people to remember me and what I've done."

SELECTED RECORDINGS

Knee Deep in Blue Grass, 1958
The High Lonesome Sound of Bill Monroe, 1966
Bill Monroe and His Blue Grass Boys, 1970
Bill Monroe's Country Music Hall of Fame, 1971
Uncle Pen, 1972
Bean Blossom, 1973
Best of Bill Monroe, 1975
Bill Monroe and Friends, 1983
Country Music Hall of Fame Series, 1991
The Essential Bill Monroe, 1992
The Music of Bill Monroe from 1936 to 1994, 1994 (4 CD compilation)

HONORS AND AWARDS

Country Music Hall of Fame: 1970
Nashville Songwriters Association International Hall of Fame: 1971
Music City News Award for Best Bluegrass Group: 1980, 1981
National Heritage Fellowship: 1982
Grammy Award: 1989, for Best Bluegrass Recording
Lifetime Achievement Award: 1993, National Academy of Recording Arts and Sciences

National Medal of the Arts: 1995
Rock and Roll Hall of Fame: 1996 (inducted)

FURTHER READING

Books

Nash, Allana. *Behind Closed Doors: Talking with the Legends of Country Music,*
    1988
Who's Who in America 1996

Periodicals

American Heritage, Nov. 1994, p.40
Atlanta Constitution, Sep. 10, 1996, p.A1
Chicago Tribune, Sep. 11, 1988, Arts, p.24
Entertainment Weekly, Sep. 20, 1996, p.81
Lexington Herald-Leader, June 4, 1990, p. B2; Sep. 8, 1996, p.B5; Sep. 10,
    1996, p.A1
Los Angeles Times, Jul. 31, 1987, Calendar, p.1
New York Times, June 9, 1994, p.C1; Sep. 10, 1996, p.A22; Sep. 22, 1996,
    p.A30; Nov. 4, 1996, p.A8
Newsweek, Sep. 23, 1996, p.75
People, Sep. 1, 1986, p.49; Sep. 23, 1996, p.130
Philadelphia Inquirer, Sep. 10, 1996, p.B6
Rolling Stone, June 16, 1994, p.25; Sep. 22, 1994, p.54; Oct. 31, 1996, p.20
Smithsonian, Mar. 1993, p.69
Wall Street Journal, Sep. 16, 1996, p.A14
Washington Post, Sep. 10, 1996, p.A1

Other

National Public Radio, transcript, "Morning Edition," Sep. 10, 1996

Alanis Morissette 1974-

Canadian Singer and Songwriter
Creator of *Jagged Little Pill*, the All-Time Best-Selling
Recording by a Female Artist

BIRTH

Alanis Nadine Morissette was born on June 1, 1974, in Ottawa,
Canada. Her father was Alan Morissette, a French-Canadian
teacher and principal, and her mother was Georgia (Feuerstein)
Morissette, a Hungarian-born teacher. Alanis has an older
brother, Chad, and a twin brother, Wade.

Alanis's mother, Georgia (Feuerstein) Morissette, fled from her
native Hungary to Canada in 1956 at the time of the anti-

Communist revolt, when many Hungarians rose up to protest against Communist rule imposed by the then-Soviet Union. Georgia and Alan met at school in Ottawa, according to Alanis. "My parents are outgoing, worldly, direct people who are very cute together," she says. "For instance, my father went up to my mother in an Ottawa schoolyard when he was 12 and told her, 'I'm gonna marry *you*'." Years later, after his prediction proved true, the family lived mostly in Ottawa. But they did spend three years, beginning when Alanis was three years old, in the former West Germany, where Alan and Georgia Morissette taught the children of U.S. military forces.

YOUTH

Alanis Morissette came to superstardom at an amazingly young age—she was only 21 when her hit record, *Jagged Little Pill* (1995), was released. But she had been part of the entertainment industry for over 10 years by then, since about age 10. In fact, Morissette really didn't have a typical childhood, because she was working the whole time. She's been preparing for success her whole life.

At age six, Alanis began studying piano, and at age nine, she began writing poetry and songs. But then the acting bug struck. After auditioning along with 600 other kids, she landed a role on the Nickelodeon series "You Can't Do That on Television," which was filmed in Canada. "It was a good, stupid, sarcastic kind of show. Very obnoxious and very tongue in cheek," she now recalls. "I got hate mail [from female viewers] because I played the girlfriend of the two lead guys on the show, so I represented a threat to them ever having these guys. It wasn't the best experience." Other small acting jobs followed, including a part opposite Matt LeBlanc, now a star on "Friends."

But her first love was always music. In fact, Alanis saved her earnings from her acting jobs to create her own record label, Lamor Records. Her 1987 single, which she financed and released independently when she was 12, featured two songs, both written by Alanis: "Fate Stay with Me" and "Find the Right Man." Also at about age 12, Alanis hooked up with a local entertainment promoter, Stephan Klovan, who was auditioning kids to perform at a spring pageant. He asked her to do a cartwheel like the other kids, but she refused. Instead, she sang "Find the Right Man." Klovan was bowled over by her talent and maturity, and he made her the star of that performance.

Klovan started booking dates for her to sing the national anthem at high-profile sports events, beginning with the 1988 World Figure Skating Championships, which were held in Ottawa. As he later recalled, "There was an RCMP (Royal Canadian Mounted Police) officer next to her as she sang it and there were tears coming down his eyes. So I knew right then that was a good vehicle for her." Klovan also helped her to hook up with Leslie Howe, who became her musical collaborator, as producer and songwriter. Alanis continued to perform locally, and she even flew to Paris to film a promotional video for one of her songs — she thought the Paris scenery would make her seem more worldly. At age 14, with the help of the video, she landed a song-publishing contract with MCA Music Publishing in Toronto, Ontario.

EDUCATION

Morissette was raised a Roman Catholic, and early on she attended Ottawa Catholic schools, including Immaculata High School. She transferred from there to Glebe Collegiate High School. There, she excelled in music and drama classes. Morissette graduated from Glebe Collegiate High School in 1992, when she was 17.

FIRST JOBS

By the time she graduated from high school, though, Morissette was already a star across Canada. Her 1991 debut recording, *Alanis*, sold over 100,000 copies and earned her a Juno Award, the Canadian equivalent of a Grammy Award. At that time, her music and her image were very different from what they are today. In her early years she'd been called a Canadian version of singer Debbie Gibson or the mall-star Tiffany. Her record *Alanis*, which featured a disco-influenced style of dance-pop music, has been called polished though formulaic. And her look was different too — more makeup, more hair, and an all-around more glamorous look, a teenaged disco diva. In 1992 she followed up with *Now Is the Time*, another dance-pop recording, which sold 50,000 copies. Today, Morissette has this to say about those early albums: "There was an element of me not being who I really was at the time. It was because I wasn't prepared to open up that way. The focus for me then was entertaining people as opposed to sharing any revelations I had at the time."

After that early success, though, came a bit of a letdown. It was a stressful time for the young singer. Her friend Louis Reny recalls the tremendous pressure Morissette was under. "She's got the record company and people telling her 'you've got to be thinner, you've got to look better. We want you to look like a little pop queen.' They want everybody to have boob jobs and be skinny and beautiful. . . . [You] have to be so self-confident to get over that."

After finishing high school in 1992, Morissette left her family's home in Ottawa and moved to Toronto. There she had what she has called a couple of breakdowns, as she tried to reconcile her feelings about religion, spirituality, and sexuality. But she also continued writing songs throughout this time, and she spent a lot of time unsuccessfully searching for a song-writing partner. The people she met, Morissette has said, tried to force her writing in a commercial direction, while she was trying to do something both more personal and more adventurous. "There was really no one I was connecting with in a cerebral, creative way at all," she later explained. "It became very disheartening. The whole collaborative process, I almost threw it out the window." Ultimately she decided to move to Los Angeles, and almost as soon as she arrived she was held up at gunpoint. Still, the move soon proved to be her best decision yet.

CAREER HIGHLIGHTS

In Los Angeles, Morissette tried collaborating with many different songwriters before she teamed up with Glen Ballard. A well-known songwriter and record producer, Ballard had worked with a host of top names, including Quincy Jones, Michael Jackson, Aretha Franklin, Barbra Streisand, and Paula Abdul, among others. As soon as Morissette and Ballard met in 1994, they clicked. "It was like a sanctuary for us," she said. "We were finally in this environment where we could do whatever the hell we wanted because there was no expectation." As Ballard explained, "What struck me about Alanis was that she was so incredibly self-possessed. I just connected with her as a person, and, almost parenthetically, it was like 'Wow, you're 19?' She was so intelligent and ready to take a chance on doing something that might have no commercial application. Although there was some question about what she wanted to do musically, she knew what she didn't want to do, which was anything that wasn't authentic and from her heart."

Their collaboration worked like this. Sitting around Ballard's home studio, they would play acoustic guitars, messing around with melodies and lyrics. They would either finish a song right away, or drop it and move on. They recorded the songs as they went along, and much of what ended up on the final release was actually taped during the process of collaboration. By recording the songs immediately they captured Morissette's unfiltered voice, alternately gentle or cutting, or searing with anguish and passion. "It was the most spiritual experience either of us ever had with music," Morissette says. "The whole thing was very accelerated and stream of consciousness."

Jagged Little Pill

The album that they put together was *Jagged Little Pill*. Powerful and intensely emotional, the tautly written lyrics surprised listeners with their honesty and autobiographical revelations. The frank tales of love and betrayal cover a wide range of emotional territory, from sympathy to sarcasm to raw anger. Yet the vulnerability uncovered here is leavened with a sense of empowerment, self-awareness, and strength.

Jagged Little Pill was released in 1995 by Maverick Records, the label owned by Madonna. The first single, "You Oughta Know," was initially picked up by the influential alternative rock station KROQ in Los Angeles. As soon as they

played it, "the phone lines completely lit up," according to music director Lisa Worden. "So we played it again an hour later. The girls look up to her, and the guys just dig her." In Los Angeles and across the country, listeners immediately responded to the confrontational lyrics and fierce, sneering tone. The single—and then the album—climbed to the top of the charts. To date, *Jagged Little Pill* has sold over 25 million copies worldwide, becoming the all-time best-selling recording by a female artist. It was an amazing achievement for a singer who was then just 21, and one her fans hope she can duplicate next time around.

Evolving as an Artist

Morissette has expressed frustration at people's misunderstanding of her music. "[Many people] saw me as 'the ever-depressed, ever-angry Alanis Morissette, who is the poster girl for rage, [the] alterno-girl who was the Debbie Gibson of Canada in her youth.' It's so one-dimensional and so selling me short. It's funny, though, because I had a similar discussion with someone the other day who found it hard to believe that anyone could go from writing dance pop to cutting a record like 'You Oughta Know.' I said, 'Well, weren't you a different person at 15 than you were at 21?' But, once a person steps out into the limelight — you're not allowed to evolve, you're not allowed to change. Especially if it's a drastic one.

"When I was younger and started doing music, I was immersed in the mid-1980s, when music was more for its sense of entertainment. I wasn't writing to communicate anything, and I was definitely not ready on the self-esteem level to indulge myself and all my personal turmoil. I wasn't prepared to be unadulterated; I saw music as a way to perform and entertain people. Make them smile, and take them away from reality.

"Also the environments that I was in sort of tried to lead me to believe that songwriting was a black-and-white thing. You were writing a song, and there was nothing spiritual or overly emotional about it. It was a very menial thing, really. There was a part of me that disagreed with that, but because I was 14 or however old I was and didn't have the experience, I wasn't able to stand up for myself and say, 'Listen, I disagree with this way of writing, and I'm going to do it my own way. See you later.' . . .

"I eventually moved to Los Angeles and wrote with so many different collaborators. The only thing I learned out of writing with those people is what I didn't want. I continued to run up against the 'You know you can't write that, young lady,' you know? 'You're too young to say that.' I just kept thinking no, this isn't right. And when I met Glen [Ballard], it was like, without saying it, he just said to me, 'You can be whatever you want.' And I thought, 'Wow. OK.' Musically and lyrically, it was just so pure and so spiritual for me. I felt that he wasn't judging me. . . . With that encouragement, and with that belief, and with that openness to the spiritual approach that we took, it just sort of wrote itself."

Self Image and Self-Esteem

The issue of her physical image is an important one for Morissette. Here, she talks to a reporter for the London *Times* about her feelings about her looks, as a teen star in Canada and today. "Oh, I could talk on this issue for hours." she said. "But let's start by acknowledging that maybe only 3% of the population meet what has become the prescribed standard for physical beauty, thus leaving the other 97% of us in the ludicrous situation of feeling unattractive or, at best, quirky.

"Rationally, we know we're all different and so should be able to figure out that the prescribed standard is just one more obstacle to be transcended on the path to self-acceptance. But I gave in to its tyranny for a long time — very easy to do when you have low self-esteem and judge your worth in terms of external success and what you look like. And that's really unfulfilling, you know? . . . If I'm honest, there wasn't a really constant pressure from outside — just little bits, here and there. But along the way I met some people against whom I still harbour resentment — and I hate it that I do — for not knowing better. The

Morissette receiving a Juno Award in 1992

image advisers and stylists. The hints that it would be preferable if I did this, did that, tried a nose job, whatever. I was just 15, for God's sake. . . .

"You could say that I've had an easier time than most, because I happen to fall somewhere close to that prescribed standard we've talked about — something I think about a lot. And I believe that, regardless of where I found myself on that continuum, I still would have been able to transcend it at some point. But even so, it was a real struggle for me, one that lasted many years."

HOME AND FAMILY

Morissette is unmarried and is based in Los Angeles. After the release of *Jagged Little Pill*, she and her four-piece band went out on an extended tour. Currently, she's taking a break before recording her next album.

RECORDINGS

"Fate Stay with Me" / "Find the Right Man," 1987 (single)
Alanis, 1991
Now Is the Time, 1992
Jagged Little Pill, 1995

HONORS AND AWARDS

Juno Awards: 1992, Most Promising Female Vocalist of the Year, for *Alanis*; 1996 (five awards), Female Vocalist of the Year; Single of the Year, for "You Oughta Know"; Songwriter of the Year (with Glen Ballard); Album of the Year, for *Jagged Little Pill*; and Best Rock Album of the Year, for *Jagged Little Pill*; 1997 (3 awards), International Achievement Award; Single of the Year, for "Ironic"; and Songwriter of the Year (with Glen Ballard), for "You Learn" and "Ironic"

Grammy Awards: 1996 (4 awards), Album of the Year, for *Jagged Little Pill*; Best Female Rock Vocal Performance, for "You Oughta Know"; Best Rock Song, for "You Oughta Know"; and Best Rock Album, for *Jagged Little Pill*

The BRIT Award (British Phonographic Industry): 1996, for Best International Newcomer

American Music Awards: 1997 (2 awards), Favorite Female Pop/Rock Artist; Favorite Pop/Rock Album, for *Jagged Little Pill*

FURTHER READING

Books

Grills, Barry. *Ironic: Alanis Morissett, the Story*, 1997
Rogers, Kalen. *The Story of Alanis Morissette*, 1996

Periodicals

Billboard, May 13, 1995, p.7; July 15, 1995, p.1
Details, Oct. 1995, p.174
Entertainment Weekly, Oct. 20, 1995, p.20
Interview, Oct. 1995, p.114
Los Angeles Times, July 30, 1995, Calendar section, p.3
Maclean's, Dec. 11, 1995, p.64
New York Times, Feb. 28, 1996, p.B1
Ottawa Sunday Sun, Dec. 17, 1995, Showcase p.9
Rolling Stone, Nov. 2, 1995, p.42
Spin, Nov. 1995, p.48
The Times (London), June 15, 1996

ADDRESS

Maverick Music Company
8000 Beverly Boulevard
Los Angeles CA 90048

Sam Morrison   1936-
American Librarian
Head of Broward County Library,
"1996-97 Library of the Year"

[Editor's Note: Sam Morrison, who heads Broward County's library in Broward County, Florida, kindly granted a private interview to the Editor of Biography Today. *He explained how he became a librarian and encouraged young adults, especially African-American students, to become librarians. He also talked about his planned African-American Library, which will house one of the most distinguished collections of African-American art, artifacts, and print collections in the country. We are grateful for his time and for his willingness to share his insights with us.]*

BIRTH

Samuel F. Morrison was born December 19, 1936, in Flagstaff, Arizona. His parents were Travis and Ruth Morrison. Travis worked in munitions plants throughout the Western portion of the country, and the family moved often. Morrison had one sister who died in an accident many years ago.

YOUTH

Morrison remembers that he lived "up and down the West Coast" for his dad's job. He lived in Arizona, Washington, Nevada, and California, all by the fourth grade. That's a lot of moving, but Morrison remembers that his family was very close, and his parents were always strict. He was expected to do well in school, and he did. And he always loved to read.

EDUCATION

Morrison went to a number of different schools as his family moved around. He started school in Hanford, Washington, went to the third grade in Nevada, and attended fourth grade in Phoenix, Arizona. He was in an accelerated program for students.

In 1952 the family moved to Los Angeles. Going from his small, segregated high school of 200-300 students in Phoenix to LA's Compton High School, with 5,000 students, was a "big shock" for Morrison. He had always been considered one of the best students at his school; now he had a lot of competition. He was smaller, younger, and less mature than his fellow students, which, he remembers, caused some "social difficulties." Still, he considers it a positive experience overall. The years of accelerated studies paid off when he graduated from Compton High School in 1952, two years early.

School, Service, and Work

After high school, Morrison started taking classes at the local community college, while also working as a stock boy in a supermarket. His parents had raised him with high expectations: they wanted him to be an engineer or a doctor. But Morrison found the course work for those professions harder than expected. His first semester he did alright, but in his second semester, he learned how to play chess, and spent a great deal of time playing chess instead of going to class. In his third semester, about to flunk out, he decided to quit college. He knew that college was not right for him at that time. He says it was time for him to "stop, think, and grow up."

Morrison also wanted to take advantage of the G.I. Bill, a government program that provides educational and other benefits for people who serve in the armed forces. So he enlisted in the Air Force, where he served for five years.

For three of those years, he was stationed in Morocco, on the east coast of Africa. During those years, he ran the library at the Air Force base, getting a taste of what he would do later in life. He also attended college classes while in the Air Force, earning his associate's degree—the first two years of a Bachelor's degree.

After he got out of the service, he went back to working at the supermarket and back to school, at California State University in Los Angeles. He spent the next six years combining school and work. When the supermarket chain was bought out, Morrison decided to go back to school full time.

By this time Morrison had enough credits to be in his senior year. But he hadn't buckled down and studied— he was on academic probation, and had to get all A's in his last two semesters to graduate. He likes to tell the story to children that he made the Dean's List while on academic probation—a story that, in his words, tells kids, "You can make it!"

Morrison graduated from California State University in Los Angeles with a degree in English in 1970, and applied to graduate schools in English and library science. He decided to attend the University of Illinois graduate program in library science, in large part because they gave him a full scholarship.

CHOOSING A CAREER

Morrison remembers that he chose library science because he had worked in the school library as a child, and again at the Air Force base in Morocco. He was a lifelong reader, and he has kept his first library card.

CAREER HIGHLIGHTS

During the last year of his library science program, Morrison began to look for a job. Up to that point, he hadn't even looked into the starting salary of a librarian. He thought he would like to work as an academic librarian, at a college or university. In fact, one of his first interviews was for a position as a librarian at the Columbia University Fine Arts library, and it's a job he almost took.

Frostproof, Florida

In early 1971, Morrison got a call about a job in Florida. The year before, CBS News had broadcast an important expose called "Harvest of Shame," which focused on the plight of migrant workers in the United States. It told of the shameful conditions under which most migrant workers labored at the time, with particular attention given to the workers based in Florida picking crops for the Coca Cola Company. (Coca Cola owns several large companies that raise and market fresh produce in Florida.)

Coca Cola wanted to make amends to the migrant community in Florida, and so they set up housing, schools, medical facilities, and other community development opportunities for their workers. The migrants in one area, called Frostproof, Florida, also wanted a library. The job of setting up this library was offered to Morrison. He recalls that he thought, "I had a feeling I could do this job." He also hadn't up to that point given a thought to service to the community. But the job seemed right. He got the job.

During the last months of his degree program, he flew back and forth from Florida to Illinois, to buy books and furniture and get the library up and running. Morrison held the job for two-and-a-half years, and the success of the project reached throughout the library community.

In 1974, the Broward County Library was looking for an assistant to the director. At that time, the library system consisted of 2 libraries and 100 employees. For the next 13 years, Morrison worked for the Broward system, helping it to grow to 25 branches and becoming Project Manager for the new Broward County Library in downtown Fort Lauderdale.

Chicago

In 1987, Morrison was recruited to become the chief librarian to plan the Harold Washington Library Center of the Chicago Public Library system, which is the largest municipal library in the United States. Because they were contemplating building a major new library, they wanted someone with experience and a proven track record to get the job done. Morrison found the work challenging and enjoyed Chicago. But Chicago is an intensely political town, and when Mayor Washington died during his second term, Morrison knew his time would be up shortly.

In 1990, he was offered the Director position at the Broward Library, and "went back home again." Under his stewardship, the Broward system has grown to 33 branch libraries. Its outstanding growth and development was honored in 1996 when it was named "Library of the Year" by *Library Journal* and Gale Research. Morrison enjoys south Florida and sees that the library has "good years ahead of us." He praises the "good financial support" from

the state and local funding sources and notes the outstanding public and private support the library enjoys.

African-American Project

Morrison is now at work fundraising for his latest goal, the African-American Research Library and Cultural Center. He plans to build a 52,000 square foot library in a predominately black area of Fort Lauderdale, which will showcase the culture and history of African-Americans. Morrison was moved to undertake the project because of the large black population in the area, which has grown in part due to a large influx of immigrants from the Caribbean and South America. The library will contain art, artifacts, papers, and other types of archival material detailing the African-American experience. The library will be a research facility, a home to art exhibits, and a cultural center, with an auditorium for performances. The project is already underway, and Morrison is busy collecting art and planning early exhibits. He plans to break ground for the new facility in late 1997, with a tentative completion date of late 1999. "Part of our responsibility as human being is to leave the world a better place," he says. "This library will help make the world a better place."

ADVICE TO YOUNG PEOPLE

Morrison wants to encourage young people, particularly young African-Americans, to consider a career in libraries. It is a career that blends two of the most important areas of our world, according to Morrison, "knowledge and technology." The job is rewarding in many ways, he says.

MARRIAGE AND FAMILY

Morrison married in 1964 but is is now divorced. He and his former wife had no children.

HOBBIES AND OTHER INTERESTS

Morrison is a member of numerous civic and library associations, including the National Association for the Advancement of Colored People (NAACP), the Urban League, and the National Forum for Black Public Administrators. He is also a tireless advocate for free access to libraries for the disabled, particularly for children with disabilities. In his limited free time, he likes to listen to jazz, particularly the "cool school" of the 1950s. The works of jazz greats like Miles Davis and John Coltrane are special favorites.

HONORS AND AWARDS

NAACP Freeman Bradley Award: 1993
Urban League of Broward Service Award: 1993
The National Conference Silver Medallion Brotherhood Award: 1995
Library of the Year (*Library Journal* and Gale Research): 1996
Leadership Broward Leader of the Year Award: 1996
Excellence in Librarianship (DEMCO/BCALA): 1997

FURTHER READING

Books

Who's Who in America 1997
Who's Who Among Black Americans 1996-97

Periodicals

Chicago Tribune, Feb. 5, 1987, Chicagoland Section, p.3; Apr. 14, 1987, Chicagoland Section, p.1; Dec. 9, 1989, News Section, p.5
Fort Lauderdale Sun-Sentinel, Dec. 18, 1989, p.B1; Jan. 20, 1997, p.B1; Apr. 1, 1997, p.B1; Apr. 17, 1997, p.B3
Library Journal, June 15, 1996, p.28

ADDRESS

Broward County Library
100 S. Andrews Ave.
Fort Lauderdale, FL 33301

Rosie O'Donnell 1962-

American Comedian and Actress
Host of Her Own Talk Show, "The Rosie O'Donnell
Show"

BIRTH

Roseann O'Donnell, later known as Rosie, was born on March
21, 1962, in Commack, New York, on Long Island. (Some
sources list her birth place as Huntington, New York.) Her father, Edward, was an electrical engineer who designed cameras
for spy satellites, while her mother, Roseann, was a homemaker.
Her father was secretive about his job, and Rosie jokes that "I'm
still not really sure what he did. But he always used to tell us,

'Right now in Russia, they can read your license plate.' I'm like, 'Well, thanks, Dad. That's a comforting thought for an eight-year-old.' I'm in the bathroom thinking, 'They can probably see this in Russia, you know?'" Rosie was the third of five children, with two older brothers, Eddie and Danny, a younger sister, Maureen, and a younger brother, Timmy, who was named after Timmy the Turtle, the main character in the children's book of the same name.

YOUTH

O'Donnell's earliest years with her family were happy ones. Rosie's favorite childhood memory is sharing lemon drops with her mother in the balcony of Radio City Music Hall. She was very close to her mother, from whom she learned to love Broadway musicals, especially the singing of Barbra Streisand, and humor. "My mother was very funny," Rosie recalls. "She was president of the PTA, and at the meetings she made all the teachers laugh. When she came to visit the school and walked down the halls, all the teachers would come out of their classrooms to talk to her. So I knew she had this thing people wanted, that people would go to her because of this comedy thing." Early on, Rosie learned to use humor, just like her mom. She even used to do Streisand imitations while her mom was cooking dinner to crack her up. With her mom, Rosie learned to love show business.

Soon, Rosie was imitating her idols. In second grade she made her first appearance on stage, playing Glinda the good witch in *The Wizard of Oz,* and from then on she was hooked on performing. When other kids her age were bringing their Barbie dolls for Show and Tell, O'Donnell would belt out a number from a Broadway musical.

But Rosie always loved sports, too, Growing up, she played baseball, basketball, field hockey, touch football, kick ball, hide-and-seek, and kick the can. She was especially good at baseball, playing pitcher and shortstop. At that time, girls weren't allowed to play organized baseball with the boys, but Rosie always joined in before and after the games. "I was always the first girl picked for the neighborhood teams," she recalls with pride. "I got picked ahead of my three brothers, which I think still affects them."

Her Mother's Illness

Everything changed, though, when O'Donnell was only 10. Her mother was diagnosed with liver and pancreatic cancer. But no one in the family, which Rosie calls "a very Irish Catholic sort of repressed family," would talk about it. Instead, they were in a state of denial. "They told us at first she had hepatitis," she recalls. "They thought that was a big word and kids wouldn't know. But I went to the library and looked it up, and it said it was a disease that you got from dirty needles. I thought to myself it was from sewing. That's the kind of household it was, that you had to draw your own conclusions and answer your own questions, because you weren't really allowed to ask." Rosie's mother died on St. Patrick's Day in 1973, just four months after being diagnosed. It wasn't until six years later that Rosie learned, from a neighbor, that her mom had had cancer.

The death of her mother was "the defining event of my life," O'Donnell has said, "and it remains so." It changed everything. Her father was grief-stricken by his wife's illness and death, Rosie says, and he responded by becoming distant and withdrawn from his children. His wife's death, as well as other important issues, just weren't discussed. "My father told me, 'Your mother passed away,' and I didn't know what that meant. And that was the end of the discussion." Because she hadn't been able to attend the funeral, and because no one would ever talk about it, Rosie began to fantasize that maybe her mother really was still alive. For a long time she fantasized that her mom had been kidnaped, or maybe had just run away from home. Now she speaks very frankly about these difficult early years, saying that it has taken her years of therapy to come to terms with her mother's death and her father's emotional withdrawal.

Rosie and her brothers and sister soon learned to rely on each other. "After my mother died," she says, "the five children fused together and became one functioning parent/child unit. We took turns being those roles for each other." Her older brother did a lot of the household chores, and Rosie would be the one to defend any of the kids who got into a fight at school.

EARLY MEMORIES

The kids had another coping strategy as well: watching TV. For Rosie, many of her earliest memories revolve around the TV. "No other family was as obsessed with TV in my neighborhood as mine was. We were allowed to watch 24 hours a day, and we did. My favorite shows were Merv Griffin and Mike Douglas. I would literally run home from school and open a bag of chips and watch them," Rosie recalls. "My whole family knew the entire fall schedule before it even went on the air. We'd get the TV guide . . . and we'd read that and memorize the entire schedule of what was on, and when. We were a huge, huge, huge TV family."

But for Rosie, watching TV was much more than entertainment; she was looking to the shows to give her a semblance of family life. "I think that in my house it took the place of parenting. Because, you know, my mom had died, and my father was bereft, and there was really a lack of interaction with all the children." Entertainment celebrities had such a powerful role in her life when she was young, and she knew that someday she wanted to do the same for other kids. "I think kids use celebrities and, you know, their heroes on TV or in the movies or on CDs, to dream, and to dream of a better life than the one they know. . . . I understand the effect and the power that movie stars have on little children, and if a child can use me to be inspired to live a bigger or a better or a happier life than the one that they know, I'm all for it. I think that to use my celebrity to inspire or help or encourage children is really payback for all the celebrities who helped me so much through [my childhood]."

But she also recognized early on that celebrities could have a different kind of power, too. "I definitely wanted to be one of those people that had the kind of life and the kind of access and the kind of power that [celebrity] brings," she recalls of her childhood. When her mother got sick, Rosie thought that "if Barbra Streisand's mother was sick, she could go on television, on 'The Tonight Show' or Merv Griffin—now mind you Barbra Streisand was God to me as a child—and that she could tell everyone to send in ten dollars 'cause her mom was sick, and they would make a cure. Now I was eight or nine years old, but I remember even at that age knowing that there was power somehow in celebrity. There was availability to things that weren't available to me."

EDUCATION

O'Donnell attended Commack South High School on Long Island. There she was "Little Miss Overachiever," in her own words. She was elected homecoming queen, prom queen, senior class president, and most school spirited—plus she was active in the theater club and in sports. She graduated from high school in 1980.

After high school, O'Donnell won a scholarship to Dickenson College in Pennsylvania. She spent one year there, but she always felt out of place. "It was a school for people much smarter than me," she now says. She then transferred to Boston University's School of Theater Arts in 1981, but she was discouraged when a theater professor told her that she would never make it as an actress. She dropped out of Boston University after less than a year there. But by that point, she had already started to build a career in show business.

GETTING STARTED

O'Donnell got her start as a comedian when she was still in high school. She began performing at the local clubs on open-mike nights, when anyone in the audience is allowed to come up on stage and try out their act. At age 17, she got her first actual date in a comedy club in Huntington, New York. Her debut engagement was a killer show—the audience loved her! This was not surprising, considering that she had stolen all her jokes from the hot new comic Jerry Seinfeld, whom she had just seen on TV. As she recalls, "I walked off the

From the Flintstones

stage and all the comics surrounded me. They said, 'Where'd you get those jokes? I said, 'Jerry Seinfeld from 'The Merv Griffin Show.' They said, 'You can't do that!' I was totally devastated. I went home thinking, 'How am I going to do this if I have to make up my own jokes?' When you're 16, you haven't lived enough to have any observations. So I ended up doing, 'Nice shirt. Where'd you get it, Kmart?'"

FIRST JOBS

During her years in college and after she dropped out, O'Donnell continued touring around the country. She spent several years on the comedy club circuit, creating and polishing her routine. It was a lonely and depressing time. "You fly to some city you don't know and some stranger picks you up," she recalls. "You drive to this condo in the middle of nowhere. There's mildew on the shower curtain and a lock on the phone because the comic who was there last week ran up the bill. And it's what I did for years." Most of the other comedians in the clubs were older men, and there was a lot of drinking and drugs. It made her feel very young and scared to be on her own. But all the hard work paid off in 1984 when she was invited to appear on "Star Search," where she won about $15,000 to $20,000, according to various sources. With that money she was able to move to Los Angeles, the center of the entertainment industry.

O'Donnell was set to perform in an LA comedy club one night when, coincidentally, fellow comedian Dana Carvey was there auditioning to appear on "Saturday Night Live." He warned her that the audience that night included Brandon Tartikoff, who was then the head of the entertainment division at NBC. Tartikoff might have left before Rosie appeared on stage if it weren't for a cocktail waitress at the club whom Rosie had befriended. The waitress refused to give Tartikoff his bill until he had seen O'Donnell's act. He liked her act so much that he cast her in the TV sit-com "Gimme a Break" as the neighbor Maggie O'Brien. That led to a show as a VJ on the cable music station VH-1. Actually, she had first sent a tape to MTV auditioning to be a VJ, but they rejected it. O'Donnell sent a nice thank you note to the producer at MTV anyway. Impressed by the gesture, he sent the tape on to VH-1, who hired her. For O'Donnell, being nice works!

CAREER HIGHLIGHTS

During the late 1980s and early 1990s, O'Donnell spent several more years working hard—and paying her dues—before becoming the big success that she is today. She started out at VH-1 as a VJ in 1988. There she created and hosted "Stand-Up Spotlight," a weekly comedy special on VH-1 that showcased comics from around the country—mostly people she knew from her years on the road. She was also the show's executive producer for about four years. In addition, she appeared on several cable comedy specials in the late 1980s and early 1990s. Her first movie role, a small part in *Car 54, Where Are You*, was filmed in 1990, although this critically panned movie was not released for several years. In 1992 O'Donnell returned to TV in the short-lived sit-com "Stand by Your Man" with Melissa Gilbert-Brinkman.

Success in the Movies

O'Donnell's first big success came in 1992. That year she appeared in the hit film *A League of Their Own*, co-starring with Madonna, Geena Davis, and Tom Hanks. Those childhood years of playing baseball paid off when she won a part in this film about the All-American Girls Professional Baseball League, a real baseball league that existed in the 1940s, when many American male players left baseball to fight in World War II. O'Donnell played a role that she would repeat in several later films, that of a wisecracking, sassy best friend. Her comment in the film to Madonna, "You think there's a man in this country who ain't seen your bosoms," made audiences roar and made critics and filmmakers sit up and take notice. In reality, she and Madonna went on to become close friends, which they attribute to the shared sense of loss. Madonna, too, had lost her mother when she was young.

O'Donnell followed up her strong start in *A League of Their Own* with even greater success in the romantic comedy *Sleepless in Seattle* (1993). In this film about love and fate, she played the friend (and boss) of Meg Ryan, who falls in love with Tom Hanks, a widower, after hearing him on a radio call-in talk show reminiscing about his wife. Next up for O'Donnell was a role as a district attorney in the farce *Another Stakeout* (1993), playing opposite Richard Dreyfuss and Emilio Estevez. Her next big part was as Betty Rubble in *The Flintstones* (1994), the film version of the animated cartoon classic. She co-starred with Rick Moranis as Barney, John Goodman as Fred, Elizabeth Perkins as Wilma, and

From Harriet the Spy

Elizabeth Taylor as Wilma's mother. O'Donnell's rendition of Betty's characteristic laugh brought the character to life.

In 1994, O'Donnell took a brief break from her movie roles to appear in *Grease!* In this revival of a Broadway musical about teenage life in the 1950s, she played the gum-popping, yoyo-snapping, tough-talking Rizzo, leader of the Pink Ladies. For Rosie, after her early years enjoying Broadway musicals with her mother, it was a dream come true. She returned to the movies in *Now and Then* (1995), a touching movie about the friendships among a group of four girls, both when young and later, as adults; and in *Beautiful Girls* (1996), where she plays a beautician who dispenses advice to a group of high school friends who get together some 10 years after graduation.

Harriet the Spy

In 1996 O'Donnell appeared in *Harriet the Spy*, the first feature film put out by Nickelodeon. Fans of the 1964 novel by Louis Fitzhugh will know the story about Harriet, an inquisitive sixth-grader who likes to spy on people and write down her sometimes mean observations in her notebook (marked PRIVATE) — until the other kids catch her doing it, read the comments in her notebook, and start to reject her. Michelle Trachtenberg from the Nickelodeon show *The Adventures of Pete and Pete* played Harriet, and O'Donnell played Ole Golly, her nanny. In a small but crucial role, O'Donnell as Golly encourages Harriet to stick with her writing — to stick with being an individual — even when she feels like the whole world is against her.

It was her work on *Harriet the Spy* that convinced O'Donnell to give up her growing film career for something new. Shortly before beginning work on *Harriet the Spy*, she had adopted a baby boy, Parker Jaren. She was frustrated that while filming the movie she was able to see her son only an hour a day, at most. After growing up without a mother, she knew that that was not the type of mom that she wanted to be. She had this to say about her experiences while making *Harriet the Spy*. "During the 23-day shoot in Toronto, I hardly ever saw my son," she said. "I felt horrible. By the second day, I knew it wouldn't work. This was not the kind of parent I wanted to be. I want to be the one to put him to bed, to wake him up in the morning, and to be there when he takes his first step and says his first word. . . . I wanted to find a job in the entertainment industry that could accommodate my desire to be a full-time parent."

O'Donnell started to think about a new line of work, something that would allow her to spend a lot of time with Parker. One option was a talk show. Rosie had done some substitute hosting on "Live with Regis and Kathie Lee," and the preparation and screen time really hadn't taken that much out of her day. A talk show seemed like a good alternative—especially when Warner Brothers agreed to pay her about $4.5 million and to locate the show in New York, so Rosie could live near her sister and her family.

Creating a Talk Show

"The Rosie O'Donnell Show" debuted in June 1996. The show features a mix of comedy and conversation with celebrities. It usually opens with Rosie doing a few jokes, then showcases a mix of guests—including actors, musicians, and others—along with a human interest piece. It's really an old style variety show, Rosie says, patterned after the daytime shows during the 1960s and 1970s by Mike Douglas and Merv Griffin—shows that she had loved to watch as a kid. But she also cites the influence of late night host Johnny Carson, whom she considers the best ever at really listening to his guests and encouraging them to talk. "The Rosie O'Donnell Show" was an immediate hit with reviewers and audiences fed up with daytime trash TV. For many, Rosie's approach—"The Queen of Nice" is what some called it—was a welcome relief.

Unquestionably, the best part of the show is Rosie herself. Commentators have applauded her realness, honesty, and good humor. She's considered funny, friendly, playful, confident, self-assured, able to improvise, clever, and a gifted interviewer. Unlike some hosts who seem to mock their guests, O'Donnell shows a gushing enthusiasm for show business and a genuine reverence for celebrities, which always makes her guests feel at ease. "She's Everywoman as talk-show host, and it's her unabashed commonness that makes her so unique. She's like your best girlfriend in junior high school who could always make you laugh," Renee Graham explained in the *Boston Globe*. It's just that quality that draws millions of viewers every day.

MAJOR INFLUENCES

In addition to her mother, O'Donnell cites Barbra Streisand and Bette Midler as two of her biggest influences when she was young. As she got older, she also admired the talents of Carol Burnett, Gilda Radner, and Lucille Ball.

MARRIAGE AND FAMILY

O'Donnell, who is unmarried, adopted a baby boy, Parker Jaren, soon after his birth in May 1995. They live just outside New York City, where her TV show is based. They also live near her sister Maureen, with whom Rosie is very close.

CREDITS

"Gimme a Break," 1986-87 (TV show)
"Stand by Your Man," 1992 (TV show)
A League of Their Own, 1992
Sleepless in Seattle, 1993
Another Stakeout, 1993
Fatal Instinct, 1993
I'll Do Anything, 1993
Car 54, Where Are You, 1994 (filmed in 1990, although not released until 1994)
The Flintstones, 1994
Exit to Eden, 1994
Grease! 1994 (Broadway musical)
Now and Then, 1995
Beautiful Girls, 1996
Harriet the Spy, 1996
"The Rosie O'Donnell Show," 1996- (TV show)

HONORS AND AWARDS

Kids' Choice Award (Nickelodeon): 1995, for Favorite Movie Actress, for *The Flintstones*
Entertainer of the Year (*Entertainment Weekly*): 1996
American Comedy Awards: 1997, for Funniest Female Performer in a TV Series

FURTHER READING

Books

Parish, James Robert. *Rosie: Rosie O'Donnell's Biography,* 1997.
Who's Who in America, 1997

Periodicals

Boston Globe, Jan. 16, 1994, Arts and Film Section, p.49; July 5, 1996, Living
    Section, p.37
Chicago Tribune, Aug. 22, 1993, Womanews section, p.4
Cosmopolitan, June 1994, p.72
Current Biography Yearbook 1995
Entertainment Weekly, June 28,1996, p.89; July 26, 1996, p.24; Dec. 27, 1996,
    p.16
Ladies' Home Journal, Feb. 1997, p.104
Los Angeles Times, Mar. 24, 1994, OC Live Section, p.4
Mademoiselle, Aug. 1993, p.160
Mirabella, June 1993, p.50
New York Times, May 8, 1994, Section 2, p.8
Newsday, May 8, 1994, Fanfare Section, p.10; June 9, 1996, Fanfare Section,
    p.10
Newsweek, Aug. 16, 1993, p.60
Nickelodeon, June/July 1996
People, July 20, 1992, p.65
TV Guide, June 15, 1996, p.28

ADDRESS

The Rosie O'Donnell Show
30 Rockefeller Plaza
New York, NY 10112

WORLD WIDE WEB SITE

http://www.rosieo.com

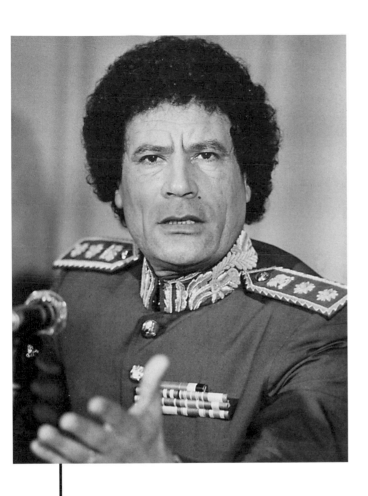

Muammar el-Qaddafi   1942-
Libyan Leader
Chairman of the Revolutionary Command Council
of Libya

BIRTH

Muammar el-Qaddafi (MOH-mar el kuh-DAHF-ee) was born
in 1942 to Mohammad Abdel Salam ben Hamed ben Moham
mad Qaddafi and Aisha Ben Niran. They were a Bedouin family of the nomadic Ghadaffa Berber tribe in northern Africa. The
Ghadaffas, who were an an Arabic tribe, had roamed the Sirte
Desert since the 15th century, scraping out a meager existence as
herders of sheep and goats. The people of the tribe were follow-

ers of the religion of Islam. The exact date and place of Qaddafi's birth are unknown, in part because his tribe was constantly on the move, traveling from one seasonal water source to another. Some sources speculate that he was born in the coastal city of Misurata or in the country's eastern provinces, but most people — including Qaddafi himself — believe that he was born in a goatskin tent somewhere out in the Sirte Desert. Qaddafi was the only boy in the family, and he had three sisters. Long after Qaddafi assumed power, his family continued with their nomadic lives out in the Sirte Desert region.

The Qaddafi family name has been translated from the Arabic language in many different ways since Muammar el-Qaddafi rose to rule Libya. Common spellings of his name include Gadaffi, Gaddafi, Kazzafi, Khadafy, and Qadhafi.

LIBYAN INDEPENDENCE

Qaddafi grew up during a time of great change in North Africa. In 1911 Italy had taken control of the region now known as Libya from the people who had long lived there, and the Italians had maintained their hold on the region even though many natives of the area fought them. Several members of Qaddafi's family, in fact, were killed or imprisoned by the Italian occupiers during the first half of the 20th century. During his childhood, Qaddafi heard many tales of his ancestors' heroism and the Italians' cruelty. After World War II — in which Italy was defeated — control of the region passed to Great Britain and France. In 1951, when Qaddafi was only nine years old, the region was finally granted independence. Ruled by King Idris I, the new country was named the United Kingdom of Libya.

YOUTH

Years after Qaddafi became the controversial ruler of Libya, one of his childhood friends remarked to biographer Mirella Bianco that "if one wants to understand [Qaddafi] one must always keep in mind the essential: he is a son of the desert. It was in the desert that he learned his first lesson, much more than at any school. It was the desert which taught him patience, endurance, generosity and faith in God; and it is in the desert that he learned self-sufficiency, facing up to such difficulties as its storms, its immense distances, and the privations it inflicts."

Indeed, Qaddafi did not have many luxuries as a young boy. Life out in the desert was hard, and even the youngest members of the Bedouin people had to pitch in and help with chores. As biographer George Tremlett noted, Qaddafi's childhood days "were spent guarding the family's goats and sheep, drawing buckets of water at their wells, [and] shooing away jackals." As he grew older, his parents saw that he was different than other children his age. They noticed that he sometimes did not participate in the games that the other children played. Instead, he often seemed "lost within his own thoughts, listening to the legends told around the fire at night while a kettle simmered on a fire of twigs, camel dung, and heated stones, waiting for yet another cup of green tea," wrote Tremlett. "They always thought he seemed older than his years."

As his son grew older, Qaddafi's father arranged for him to learn to read and write. After going on a trading trip, he brought a teacher back to teach Qaddafi about the Koran, a book of teachings that is regarded by Muslims as sacred. The Koran is a cornerstone of Islam, a religion based on the worship of the Supreme God Allah and a belief in the prophet Muhammad.

Qaddafi was very interested in gaining an education, and he proved to be an enthusiastic and smart student. "He would follow his teacher like a shadow," recalled Qaddafi's father. By the time Qaddafi was about ten years old, his father had decided to send him to a regular school, even though this plan would involve big sacrifices for their poor family. His absence would create more work for the other members of the family, and the cost involved would further strain an already tight family budget. Despite the drawbacks, however, Qaddafi's father remained determined to send his son on to school. "I did not want him to continue in our sort of life," he said.

EDUCATION

The nearest school was about 30 miles away, but for five years Qaddafi walked to the school each Saturday. After attending classes all week, he would then slog through the hot desert terrain to return home for Friday prayers (Friday has special significance for people of the Islamic faith).

Classmates recalled that Qaddafi had great confidence in himself, even though he was poor and had started school at a relatively late age. "There were three or four of us Bedouin at the school," said one of Qaddafi's school friends, "and we were held in utter contempt. We were so poor that we often had nothing to eat at break . . . we felt ourselves to be outsiders in some way, and I believe that had it not been for [Qaddafi] we would have been ashamed of our origin. But he was proud of it. 'We are equal to anyone else,' he would say. 'And we can learn as well as anyone.'"

Soon after Qaddafi began school, it was clear to his teachers that he was extremely intelligent, and most of the other students looked up to him. He performed so well that his instructors had him skip a number of grades, and at the age of 14 he moved on to a secondary school in Sebha, one of Libya's larger cities. Again, Qaddafi emerged as a leader among the students, who admired his quiet confidence and strong religious faith.

Qaddafi's interest in politics surfaced for the first time during his years in Sheba, where he organized and participated in a number of anti-Israel and pro-Nasser demonstrations. Israel had been at war with a number of Arab nations ever since it had achieved independence in 1948, in large part because the Arabs felt that the land on which Israel was situated belonged to them; Qaddafi subsequently viewed Israel as an enemy of the Arab world. Gamal Nasser, on the other hand, was one of Qaddafi's heroes. Nasser was the nationalist leader of the Egyptian revolution that had overthrown Egypt's King Farouk in 1952. Indeed, Nasser's actions in Egypt inspired Qaddafi. While at Sheba he formed a secret society dedicated to the overthrow of Libya's King Idris, who he thought was betraying Arab ideals. Many of the young men who joined him in this secret organization would later form the nucleus of the Revolutionary Command Council, the group that would take control of Libya in 1969.

Qaddafi and his fellow conspirators sought to overthrow King Idris for a number of reasons. They worried that Western powers such as the United States and Britain had become too influential in Libya's affairs, and that basic rules of appropriate Islamic conduct (such as refraining from drinking, gambling, and smoking) were being ignored in the country. Qaddafi and his allies also favored greater Arab nationalism and an economic structure built along socialist lines.

Qaddafi's days at Sheba helped lay the groundwork for his future success, but at least one of his teachers at the school later admitted that the instructors did not fully recognize his ambition. "All his teachers noticed him, of course, for it was impossible not to notice him. He was so different from the other pupils, but even when he began his activities as an agitator, organizing political demonstrations, with or without authorization by the school, I don't think any of us really took him seriously. . . . We thought of him as a dreamer, a hothead; in any case, we did not imagine that his dreams could come true."

In October 1959 Qaddafi was expelled from Sebha for his increasingly vocal protest activities. He subsequently attended a school in Misurata, where he finished his secondary school education. Qaddafi was then accepted to the University of Libya, from which he graduated in 1963 with a degree in history. From there he entered the Libyan Military Academy in Benghazi, where he struck up friendships with other young Libyan officers who held political philosophies similar to his own. In 1965, Qaddafi graduated from the military academy as a commissioned officer.

CAREER HIGHLIGHTS

After graduation, Qaddafi was sent to England to take a six-month course in armored warfare. Upon his return, he resumed his efforts to build a network of conspirators who would support him in his quest for revolution. He was spectacularly successful in these efforts, and some sources estimate that he may have convinced a majority of Libya's 7,000-member military force to support him. By 1969, Qaddafi had risen to the rank of captain and formulated a strategy for the overthrow of King Idris. A number of missions designed to seize control of the government had to be scrapped for one reason or another, though. Qaddafi grew concerned, for he knew that suspicions about him and his allies were growing. But Idris's government was weak and distracted by widespread unhappiness with his rule, and Qaddafi was able to wait until the moment was right to strike.

The Revolution

On September 1, 1969, when Muammar el-Qaddafi was 27, he launched his revolution. He ordered his lieutenants, known as the Free Union Officers, to take control of the government offices, military bases, and royal palaces. He also seized command of Libya's television and radio stations, newspaper offices, and other media centers, and he personally led the forces that took control of the Benghazi radio station. The leaders of Libya were so surprised by the well-organized revolt that only one death was recorded during the entire coup. The government surrendered to Qaddafi without a fight. King Idris, who was in Turkey at the time, recognized that his days of rule were over. He abdicated his throne within days of the revolt. He lived in exile in Egypt until his death in 1983.

Qaddafi and his aides, all of whom were under the age of 30, quickly dissolved the government and the constitution and set up their own system of government. The newly named Libyan Arab Republic was placed under the total control of Qaddafi and his Revolutionary Command Council. At the same time, Qaddafi promoted himself to the rank of colonel and took control of the country's military forces.

The young officers who had seized the helm of Libya dramatically changed the country's social and political direction over the next few months. Qaddafi and his allies pledged to support other Third World nations. They felt that these countries, termed "Third World" because of their underdeveloped economies and industries, were being hampered by racism, colonialism, and other factors that originated with the capitalist nations of the West. Qaddafi also advocated a return to the strict religious laws of Islam, and he quickly became known throughout the Arab world for his strong statements supporting Arab unity and condemning Israel.

Qaddafi also recognized that Libya's allies and trading partners, as well as its own people, wondered whether the change in leadership was good news or not. In the months after the overthrow of King Idris's government, Qaddafi tried to ease the fears of the Libyan people and other nations in the Middle East and around the world. He promised to respect all property rights, and he assured other countries that he would honor Libya's agreements with them. These promises began to fall by the wayside, however, as he tightened and strengthened his power.

In 1970 Qaddafi assumed total control by naming himself Libya's premier and minister of defense. He then closed British and American military bases within its borders and began to transfer control of the oil industry — easily the most important industry in Libya — out of the hands of private operators and into the hands of the government. This transfer gave Qaddafi total control of the country's major moneymaking resource, and he used the oil revenue to launch construction of a wave of industrial plants, hospitals, highways, and irrigation projects. He also confiscated the properties of Italian and Jewish residents of Libya as part of his effort to rid the country of both ethnic groups. Other nations criticized him for this, but he ignored them. He had long hated both Italians and Jews, and his power gave him the opportunity to do something about it.

The Green Book

Once he became ruler of Libya, Qaddafi dramatically changed the way the people of his country lived. He published much of his guiding political philosophy in the three-volume *Green Book,* which has become a dominant part of Libyan life. As George Tremlett noted, "all children in Libya spend two hours a week studying *The Green Book* as part of their school curriculum. Extracts from *The Green Book* are broadcast every day on television and radio; there are constant lectures and seminars relating to *The Green Book* in colleges and universities, and its slogans are to be seen wherever one goes — on the outer walls of public buildings, on roadside billboards, over the entrance to Tripoli Airport."

Qaddafi's political theories are based on his belief that all government institutions eventually become corrupt. He argued that Libya should have no traditional institutions, no legislature, no constitution, no political parties, and no organized court system. According to *The Green Book,* everything from business to government should be run by "people's committees," which are elected by the workers. According to Qaddafi, the people of Libya should look on his *Green Book* as a sort of instruction manual for living within this system. When asked about his position in the Libyan government, Qaddafi claims that he is simply "the leader of the Revolution."

Traditional Islamic principles are also a part of life in Libya, though Qaddafi placed greater emphasis on certain aspects of those principles. Qaddafi has held to the Islamic ban on gambling, alcohol, and drugs, and he has even fol-

lowed the Islamic code of cutting off a person's hand for the crime of theft. But while he views himself as a devout Muslim, Qaddafi has granted women much greater rights than they enjoy in some other Arab countries, and he has consistently opposed Islamic fundamentalism in the Middle East. Some fundamentalists, who believe in an extremely strict observation of religious codes, have favored violence against "nonbelievers" who do not share their views. But Qaddafi does not favor strict adherence to Islamic religious teachings as the sole basis for law and government. Qaddafi has described fundamentalists who favor such arrangements as "maniacs" who have no place in the new socialist Arab world.

Branded as Terrorist

While working to reform Libya, Qaddafi also began to flex his muscles in other parts of the Arab world. Less than two years after seizing power, he called for Arab nations to unite as a "Federation of Arab Republics." This loose group, initially comprised of Libya, Syria, and Egypt, welcomed any Arab country that supported democratic socialism and opposed Israel. But Qaddafi's dream of a united Arab confederation never really became a reality. The various Arab nations disagreed on many issues, and Libya itself became unpopular with many Arab countries because of its growing sponsorship of terrorist groups and its persistent meddling in the affairs of nations in the Middle East and elsewhere.

Qaddafi continually interfered in Chad, a country with two large population groups—Muslims and blacks—that have often fought each other for control of the nation. He openly supported a revolt against Morocco's King Hassan because of Hassan's friendship with such Western nations as the United States, and in the 1970s he helped the brutal Ugandan dictator Idi Amin stay in power. He emerged as a big supporter of the Palestinian Liberation Organization (PLO), which was locked in a struggle with Israel over disputed land. Qaddafi also used Libyan oil money to help finance the Irish Republican Army and militant groups in the United States. In addition, he provided funds to the Sandinistas in Nicaragua, Marxist rebels in the Phillipines, and rebel groups in central and western Africa. Qaddafi's sponsorship and bankrolling of rebel and terrorist groups infuriated the United States and other Western nations. Their relations with Libya were already poor because of Qaddafi's alliance with the Soviet Union, which provided economic and military aid to his country. Qaddafi's involvement in terrorist activities worsened relations with the United States and its allies even more.

By the mid-1980s, governments in the United States and Western Europe had concluded that Qaddafi was a dangerous figure. His record of aiding anti-Western and anti-Israel terrorist groups was well-known, and no one knew what he might do next. American Vice President George Bush called Qaddafi "mad and unpredictable," and President Ronald Reagan charged that Libya had become "an outlaw state." America's Central Intelligence Agency (CIA) began to investigate ways in which Qaddafi could be removed from power.

Concerns about Qaddafi's actions became even more intense in the spring of 1986. Libya was accused of playing a role in a number of bombings around Europe, including an attack on a nightclub in Berlin, West Germany, that killed an American servicemen and a Turkish woman and wounded 230 others. On April 15, the U.S. military responded to the Berlin explosion by conducting bombing raids on targets in Libya. Their targets included several places where U.S. officials thought Qaddafi might be. Qaddafi was not harmed in the assault, but his 15-month-old adopted daughter was killed. In the days after the U.S. attack, diplomats and politicians around the world debated whether there had been enough evidence to justify such an action. Reagan insisted that "we have done what we had to do. If necessary we shall do it again." Even some of America's allies, though, thought that the bombing raid was an overreaction.

The 1986 raid, along with occasional attempts on his life by people inside of Libya over the years, have made Qaddafi cautious about staying in one place too long. It is widely believed that he never sleeps in the same place two nights in a row out of fear of assassination.

In 1988, after years of throwing troops and financial aid behind the Muslim forces in Chad, Libya was forced to retreat from the country. A few months later, a bomb exploded in a Pan Am passenger flight over Scotland, killing 270 people. This terrorist act incited worldwide outrage. Two Libyan security officers became the prime suspects in the bombing, but Qaddafi refused to turn them over to international authorities. The United Nations subsequently imposed a range of penalties, known as sanctions, against Libya. "Colonel Qaddafi is cornered," said one European diplomat. "If he fulfills the United Nations sanctions [and turns over the suspects], he can combat the growing discontent among the populace. If he extradites the two suspects, the security apparatus, the very pillar of his rule, will turn on him."

Indeed, by the late 1980s and early 1990s, many of Libya's people seemed unhappy with Qaddafi's rule. The country's poor economy, lack of organizational structure, and intimidating security forces, along with its growing isolation from the world community, spurred previously unseen levels of anger and frustration among its citizens. As Chris Hedges noted in 1992 in the *New York Times*, "many Libyans live without basic services like water and sewer systems. Hospitals lack equipment and qualified staff. Schools teach from the *Green Book* . . . but they have no desks or chalk."

Qaddafi's defense of Iraq's President Saddam Hussein in the wake of the 1990 Gulf War was intensified by Libya's isolation from the rest of the international community. On August 2, 1990, Hussein had directed an invasion of Iraq's neighbor Kuwait, an oil-rich land with easy access to the Persian Gulf. But Hussein invaded Kuwait for other reasons as well. Iraq owed Kuwait a great deal of money because of loans that it had taken out to finance an earlier war against Iran, and its government noted that at times in the past both Kuwait and Iraq had actually been part of a larger kingdom known as the Ottoman Empire. But most other countries recognized that the invasion was basically a brazen bid by Hussein to increase his power, and they angrily denounced the aggression. Within hours of the invasion, the United Nations Security Council passed a resolution criticizing Iraq, and within a matter of days a huge anti-Iraq military coalition of nations led by the United States had been formed. A trade embargo against Iraq was imposed, and the coalition warned Iraq to leave Kuwait by January 15, 1991. Hussein was defiant, though, so on January 17 the coalition launched a bombing campaign against Iraqi military targets. A month later, on February 24, the United States and its allies initiated a massive ground offensive against Iraqi positions in Iraq and Kuwait, and within days Iraq was forced to retreat from Kuwait and accept severe penalties for its aggression as part of a cease-fire agreement.

Libya was one of several Arab nations that criticized the coalition for interfering in Arab affairs. Indeed, many poor Arabs actually supported the Iraqi invasion, swayed by Hussein's claims that he wanted to redistribute the wealth of major oil-exporting nations such as Kuwait. Qaddafi's public condemnations of the U.S.-led coalition only widened the chasm between Libya and most of the rest of the world.

Perhaps because of the difficulties facing his country, Qaddafi has made some attempts to repair his damaged reputation in recent years. He initiated a number of reforms in Libya, toned down much of his anti-Western rhetoric, and suspended his financial support to a number of militant organizations around the world. In light of these steps, some Arab leaders have encouraged the West to reconsider their opposition to him. They believe that Qaddafi has played an important role in slowing down the progress of Islamic fundamentalism, which they view as dangerous. Some observers claim that Western nations are so determined to get rid of him that they have leveled false charges against him.

The United States and its allies, though, continue to view Qaddafi as a supporter of terrorism. United Nations sanctions against Libya remain in place, and in August 1996 the United States passed a law to punish foreign firms that invest in energy projects in Libya. After signing the bill, President Bill Clinton said that "you cannot do business with countries that practice commerce with you by day while funding and protecting the terrorists who kill you and your innocent civilians by night."

MARRIAGE AND FAMILY

Qaddafi was first married in 1969 to Fatiha Nouri Khaled, a schoolteacher and daughter of a Libyan army officer. While this marriage only lasted a short time, they had one son, Mohammed. In July 1970 Qaddafi married a nurse named Safiya, with whom he has had six sons and a daughter, who was killed in the 1986 U.S. bombing raid. Despite his years as leader of Libya, Qaddafi's supporters like to point out that he still remembers his Bedouin roots. They note that he leads a nomadic existence within Libya's borders, and that he often goes out into the desert to sleep in a tent underneath the stars.

WRITINGS

The Story of the Revolution, no date
The Green Book, published in English in three parts between 1967 and 1981
Discourses, 1975
The Village, the City, the Suicide of the Astronaut, and Other Stories, 1995

FURTHER READING

Books

Bearman, Jonathan. *Qadhafi's Libya,* 1986
Bianco, Mirella. *Gadafi: Voices from the Desert,* 1974
Blundy, David, and Andrew Lycett. *Qaddafi and the Libyan Revolution,* 1987
Encyclopedia Britannica, 1997
International Who's Who, 1996-1997
Kyle, Benjamin. *Muammar el-Qaddafi,* 1987
Lawson, Don. *Libya and Qaddafi,* 1982
Tremlett, George. *Gadaffi: The Desert Mystic,* 1993
World Book Encyclopedia, 1996

Periodicals

Current Biography Yearbook 1973
Economist, Sep. 10, 1994, p.45
Los Angeles Times, Jan. 27, 1986, p.2; June 29, 1992, p.8
New Republic, May 31, 1993, p.19
New York Times, Apr. 12, 1987, sec.1, p.1; Jan. 13, 1988, p.A4; Sep. 2, 1988,
    sec.1, p.10; Sep. 2, 1989, sec.1, p.3; June 24, 1992, p.A3; Sep. 10, 1995,
    p.N7; May 25, 1996, p.3; Aug. 28, 1996, p.A7
New York Times Magazine, Feb. 6, 1972, p.2
Time, Apr. 2, 1973, p.101; Apr. 1, 1996, p.46
U.S. News & World Report, Feb. 21, 1994, p.55; Oct. 31, 1994, p.58
Washington Post, May 20, 1973, p.3

ADDRESS

Office of the President
Tripoli, Libya

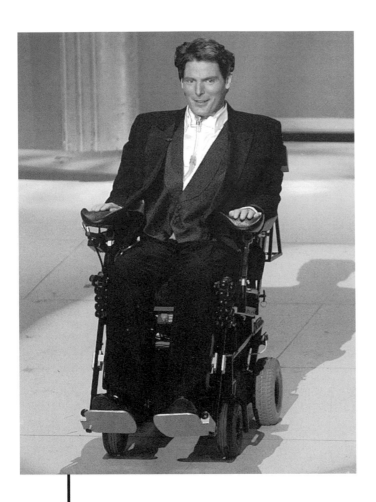

Christopher Reeve   1952-

American Actor, Director, and Spokesman for People
with Spinal-Cord Disabilities

BIRTH

Christopher Reeve was born on September 25, 1952, in
Manhattan, New York. His father, Franklin D'Olier Reeve, was
a distinguished poet, novelist, translator, and university professor. His mother, Barbara Pitney Lamb, was a writer for the
newspaper *Town Topics* in Princeton, New Jersey. Christopher
had a younger brother, Benjamin, and several stepbrothers and
stepsisters.

246

YOUTH

When Reeve was just four years old, his parents divorced and he moved with his mother to Princeton. Since his parents were not on speaking terms with one another, Reeve and his brother got stuck in the middle. "I felt torn between them," he admitted. "They had a tendency to use me as a chess piece." Both his parents eventually remarried and had more children, and Reeve managed to maintain a good relationship with his extended family.

As a child, Reeve was tall, thin, and awkward. He also suffered from a number of childhood diseases that made him uncoordinated and caused his hair to fall out. "I was 6' 2" by the time I was 14. And I moved like a building," he recalled. "Even though I was attractive, I lacked self-confidence." As a result, Reeve often chose activities that involved spending time alone, like playing the piano, swimming, and sailing. His stepfather bought him a 12-foot sailboat one year, and he spent a great deal of time in the summers sailing with his brother along the New Jersey shore.

Reeve received his first acting role by chance when he was in the fourth or fifth grade. A representative from the local McCarter Theater came into his classroom looking for a child to sing in a production of Gilbert and Sullivan's *The Yeoman of the Guard.* Reeve, who was bored with his lessons, volunteered. He soon found that he enjoyed acting, which provided him with a temporary escape from being himself. "I found relief in playing characters. You knew where you were in fiction. You knew where you stood," he explained. From then on Reeve played a variety of roles in local stage productions and became determined to make acting his career.

EDUCATION

Reeve went to the Princeton Day School, an exclusive private school in New Jersey. He was a good student, and he also participated in many activities. For example, he was the assistant conductor of the school orchestra and the goalie on the school hockey team. "I took a whack at everything that interested me, but more and more I felt that the theater was my home—acting was what I did best," Reeve stated. Besides playing the starring role in all of his school's theatrical productions, he spent his summers studying acting or working as an apprentice in local theaters.

Though this hectic schedule did not leave much time for a social life, Reeve did not seem to mind. "It solved the problem of Friday and Saturday nights. I didn't have to worry about how I was going to ask little Suzy out for a date, because I was too busy in the theater anyway," he recalled. "The whole dating game was painful. It really was, because I was also a very serious kid, and a lot of girls weren't ready for that. I don't mean serious about 'I love you,' but about World War III and the latest article in the *New Statesman.* I was not a whole lot of laughs." By the age of 16, Reeve had joined the Actors' Equity Association and hired an agent.

After graduating from the Princeton Day School in 1970, Reeve decided to attend college at Cornell University in Ithaca, New York — breaking a long tradition of men in his family going to Princeton University. While at Cornell, Reeve learned to ski in the mountains of upstate New York and continued to pursue an acting career. "I had an understanding agent who'd set up auditions and meetings around my class schedule," he noted. "Somehow, I managed to balance the academic and professional sides of my life." After earning a bachelor's degree in English and music theory with honors in 1974, Reeve enrolled at the prestigious Juilliard School for Drama in New York City. His roommate there was comedian Robin Williams, and the two young actors became close friends.

To help pay for his studies at Juilliard, Reeve took a role as Ben Harper in the television soap opera "Love of Life." Before long, however, his character became so popular that he was forced to drop out of school. "At first the character was set to appear just once or twice a week, and I could study the rest of the time. But he caught on and I was in almost every episode after a while," Reeve related. "The guy was a scoundrel — no moral scruples whatsoever. He was married to two women at the same time, one of whom was pregnant, and the Mafia had a contract out on him because of some blackmail-extortion scheme." One time, while Reeve was eating dinner in a restaurant, a woman came up to him and whacked him over the head with her purse. She had apparently assumed that he actually *was* Ben Harper, rather than an actor who played the character on TV.

CAREER HIGHLIGHTS

Reeve graduated from the soap opera to his first Broadway play in 1975, playing Katharine Hepburn's grandson in *A Matter of Gravity.* The play received good reviews, but Reeve was overshadowed by the legendary Hepburn. He later admitted that he was too nervous to perform well, but said he learned a great deal from his famous co-star. "I'd always thought of acting as a way to lose yourself, disappear into a part and thus find a kind of freedom," he stated. "[Hepburn] taught me that quite the opposite is supposed to happen. You must bring your own convictions, things you really love and hate to the character and then adjust after that." Reeve's Broadway debut also led to some positive changes in his family. "I said, 'What the hell,' and got my parents and stepparents tickets all together in the same row," he remembered. "They buried the hatchet" after not speaking to each other for 15 years.

When the play closed a year later, Reeve went to California to try his luck in the movies. His first film role was a small part in the disaster movie *Gray*

Lady Down, which did very poorly at the box office. Discouraged, Reeve spent the next five months bumming around Santa Monica. "I absolutely wrote myself off," he admitted. "I was sponging off friends, sleeping on couches, turning into a vegetable, and then one day I said this isn't right." He then returned to New York, acted in a variety of theater productions, and worked toward his big break to stardom.

Superman

The break came in 1977, when Reeve was chosen over 200 other actors to play the role of Superman in a blockbuster movie about the comic-book super-hero. The movie's producers, Alexander and Ilya Salkind, had begun search-ing for a big-name actor to play Superman in 1975, but all the stars they talked to either turned down the role or did not audition well. After they managed to cast Marlon Brando as Superman's father and Gene Hackman as the villain Lex Luthor, the Salkinds decided that they could afford to con-sider unknown actors for the starring role. Initially, Reeve was not certain he wanted the part. He wanted to act in serious films, and he worried that people would discount his talent if he appeared as an action hero. After reading the script and liking it, however, he changed his mind and spent two weeks preparing for his screen test. He got the job and a contract for $250,000. "The part came to me because . . . I have the look," Reeve admit-ted. "It's 90 percent look. If I didn't look like the guy in the comic book, I wouldn't be here. The other 10 percent is acting talent."

In the months before filming began, Reeve ate a high-protein diet and trained with weights for three hours each day in order to make his body re-semble the muscle-bound superhero. He got into such good physical condi-tion that he ended up performing all his own stunts, including "flying" over the East River in Manhattan by dangling from a 240-foot crane. The movie— which follows Superman from his birth on the planet Krypton, through his boyhood on a midwestern farm, to his days as a crime fighter in Metropolis— opened in December 1978. *Superman* was a phenomenal success, grossing $12 million in box-office receipts in its first week alone, although it was dis-missed by some critics as a fluff piece.

The sudden fame was a mixed blessing for Reeve. Though he lost his privacy and worried about being identified with Superman for his entire career, he also received many offers to play starring roles in high-profile movies. Reeve was offered the leads in *American Gigolo* and *Body Heat,* but he turned down these parts to star in *Somewhere in Time* (1980). In this love story, Reeve played a man who falls in love with a woman he sees in a 1912 photograph and goes back in time to meet her. In 1981, Reeve appeared in the sequel to his first hit, *Superman II,* which set a new American box-office record by grossing $5 million in one day. Critics generally considered it better than the first movie, with more action and special effects.

After a brief return to the theater, Reeve played a charming but deranged man in the 1982 thriller *Deathtrap.* After collecting $3 million to star in *Superman III* the following year, Reeve decided to take a break from the character for a while. "I don't want to knock Superman, but from then on it was all about trying to be recognized as someone else apart from a guy in a cape and tights," he explained. Although he reprised the role in *Superman IV* in 1987, he passed up a number of lucrative action-hero roles in favor of smaller parts that would provide him with a challenge and expand his range as an actor. "I wanted to be an actor, not run around with a machine gun. I've stuck to what I wanted to do and feel rewarded by that," he stated. For example, Reeve received good reviews for his performance opposite Emma Thompson and Anthony Hopkins in the drama *The Remains of the Day* in 1993.

The Accident

By 1995, all the aspects of Reeve's life seemed to be falling into place. He had evolved into a highly regarded veteran actor, with numerous roles in movies and on television, and he planned to direct his first film. He had also settled down personally and become a committed family man, marrying his long-time girlfriend Dana Morosini. In addition, he had begun to earn a reputation as a passionate political activist, using his position in the public eye to support environmental and human rights causes. For example, Reeve helped Vice President Al Gore and a group of volunteers clean up a beach in New Jersey, and he traveled to Chile to speak out on behalf of people who had been imprisoned for their political beliefs. He also helped found the Creative Coalition, a group of celebrities concerned about various environmental and social causes.

Despite his busy schedule, Reeve remained very active in sports. He learned to fly and bought his own plane, and he continued to sail and play tennis. But his latest passion was horseback riding. He bought and trained horses and began competing in equestrian (cross-country horse-jumping) events. "I trained six days a week. When I do a sport or a hobby I take it to as high a level as I can go," Reeve explained. "I don't do things carelessly or recklessly." He also encouraged other riders to take safety precautions, posing for a helmet-safety poster and volunteering to narrate a video on head-injury prevention.

Reeve had learned about the perils of head, neck, and spinal-cord injuries while researching his role in a 1995 TV movie, *Above Suspicion.* Reeve played a police officer who, after being shot in the line of duty, struggled to cope with being paralyzed and confined to a wheelchair. In preparing for the role, Reeve spent several days at a hospital that specialized in spinal-cord injuries, talking with patients and their families. "A couple of days spent out at the spinal-cord trauma unit and you see how easily it can happen," he stated. "You think, God, it could happen to anybody. It is frightening how easily life can change. One moment everything is fine and then the world falls apart."

Reeve (right), with wife, Dana, and Katie Couric of NBC's Today Show

Just a few days after the movie aired, the unthinkable happened to Reeve. On May 22, 1995, he competed in a horse-jumping event in Culpeper, Virginia. During the approach to a routine, three-foot jump, his horse — a seven-year-old Thoroughbred gelding named Eastern Express — stopped suddenly. Reeve lost his balance and tumbled forward over the horse's head. "I went over his ears like a football through the goalposts and ended up on the other side of the jump," he recalled. "And I landed straight on my head because my hands were entangled in the bridle and I couldn't get an arm free to stop my fall. Had I done that, I'd be looking at a sprained wrist." Instead, Reeve fractured the first and second cervical vertebrae in his neck, at the base of his skull. He lay unconscious and not breathing until a spectator cleared his air passage and performed mouth-to-mouth resuscitation. He was rushed to a hospital by helicopter, where doctors gave him a 50 percent chance of survival. Even if he pulled through, they said, he would be a quadriplegic — paralyzed from the neck down.

Reeve's family rushed to his bedside and spent an anxious week waiting for him to regain consciousness. When he first woke up and realized that he was paralyzed, Reeve suggested to his wife that it might be better if he died. "I remember saying to Dana that maybe it wasn't worth the trouble, maybe we should just let me go," he remembered. "If Dana had looked at the floor or taken a pause, it would have been difficult because I would have thought, *She's just being noble.* But without missing a beat, she looked me right in the eye and said, 'But you're still you and I love you.' And that saved my life right there. That put an end to any thought of giving up." Reeve was also cheered up by a surprise visit from his longtime friend Robin Williams. "I was hanging upside down [in a special hospital bed], and I looked and saw a blue scrub hat and yellow gown and heard this Russian accent," he stated. "There was Robin Williams being some insane Russian doctor. I laughed, and I knew I was going to be all right." After details of his condition were made public, Reeve received a total of 100,000 cards and letters from fans wishing him well.

As his recovery progressed, Reeve was sent on June 27 to one of the premier facilities for spinal-cord injuries in the United States, the Kessler Institute for the Disabled in New Jersey. During six months of rehabilitation that he described as being "a little bit like boot camp," he learned to use a special wheelchair that he controlled by sipping or puffing air into a straw with his mouth. Even after he was able to return home in December, Reeve depended on a respirator to breathe and required round-the-clock nursing care. Many of the everyday actions people take for granted became major ordeals for him. "You have to become knowledgeable about your body because you have lung problems, skin problems, bowel problems, bladder problems all caused by the spinal cord," Reeve explained. "The brain can't get messages through to control all those things." For example, aides had to force him to cough several times per day in order to clear his lungs. They also had to turn him over in bed every two hours so that he did not get sores on his skin. He even was unable to go outdoors on some summer days because he lost the ability to perspire and would become overheated.

Speaking Out About Paralysis

Though every day was a trial for him, Reeve refused to feel sorry for himself. "Yes, it was terrible what happened to me," he admitted. "But why should I be exempt? I had one very unlucky and unpredictable moment. The choice is whether to wallow in self-pity and musings about the past or to take a proactive stance about the future." Building on his past political activism, Reeve soon joined the board of the American Paralysis Association and became involved in several issues that affect people with spinal-cord disabilities. For example, he spoke out about the need to fund medical research in order to find a cure for paralysis.

Over 200,000 people in the United States have been paralyzed due to spinal-cord injuries. The majority are young men who got hurt in car wrecks, sports accidents, or shootings, and their medical needs cost the government over $8 billion per year. "I hope that with a groundswell of public support we can convince Washington to spend money on research to cure people with spinal cord injuries, rather than just take care of them," Reeve noted. "A very small amount of money, say as little as $40 or $50 million [per year], if that would be spent on research, if you would invest in the research, you could cure Parkinson's, Alzheimer's, multiple sclerosis, and spinal-cord injury in the very near future. But I'll bet you, in my life, and maybe even in the next 10, 15 years, if the public will demand that the politicians spend that little bit of money, and make that investment, I'll be up and walking around again." Scientists have made some encouraging progress toward that goal in recent years. In one study, researchers severed the spinal cords of rats, leaving the rodents paralyzed. When they transplanted nerves from other parts of the rats' bodies into the area, the spinal cords began to regenerate and the rats regained some mobility. Reeve hoped that the same techniques could some-day be used to help people.

Reeve also spoke out about the need for health insurance providers to raise their maximum lifetime benefits in order to pay for the care of people with spinal-cord disabilities. He requires constant nursing care, and his own health care costs about $400,000 per year. The total amount his insurance would cover during his lifetime was $1.2 million. This meant that his insurance would run out within three years, and if he could not make enough money to pay for his medical needs, he would be forced to rely on government assistance, like welfare and Medicaid. Many people who are suddenly disabled by spinal-cord injuries face the same situation each year. To address the problem, Reeve sent a letter to every member of the U.S. Senate asking them to support a bill that would make insurance companies increase their lifetime benefit caps to $10 million. Though many major insurers complained that the bill would make insurance more expensive for average people, Reeve cited a study that found that it would only cost an average policy-holder an extra $8 per year.

As part of his campaign, Reeve agreed to appear in a TV interview with Barbara Walters on *20/20*. "I thought I had to put a human face on a condition that the scientists were not really able to dramatize," he noted. "You have to move politically, but you also have to reach the people's hearts." Reeve's strength and candor on the show impressed many viewers. "We got thousands of letters from people saying how inspired they were by the interview, but the one that mattered to me the most was the case of the 19-year-old quadriplegic who had recently been injured in a football game," Reeve recalled. "He was begging his family to let him die. He had watched the program, and the next morning he called his family and said, 'I've changed my mind. If Christopher Reeve can do it, *I* can do it.'"

Christopher Reeve with two of his children, Matthew and Alexandra and their mother Gae Exton, in 1985

Reeve has continued to make public appearances in order to bring attention to his cause. In January 1996, he joined philanthropist Joan Irvine Smith in announcing the establishment of the Reeve-Irvine Research Center, a spinal cord research program at the University of California at Irvine. In March 1996, he made a surprise appearance at the Academy Award ceremonies and received a lengthy standing ovation from his fellow actors. During the summer, he was the master of ceremonies at the Paralympic Games and made an emotional speech before the Democratic National Convention. He also began working as a motivational speaker and received a $3 million advance from a publishing company to write his autobiography. Most gratifying for Reeve, however, have been the opportunities to return to show business. He provided the voice of King Arthur in the animated feature film *The Quest for Camelot,* and he narrated the HBO movie *Without Pity: A Film about Abilities.* His most ambitious project so far has been directing another movie for HBO, called *In the Gloaming.* Scheduled for release in the spring of 1997, the film tells the story of a young man who comes home to his emotionally distant family because he is dying of AIDS. Though directing required Reeve to be on location every day, he claimed that the activity made him feel better than if he had stayed at home. "The wonderful thing about directing is I'm energized all day long," he stated.

Reeve steadfastly believes that he will be able to walk again someday, so he trains hard in anticipation of that time in a special gym he had built in the garage of his home in Williamstown, Massachusetts. The gym includes a special exercise bicycle that stimulates his leg muscles with electrical shocks to make them move. To keep his legs able to support his weight, he is often strapped to a special table that allows him to stand upright. He also challenges himself by breathing without his respirator for up to 90 minutes at a time. Through his rehabilitation, Reeve has regained some feeling in his shoulders and left leg, though he is still unable to move them. He has also maintained a positive outlook on life. "It's like a game of cards, and if you think the game is worthwhile, then you just play the hand you're dealt. Sometimes you get a lot of face cards, sometimes you don't," he explained. "But I think the game's worthwhile, I really do."

MARRIAGE AND FAMILY

Reeve met Gae Exton, a British advertising agent, in 1977 during the filming of *Superman*. They lived together for ten years and had two children, Matthew and Alexandra. Reeve recalled that it took him some time to get used to the responsibility of being a father. One time, when Matthew was just eight days old, Reeve left his son in a basket in the shade at the beach while he went snorkeling. "When I surfaced, Matthew was no longer in the shade," he recalled. "His poor little face was all red on one side. I thought— fried baby. But luckily, he was fine." Though Reeve and Exton broke up in early 1987, they maintained a friendly relationship, and he was able to spend four months per year with his children. "If the love is not in question, they can survive separation," he noted. "When we get together, we fall right into place."

Reeve met Dana Morosini, a singer and actress, in June 1987 in a nightclub where she was singing. They were married in June 1992, and one month later she gave birth to their son, Will. Reeve credits his wife for giving him the strength to survive his injury. "Dana is the one who sees all the positive sides of me, because she has gotten me to lighten up," he stated. "She is my life force."

HOBBIES AND OTHER INTERESTS

Before his accident, Reeve was actively involved in a wide variety of sports. He flew solo across the Atlantic Ocean twice in his own small plane, and he sailed from Connecticut to Bermuda with a small crew after he completed the filming of *Superman*. He also enjoyed skiing, tennis, horseback riding, and playing the piano.

CREDITS

Movies

Gray Lady Down, 1978
Superman, 1978
Somewhere in Time, 1980
Superman II, 1981
Deathtrap, 1982
Monsignor, 1982
Superman III, 1983
The Bostonians, 1984
The Aviator, 1984
Street Smart, 1987
Superman IV, 1987
Switching Channels, 1988
Noises Off, 1992
Morning Glory, 1993
The Remains of the Day, 1993
The Rhinehart Theory, 1994
Speechless, 1994
Village of the Damned, 1995
The Quest for Camelot, 1996

Plays

A Matter of Gravity, 1976
Fifth of July, 1980
The Winter's Tale, 1989

Television

"Love of Life," 1968-76 (series)
Anna Karenina, 1985
The Great Escape II: The Untold Story, 1988
The Rose and the Jackal, 1990
Bump in the Night, 1991
Death Dreams, 1991
Mortal Sins, 1992
Nightmare in the Daylight, 1992
The Sea Wolf, 1993
Above Suspicion, 1995
The Black Fox, 1995

Without Pity: A Film about Abilities, 1996 (narrator)
A Step Toward Tomorrow, 1996

HONORS AND AWARDS

Citation for Distinguished Service (American Medical Association): 1996
National Courage Award (Courage Center): 1996, for contribution to the
 health, welfare, and rehabilitation of people with disabilities

FURTHER READING

Books

Havill, Adrian. *Man of Steel: The Career and Courage of Christopher Reeve,* 1996
Who's Who in America, 1996

Periodicals

Current Biography 1982
Good Housekeeping, June 1996, p.86
Independent, June 2, 1995, p.1
Ladies' Home Journal, Apr. 1996, p.131
McCall's, Sep. 1987, p.53
New York Times, Apr. 11, 1996, p.C1; Oct. 31, 1996, p.B1
Newsweek, June 12, 1995, p.43; July 1, 1996, p.52
People, July 6, 1981, p.82; Apr. 20, 1992, p.141; June 12, 1995, p.92; June 26,
 1995, p.55; Oct. 30, 1995, p.56; Dec. 25, 1995, p.52; Apr. 15, 1996, p.116
Teen, June 1983, p.51
Time, Aug. 26, 1996, p.40
Times of London, Sep. 17, 1995, p.F1

Other

20/20 (television interview transcript), Sep. 29, 1995

ADDRESS

Wolf Kasteler Public Relations
1033 Gayley Ave., #208
Los Angeles, CA 90024

Pete Sampras 1971-

American Professional Tennis Player
Number One Ranked Men's Singles Player
in the World

BIRTH

Peter Sampras was born August 12, 1971, in Washington, D.C.
He was the third of four children—including older brother Gus,
older sister Stella, and younger sister Marion—born to Soterios
(known as Sam) and Georgia Sampras. The Greek-American
family lived in Potomac, Maryland, where Pete's father worked as
an aerospace engineer for the Department of Defense and helped
run a deli. In 1978, a new job in the aviation industry prompted
him to move the family to Rancho Palos Verdes, California.

YOUTH

Raised in a middle-class home, Sampras learned the values of decency and hard work from his quiet, somewhat old-fashioned parents. Tennis did not really find its way into his childhood world until the family moved to California when he was seven. While living in Potomac, however, Sampras did learn some basics of the game as he spent several hours whacking a tennis ball against the basement walls with an old wooden racquet he found. Wanting a normal life for their children, Sampras's parents at first decided not to pay for private lessons, despite Pete's and his sister Stella's apparent abilities. "I was not going to join a [tennis] club," Sam Sampras recalled. "I was going to put Pete and Stella with local tennis, you know, public courts." One day at just such a public court, though, two observers asked Sam about Pete as they watched the boy play. After hearing Sam's explanation that he worried private lessons would cause family animosity and jealousy among his other children, the observers told Sampras's father he was foolish not to give the young player the opportunity he deserved. Soon Pete began playing out of the Peninsula Racket Club in Palos Verdes, and then the Jack Kramer Tennis Club in Rolling Hills Estates.

So it was that Sampras, at the age of eight, got his first coach — pediatrician and amateur tennis player Peter Fischer. "Fischer taught me how to play the game," Sampras noted. "He taught me how to serve and volley, he taught me strategy." Sampras had other coaches, as well, but Fischer and the films of legendary Australian player Rod Laver, which Sampras studied for several years, shaped the young player in his early years as he adopted a classic, all-court style of playing. "He looks like he grew up playing with a wooden racket," television analyst Mary Carillo once noted. "You can tell his values are steeped in the past. He's anti-entourage; he wears white on the court. People say, 'Where did this guy come from?' He comes from the '60s, that's where."

Sampras knew early on what he wanted to do with his life. "By the age of 12," Sampras remembered, "I was determined to be a tennis pro. People said I had potential and they were right." As his career forged ahead, Sampras consistently ranked among the top 25 nationally for his age group, and he became the youngest player on the United States Junior Davis Cup team at the age of 15. The Davis Cup is an international competition in which players represent their home countries. As Sampras traveled across the country to play in junior tournaments, his father accompanied him while his mother remained at home with his siblings. Family vacations were postponed because of tennis, and tennis clothing and equipment were permanent car accessories, even when the family went to church.

The junior tour was more difficult for Sampras than for other young players because, in an effort to improve, he most often faced opponents that were older than him. "The guys I played were twice my size," he recalled. "My coach and I were more concerned with learning to play well than with winning." That's why in 1987 Sampras made an important change in his game that would be instrumental in his future success as a serve-and-volley player: under the instruction of Fischer he switched from his best stroke, a two-handed backhand, to a one-handed backhand. "It was really tough and I was losing matches that I shouldn't have lost," Sampras remembered. "[But] everything [Fischer] had done up to that point was right, so I stayed with it." Later that same year Sampras's hard work was rewarded with a second place finish in his age group at the National Hard Court Championships, as well as the under-18 International Grass Court doubles title.

EDUCATION

With tennis taking up most of his time, Sampras had little interest in Rancho Palos Verde High School. "I didn't have any close friends at school," he explained. "I didn't experience going out on dates or doing any fun things when I was young." After much family discussion, it was eventually decided that — as an experiment — Sampras would drop out of high school in 1988, after his junior year, and join the professional circuit. He never returned to school, and he has no plans to do so.

Looking back at this time in his life, Sampras has few regrets about his missed education: "I just played tennis, and the rest of the kids looked at me as that, a tennis player, not as one of the guys. Did they think playing tennis wasn't cool? Well, I didn't care. By 16, I knew I wasn't going to college. I hear people say what a good time college is, but then I look at myself and the money I make and the job I do and, well, that's fun, too. I'm not into fraternities or going to parties; maybe if I was a normal kid and not playing tennis, I would be, but I guess I'll never know." Later in his career, after winning his first Grand Slam title, Sampras once again reflected on this lack of normalcy in his youth: "Right now, it all seems worth it, I guess, the sacrifices made by my family, the way my normal childhood went right out the window. But what I also found out is my life won't be normal . . . forever."

CAREER HIGHLIGHTS

The Pro Tour

After his consistent and steady success in junior tournaments, Sampras joined the world of professional tennis in 1988 as number 311 in the world. During his first year as a pro, Sampras's best finish was at a tournament in Schenectady, New York, where he made it to the semifinals before losing. This lack of immediate success was one of the reasons the young pro decided to spend a week at the Connecticut home of 28-year-old Czechoslovakian tennis great

Ivan Lendl, who had won the U.S. Open the previous three years, in an effort to improve his game. "The guy practically killed me," Sampras stated. "Lendl had me biking 20 miles a day, talking to me about discipline and working hard and practicing until I couldn't walk home. I'll never forget that." By the end of the year Sampras had broken into the top 100 in the world, at number 97, and the 17-year-old only continued to improve.

Sampras's first taste of stardom came at the 1989 U.S. Open in Flushing Meadows, New York. The U.S. Open is one of four prestigious events that make up the "Grand Slam" of tennis, along with the French Open, Australian Open, and Wimbledon. The second round of the tournament was expected to be Sampras's last as he faced defending champion Mats Wilander, but instead Sampras handed him a five-set upset. "I just couldn't get over it," Sampras noted. "I remember driving back to the hotel around midnight, and I just couldn't believe that I was still in the tournament. I mean, everyone expected me to lose." Though he was eliminated in a later round, the experience helped Sampras to gain confidence. It was at this point in his career that Sampras switched coaches, and his new coach, Joe Brandi, led him into his breakthrough year.

Having achieved the number 81 ranking in the world by the end of 1989, Sampras won his first pro championship in February 1990 at the United States Pro Indoors in Philadelphia. Despite being sidelined for two months with a hip injury, Sampras won his second tournament, on grass, when he rejoined the tour in Manchester, England. He then entered Wimbledon with high expectations, only to be unceremoniously knocked out in the first round. "It took a couple weeks to get over [that loss]," Sampras admitted, "because that was the tournament I was really gearing up to do well in."

First Grand Slam Title

By the next major tournament, the 1990 U.S. Open, Sampras was back in top form, easily advancing through the opening rounds with his blistering 130-mile-per-hour serve. Both the quarterfinals and semifinals pitted him against past champions, Ivan Lendl and John McEnroe, but Sampras prevailed, making it into the finals on a match point ace. Facing another young American in the final, Andre Agassi, Sampras overcame his opponent with his hammering serve, ending the tournament with 100 aces and his first Grand Slam championship. "I had a great time out there, right from the first point, no nerves at all," Sampras explained in a press conference following his victory. "Today was the best I could possibly play, the best all week and all year. . . . I really don't know if anyone could have beaten me." In accepting his trophy and $350,000 check, Sampras acknowledged Fischer as the main person who had guided his development as a player: "Pete Fischer gave me exactly the game I needed to win a Grand Slam; he put his logic in my head."

With this first Grand Slam victory came a loss of privacy for which Sampras was unprepared. "I've gone from being recognized around the tennis world to being recognized by anyone around the world," he related at the time. "Your private life isn't private anymore." This newfound fame only increased as Sampras appeared on several network television morning talk shows, made a guest appearance on the "Tonight Show" with Johnny Carson, and played doubles with President George Bush. The scrutiny intensified even more in December of that same year when Sampras received a purse of $2 million — the largest single paycheck ever awarded in tennis — for winning the inaugural Grand Slam Cup. Brad Gilbert, Sampras's opponent in the final match, said of the young star: "He's taking the game to the year 2000 range. I'd like to buy some stock in him. He is the guy of the future. . . . He's got ice water in his veins. He just won $2 million and he's not even excited."

"So much has changed," Sampras pointed out after his success of 1990. "The expectations people have for me have changed. . . . It was crazy for a while. It took months for it to finally sink in, what I'd accomplished. Then, when I finally began to think about it, I was amazed." These expectations proved difficult to meet as Sampras started 1991 with chronic shin splints and continued to be plagued with other injuries, including a warped Achilles tendon, for the first half of the year. "After the Open, I didn't reflect on what I'd done, and I didn't say no to anything; instead I went off and played a ton of exhibitions and got hurt and then it seemed like I was always hurt," he noted. By the end of July, Sampras had posted a record of only 16 wins out of the 27 matches he had played, and he entered the 1991 U.S. Open feeling the added pressures of a defending champion. "I've found out what Michael Chang meant when he said being the youngest champion of a slam is like carrying a backpack full of bricks around for the next year," Sampras related. This pressure remained with the young star as he suffered a disappointing quarterfinal loss, but it began to lift in November when he came back to win the Association of Tennis Professionals (ATP) World Championship.

The year 1992 brought Sampras another new coach — Tim Gullikson. Commenting on Sampras's abilities, Gullikson stated that "Pete's serve is a blessing and a curse. He's got so much talent, it gives him a lot of choices. Sometimes too many."After winning his first Davis Cup matches at the beginning of this year, Sampras then sought to improve his playing skills on slower, clay courts, and captured his first clay title at Kitzbuhel, Austria. He then followed up with two hard court titles in Cincinnati and Indianapolis. Sampras's Grand Slam activity for the year was not as successful. He made it to the quarterfinals of the French Open, where he defeated defending Wimbledon Champion Michael Stich, but then lost to Goran Ivanisevic in the semifinals. At the U.S. Open, he battled his way to the finals only to be stricken with intestinal problems that hindered his play as he dropped the match to Stefan Edberg. This string of disappointments was buoyed by a Davis Cup victory in doubles with John McEnroe, a win that helped the United States re-claim the Davis Cup. Sampras ended 1992 with five titles for the year and led the tour with 70 match victories.

Number One Player in the World

In April 1993, Sampras solidified his spot in professional tennis by attaining the number one ranking in the world. He then maintained his new status by winning four out of the next five major tournaments, including Wimbledon in 1993 and 1994, the U.S. Open in 1993, and the Australian Open in 1994. For Sampras, his first Wimbledon victory was the culmination of a lifelong goal. "The Grand Slams have always been my top priority," he noted. "Wimbledon is very important to me. The legends who have made it there. And the way it feels. The royalty. It's nice to make money, but that's not what tennis is all about."

The excitement of his impending victory at Wimbledon was almost too much for Sampras, and he had to compose himself before each of his two match points by taking deep knee-bends. "It's all kind of a blur," he declared. "It all happened so fast, and the next thing you know, you've won Wimbledon. . . . This is the biggest one in the world, and now that I've done it, I feel as happy as I've ever felt." As his latest accomplishment sank in over the next few days, Sampras related just how important this Grand Slam win was for his future career: "If I had lost Wimbledon, it would've really set me back for a long time because I came close to winning the Open last year, and I've won a lot of nice titles since I won it the first time. But I hadn't really won the big one, you know? And that was really sort of a scary feeling going into Wimbledon. I was probably as nervous for that match as any match I've played in my career. If I had lost that, I would've been thinking, 'Now how am I going to get ready for the Open? How tough am I mentally? Geez   do I need to see a shrink?' Even my father told me after I won Wimbledon, 'You know, I knew you had the talent, Pete. But I didn't know if you had the de-sire.' I thought I did. But I didn't know."

As 1993 came to a close Sampras found himself setting more records. His 1,011 aces made him the first player to record over 1,000 aces in one year. He also had 83 match wins, the most wins for a player in one year since 1985, and earned over $3.6 million in prize money. And after winning the 1994 Australian Open, Sampras became the first man in almost 30 years to win Wimbledon, the U.S. Open, and the Australian Open consecutively. But the French Open title eluded him for the third year in a row when he was knocked out in the quarterfinals.

Following his second Wimbledon title in 1994, though, Sampras was forced to take more time off from the tour due to tendinitis in his left ankle. Because of this injury, he found himself out of match condition as he entered the 1994 U.S. Open to defend his title, and he lost in the early rounds. More injuries also hindered Sampras during the Davis Cup, but he was able to maintain his number one ranking throughout the summer and the fall of 1994 because of his large point advantage.

The beginning of 1995 brought the devastating news that Sampras's coach, Gullikson, was diagnosed with inoperable brain tumors. Fighting back tears in an emotional semifinal match against Jim Courier at the Australian Open, Sampras advanced to the finals only to fall to Agassi, who was playing at the top of his game. In the following weeks, and throughout the rest of the year, Sampras traveled back and forth from tournaments to Gullikson's Illinois home as his friend and coach went through radiation treatments. Holding up well under the pressure and strain, and working with new coach Paul Annacone, Sampras then succeeded in winning his third straight Wimbledon title, which he dedicated to Gullikson. This victory sent Sampras into the record books once again, as he became the first American to win three straight Wimbledons. In other Grand Slam activity, Sampras reclaimed the U.S. Open title and reached the finals of the Australian Open only to lose to Agassi. The end of 1995 saw Sampras setting yet another record as he became the first player to earn $5 million in one year and the biggest money winner in tennis history with $21.7 million for his career.

But 1996 started out as a sad and disappointing year for Sampras. First he had to face the death of his coach and good friend Gullikson in May. Then, in July, he was forced to withdraw from the Olympic Games due to an injury to his Achilles tendon. Entering the U.S. Open in September, it looked as though he might fail to win a Grand Slam title for the first time in four years. During a heated, five-set quarterfinal match against underdog Alex Corretja, Sampras suffered from severe cramps and dehydration. In the fifth-set tiebreaker, he stumbled to the side of the court and threw up. But, aided by thunderous applause from the crowd, he bravely continued to play and managed to defeat his opponent. After beating Goran Ivanisevic in the semifinals, Sampras went on to score a convincing victory in the finals against second-seeded Michael Chang to capture his fourth career U.S. Open title. Following the winning point, he raised his arms toward the sky in a gesture of thanks to Gullikson. "I was thinking about him all day and all during the match," Sampras recalled. "I still felt his spirit and, even though he's not with us, he's still very much in my heart. I wouldn't be here if it wasn't for his help."

A Winner

During his meteoric climb to the number one spot in men's professional tennis, Sampras never swayed from his goal of winning tennis matches. This unmoving dedication and steady vision of victory made Sampras a very

uncontroversial player in a sport known and loved for its controversy. The methodical way in which he achieves his victories has even led some critics to label him as "dull," a criticism that Sampras is quick to answer with a laugh: "That's not what I'm all about. I'm not the flamboyant type. I'm not out there to overshadow the tennis. I go out to win tennis matches. And I hope people enjoy watching that." He added, "I'm not trying to be a gentle-man on the court. It's just the way I was brought up and the way I am. I'm not concerned about too many things. I lead a very simple life. I just care about winning tennis matches and that's about it." But this does not mean that competitors should take him lightly, for Sampras warned that "under-neath it all, I'm trying to kick your ass. In a nice way."

The fame that comes with all this winning, and the responsibilities associated with it, make Sampras's image all the more important to him. "I want to try to bring to tennis the nice, clean-cut American image," he explained. "I want to be a good role model so that kids will say they want to grow up to be Pete Sampras." There is a stark contrast between this nice-guy image and the ferocity with which Sampras plays the game of tennis—always to win. As one reporter described him, Sampras "has the dark good looks of a matinee idol. He's as polite as a butler. He doesn't have the Huckleberry Finn-ish appearance of a Jim Courier, but he's as American as the hot rod and probably could have been a cleanup hitter if someone hadn't put a racket in his hands at age 7. He plays tennis like a guy dealing blackjack. All he does is beat you."

Agassi, one of Sampras's biggest rivals, summed up the winning attitude that permeates the number one ranked player in the world: "The one thing that Pete has over me, or I shouldn't say over me, but that I wish I had, is such a simple approach and raw belief that he is just better than everybody." Or, as one tennis analyst noted, "Sampras operates from an unshakable belief that he has not yet laid eyes on the man who can take him down when he is playing well."

HOME AND FAMILY

Sampras lives in Tampa, Florida, with Delaina Mulcahy, his first girlfriend. They've been involved since he was 19. The day after they met, Sampras, who had never been on a date, called and invited her to spend a week with him in Myrtle Beach, Florida. In effect, the couple's first date lasted an entire week. "Delaina was the first girl that I felt comfortable with," Sampras ex-plained. "She's independent, and she understands. I don't have to entertain her."

Another important aspect of Sampras's family life are his parents, Sam and Georgia Sampras. Always supportive of their son's career, they can't stand the stress and anxiety of attending Pete's matches. Instead, they see movies or shop at malls until a match is over. And they want none of the glory asso-ciated with their son's achievements, as Sam noted: "The only picture we want in the paper is Pete's picture. We want all the glory and happiness to be Pete's. We didn't work hard hitting balls over a net. He did. Let him enjoy it." Grateful for his parents' constant support, Sampras observed: "Growing up they didn't put a whole lot of pressure on me. They let me develop as a player and not worry about winning every junior tennis match . . . and I will always be thankful." Sampras also calls his parents his best friends, revealing that "they are the people I trust most in the world and I love them."

HOBBIES AND OTHER INTERESTS

Sampras is an avid golfer in his spare time, as well as a fan of the Los Angeles Lakers and the Dallas Cowboys. He served as Chairman of the ATP Tour Charities Program in 1992, donates money to cerebral palsy research, and participates in numerous charity tennis events.

HONORS AND AWARDS

Grand Slam Cup: 1990
U.S. Pro Indoor Champion: 1990
U.S. Open Champion: 1990, 1993, 1995, 1996
ATP World Champion: 1991
Wimbledon Champion: 1993, 1994, 1995
Number one ranked player in the world: 1993, 1994, 1995, 1996
Jim Thorpe Tennis Player of the Year: 1993
ATP Tour Player of the Year: 1993-94
Australian Open Champion: 1994

FURTHER READING

Books

Who's Who in America, 1996

Periodicals

Current Biography Yearbook 1994
Los Angeles Times, Sep. 20, 1990, p.E1; August 5, 1993, p.C1
New York Newsday, Feb. 18, 1991, p.100
New York Times, May 6, 1991, p.C7; Aug. 26, 1991, p.C1; Sep. 10, 1996, p.B1
New York Times Magazine, Aug. 27, 1995, p.46
Observer (London), Nov. 4, 1990, p.23
People, Sep. 24, 1990, p.42; July 8, 1996, p.67
Sports Illustrated, Sep. 17, 1990, p.22; Sep. 20, 1993, p.26; Sep. 16, 1996, p.22
Sports Illustrated for Kids, Aug. 1994, p.49
Tennis, Mar. 1988, p.53; Sep. 1993, p.72; Nov. 1993, p.99; Jan. 1996, p.42; Feb. 1996, p.100

Washington Post, Aug. 22, 1993, p.D1
World Tennis, Nov. 1990, p.27

ADDRESS

ATP Tour
200 ATP Tour Blvd.
Ponte Vedra Beach, FL 32082

WORLD WIDE WEB SITE

http://atptour.com

Pat Schroeder   1940-

American Politician
Retired Representative to the U.S. Congress

BIRTH

Pat Schroeder was born Patricia Nell Scott in Portland, Oregon, on July 30, 1940. Her parents were Lee Combs Scott, a pilot and the owner of an aviation insurance company, and Bernice (Lemoin) Scott, a first-grade teacher who returned to work after her kids started school. They had two children: Pat, the oldest, and younger brother Mike.

YOUTH

The Scott family moved often while the kids were growing up. After Pat was born, the family moved from Oregon to Iowa to Missouri to Texas to Ohio and back to Iowa. "I couldn't afford to be shy. Whenever we moved into a new neighborhood, I had to make friends quickly," she recalls. "I'd line up all my toys on the sidewalk and see who I could trap into becoming my friend." Although she jokes about such things now, it was tough at the time. To make matters worse, she had crossed eyes when she was a child. She outgrew it, but it made it even harder to fit in. She still remembers the other kids' taunts. "With a patch over one eye," she says now, "I wasn't exactly the No. 1 choice for kickball."

And yet Pat had a happy childhood, with loving and supportive parents who taught her and her brother some important lessons for life. Individual responsibility was important in her family. Pat and Mike always had chores to do around the house, and on school vacations they would work in their father's office. Independence was valued, too. Each child got an allowance, and from the age of 11 Pat was expected to set up a monthly budget and cover her clothing and other expenses.

Political participation was also an important part of their family life. They often discussed political issues at the dinner table, and Pat's parents would encourage her to defend both sides of an issue to sharpen her debating skills. Early on, Pat decided that she wanted to become a lawyer. That was an unusual goal for a young woman at that time, when most American women took care of their homes and their children rather than working at jobs outside the home. But Lee and Bernice Scott encouraged their daughter to believe that she could do anything she tried to do. Pat believed them. In fact, after her father taught her to fly, she earned her pilot's license at the age of 15.

EDUCATION

Pat attended grade school in Texas, junior high in Ohio, and high school in Iowa. For college, she attended the University of Minnesota, where she majored in history and minored in philosophy and political science. She worked her way through school there doing what her father had taught her to do: flying to the sites of planes crashes to assess the damages. She earned her B.A. degree from the University of Minnesota in 1961, after only three years, and graduated magna cum laude (with great distinction) and Phi Beta Kappa.

After finishing college, Pat went on to law school at Harvard University. She was one of only 19 women in a class of 554 students, and the women weren't exactly made to feel welcome. For Pat, it was her first real view of the sexism that pervaded much of society at that time. "The first time I realized there was another world, I'm at Harvard Law School," she recalls. "We have assigned seats, I go to my seat, and the young men on either side of me get up and do this total huff about how they would *never* sit next to a *woman*, why they'd *never* been in a class with a *woman* in their *entire* educational *careers*." Showing the self-confidence that has become her trademark, she goes on to say, "I was amused. It was just like, *who* are these turkeys?" One male classmate told her that she should be ashamed of herself for taking a man's place. But Pat didn't let these obstacles stand in her way.

It was at Harvard Law School that Pat met her future husband, James White Schroeder. Jim was a pilot also—he'd been in the U.S. Navy—and he and Pat really hit it off. They were married in 1962 and finished up at law school together, sharing books and professors and learning how to work as a team. Pat Schroeder earned her J.D. degree from Harvard Law School in 1964.

As she was finishing up her degree, Schroeder was ready to look for work. A law degree from Harvard, a very prestigious university, is almost a guarantee of future success. She had every reason to assume that the placement officers would be able to help her find her first job, as they routinely do with new graduates. But that didn't prove to be the case. "At Harvard, when I was ready to graduate, I went into the personnel office and they said, 'Look, you know nobody wants to hire young women. First of all, you're married. You will probably have babies and they just aren't going to be interested. We only try to put our students out that we feel really have some chance.' And I said, 'I have been paying you guys for this degree for three years. What am I supposed to do with it—hang it over the sink?' They kind of laughed and said, 'I guess so.'"

FIRST JOBS

Fortunately, Harvard's personnel officers proved to be wrong. Pat and Jim Schroeder moved to Denver, where they both found work as attorneys. She started out working for the National Labor Relations Board (NLRB) and later taught at local colleges. She temporarily cut back her work hours after the births of their son Scott in 1966 and their daughter Jamie in 1970. About a year after Jamie's birth she was back to full time, working as a hearing officer for the Colorado Department of Personnel and as legal counsel for Planned Parenthood.

Both Pat and Jim were also involved in local protests against the Vietnam War, and Jim was also becoming active in the Democratic party. In fact, it was Jim who went into politics first, when he made an unsuccessful bid for a seat in the Colorado state legislature in 1970. It was Jim's interest in politics that would soon inspire his wife to run for office.

CHOOSING A CAREER

Pat Schroeder chose what would become an almost 25-year career in politics in a rather surprising and unusual way. At that time, Jim was active in a Democratic committee that was selecting a candidate to run for the U.S. Congress. It was 1972, and President Richard Nixon was expected to win re-election in a landslide. Other Republican candidates were also expected to do well that year, particularly James D. (Mike) McKevitt, the Congressman from their district. Everyone believed that this popular Republican incumbent would win. Jim's committee was having trouble finding a Democrat willing to run what amounted to a hopeless race as a sacrificial candidate who would surely lose. Or so the experts believed.

At one committee meeting, when one of the potential candidates refused to run, Jim asked him "What about your wife?" The man responded with "What about *your* wife." Jim didn't take it seriously at first. But as he thought about it, he realized that Pat was as well qualified as any of the potential male candidates. And he talked her into it, she jokes now. "I never saw myself as a candidate. But . . . I was the only person [Jim] could talk into it!" With two tiny children—including one still in diapers—the whole thing seemed crazy. Still, she decided to go ahead with it, because she wanted to discuss important issues with the voters and also because she was so convinced that she would lose.

With Jim as her manager, they ran an inexpensive campaign relying heavily on grass-roots volunteers. They didn't have enough money to print up standard big campaign posters; they could only afford to buy small-sized paper in unpopular colors. Still, these mini-posters proved to be one of their most effective tactics. For example, one showed a field of tombstones at Arlington National Cemetery with the caption, "Yes, some American troops have already been withdrawn from Vietnam." Another, which showed a young Hispanic child on a dirt floor in a migrant labor camp, included this message: "This radical troublemaker wants something from you. Hope."

Throughout her campaign, in both her printed materials and in her public speeches, Schroeder ignored the advice of party elders, who cautioned her to avoid controversial topics. For example, many people believed that a mother of two young children should be staying home with her children rather than running for office. Instead of appeasing her listeners, Schroeder often started her campaign speeches with a funny but pointed introduction: "Hi! I'm that nut you've been hearing about, the one who doesn't shave under her arms, the one who leaps over barricades uttering obscenities, the one who keeps her kids in the freezer." Speaking forthrightly on the issues and radiating decency, good will, and humor, she opposed the Vietnam war and called, instead, for national support of education, child care, health, and the environment. Schroeder proved to be a convincing public speaker and an effective campaigner. When the votes were counted in November, Schroeder had won 52 percent of the vote. She was the first woman from Colorado to be sent to Congress.

CAREER HIGHLIGHTS

Elected to the United States House of Representatives in 1972 to represent the first congressional district of Colorado, which includes the city of Denver and surrounding areas, Pat Schroeder went on to win re-election in 11 subsequent campaigns. She served in Congress for 24 years, from January 1973 until her retirement in late 1996. At that time, she was the longest-serving woman in the U.S. House. But few would have guessed, back in 1972, that she would last that long.

Schroeder established a reputation in the House early on. Her first task was getting the right committee assignment. The main work of the U.S. House of Representatives is passing legislation, and much of the work takes place in its 19 standing committees. Each committee has its own area of expertise — like banking, agriculture, foreign affairs, and armed services. When a new bill or law is first proposed, it is sent to the committee that covers that area. Members study the bill and make any necessary changes, thereby shaping future laws. The role of the committee chairperson is crucial during this debate process. The bill is then sent to the full House, where further revisions might be made. If the bill is passed, it is sent to the Senate, perhaps for more revisions, before it is voted on there. If a bill is passed by both the House and the Senate, it must be signed by the president to become law. New members joining Congress are assigned to serve on one or more committees, and they work hard to get assignments in the areas that most interest them.

Serving on the House Armed Services Committee

Many people were surprised when Schroeder lobbied for, and won, a seat on the House Armed Services Committee, which covered military issues. In that era, it was considered a surprising choice for a young woman. But a seat on that committee was a very powerful place to be. At that time, the House Armed Services Committee controlled about 40 percent of the national budget. Schroeder wanted to join the committee in order to participate in making decisions about military issues, to expose wasteful spending in the Defense budget, and to divert some of that phenomenal amount of money to social programs. The committee chairman, Louisiana Representative F. Edward Hebert (pronounced A-bear), was opposed to her from the start. In fact, for the first year, he refused to provide a chair in the committee room for her and for Representative Ronald V. Dellums, a new African-American Congressman from California. Schroeder and Dellums were actually forced to share a seat — Hebert said they were each only worth half a seat.

At that time, under Hebert, the House Armed Services Committee was known for its willingness to support any expenditures that the military wanted. Requests for new weapons systems were virtually a guaranteed yes. But Schroeder hoped to change that. While she favored a strong U.S. military, she also scrutinized military requests closely and questioned weapons systems that she considered unnecessary. She was well informed, polite, and fearless, and she refused to back down. This made Hebert furious, as he expected unquestioning acquiescence from committee members. And Hebert tried his best to make Schroeder's life miserable, ignoring her comments, withholding information from her, and openly insulting her in committee meetings. Undaunted, she persevered. And within the next few years, Schroeder helped stage a revolt that removed Hebert from his position as chairman of the committee.

Schroeder's work in the Armed Services Committee set the tone for her demeanor and reputation in the House. She became known as a political maverick, someone who followed her own mind rather than the dictates of her party. She was viewed as outspoken and independent-minded. as well as honest, determined, and courageous. But these same qualities—her independence and tough stance—have earned her both praise and criticism. Her supporters praised her integrity and willingness to fight for what's important. But others said that when carried to an extreme, these virtues can be faults, too. The political process in the U.S. Congress requires compromise. Members must work together to get anything accomplished. Too often, Schroeder's detractors say, she refused to work with others and to make any compromises in order to get bills passed.

Articulate and plain spoken, Schroeder is graced with a sharp wit and a gift for a pithy phrase. This has shown up most often in her public speaking, where she has used humor and an irreverent style to great effect. For example, soon after arriving in Washington in 1973 she was asked how she could be both a mother and a Congresswoman. She responded, "I have a brain and a uterus, and I use both." In another famous comment, she once called President Ronald Reagan "the Teflon president," comparing him to that non-stick surface because negative political fallout never seemed to stick to him. In the words of Kathy Bonk, one of Schroeder's close friends and a member of her 1987 campaign team, "She has an uncanny gift for packaging her political messages into witty one-liners that get people's attention." Despite her use of this glib humor, Schroeder was also known for her intimate command of the complexity and detail of the issues she faced in the House.

Fighting for Issues

For over 20 years, Schroeder fought for a series of issues that she considered crucial to the future of the country. With a record as both a social liberal and a fiscal conservative, she addressed, in particular, issues relating to military policy, families, and women.

Schroeder was known as a keen critic of the military budget, drawing on her great knowledge of weaponry as she questioned the need for different weapons systems. She was also a strong proponent of arms control and disarmament. But within the military, she was perhaps best known for her support of quality-of-life issues for military personnel, working for better pay, financial security, and improved working conditions. Life for military families can be particularly difficult, because they may move around frequently. She authored the Military Family Act, which provided funds for housing, child care, health care, and moving expenses to military families. She also worked to protect the divorced wives of servicemen. It can be difficult for the spouses of military personnel to have outside jobs, because of their frequent moves and also because of their sole responsibility for the children if their spouse is sent off on a mission. But for years, divorced spouses of military personnel had no rights to medical insurance or to pension benefits to cover their retirement years, and many women were left unprotected after divorce. Schroeder felt that military spouses should be recognized for their special service, and she sponsored legislation that offered benefits to the families of American troops in the event of divorce.

Family issues for non-military people have been of equal concern for Schroeder. She has earned widespread praise for making the problems of the modern American family a national issue. She worked for the passage of the "Deadbeat Dads" act, which has forced divorced fathers to contribute financial support for their children. But her greatest accomplishment in this area is the Family and Medical Leave Act. This law, which was vetoed by President George Bush in 1992 but passed by President Bill Clinton in 1993, allows parents to take up to 12 weeks off from work to take care of a new baby, a sick child, or an elderly parent. Now, people don't have to choose between keeping their jobs and taking care of their loved ones.

Throughout her years in Congress, Schroeder has been a strong voice for women's issues, one of the most forceful advocates for women's rights on the national stage. She worked for many years for passage of the Equal Rights Amendment (ERA), a proposed constitutional amendment that would guarantee that women and men are entitled to equal rights. She has been a strong advocate for reproductive rights, as a supporter of birth control and the legal right to abortion. She has also worked for economic equity for women, which means that women should be paid the same as men for doing similar jobs. She fought for adequate day care, for programs to help battered women, and for equity in medical funding, to ensure that research on women's health issues received adequate funding. And from 1979 to 1995, Schroeder co-chaired the Congressional Caucus on Women's Issues. This bipartisan group, including both Democrats and Republicans, worked to advance women's legislation in Congress.

Running for President

In June 1987, Schroeder announced that she was mounting an exploratory campaign to consider running for the Democratic nomination for president in the 1988 election. From the start, she make it clear that she was not willing to be a symbolic candidate, the token woman. Either she would make a serious run for the presidency, or she would drop out of the race. She set a goal of raising $2 million as one criteria for deciding whether to stay in the race.

Schroeder spent the next several months traveling around the country, determining whether she could run a viable campaign. She covered 29 states and 75,000 miles, giving speeches and attending fundraisers. She called her campaign theme "Rendezvous with Reality," explaining that "I'm not going to be the Tinker Bell of this campaign, bring out the magic poofle dust, and say everything's going to be OK." Instead, she discussed the environment, arms control, foreign policy, and burden sharing, meaning that our allies abroad should be forced to contribute to our costs of providing their military defense. She also discussed issues like pay equity, job protection, improved day care, and tax reform. Although these are issues that concern the vast majority of Americans, polls at the time showed that at least 30% of voters believed that a woman — any woman — would be a worse president than any man. Despite Schroeder's years of experience facing important issues in the U.S. Congress, sexism was still a major factor in voters' response to her campaign. "I look at my qualifications," she remarked at the time, "and if my name were Patrick Schroeder, I'd be called the best qualified in the race. There's no question about it."

On September 28, 1987, Schroeder faced a group of her supporters in Denver and announced that she would not run for president. She had entered the race too late to raise enough money, she said, and to hire the most talented political organizers, who were already committed to working for other candidates. Schroeder also expressed her frustration at the dehumanizing political process of a national campaign, which left her feeling distant from her supporters. "I could not figure out how to run and not be separated from those I served. There must be a way, but I haven't figured it out yet. I could not bear to turn every human contact into a photo opportunity."

But what most people would remember best about that final speech of her brief presidential campaign was not the words that she said. At the beginning, when her supporters first understood what she planned to say, a loud groan of disappointment came up from the audience. Schroeder's eyes filled with tears, and she briefly choked up with emotion. After a moment, she turned to her husband Jim, standing nearby, and rested her head on his shoulder.

For some viewers, this brief moment seemed more important than all her years of service. They criticized her for what they saw as a dangerous display of emotionalism and interpreted it to mean that Schroeder, and all women, were unfit to be president. Schroeder would not apologize, though; she was not about, she said, to "take it like a man." But how could a woman be trusted to make the tough decisions if she would be reduced to tears? Would the country want its president to cry when sending troops into war? Schroeder responded that "I wouldn't want that person to be someone who *doesn't*

Schroeder and other female House members, (left to right) Rep. Elizabeth Furse, Paige Wagers, Rep. Nita Lowey, and Gena Hutton

cry." As she explained, "Tears signify compassion, not weakness." Soon enough, she was joking about it, saying that she could make a fortune advertising Kleenex. But Schroeder never backed down from her belief that expressing emotion is compatible with making tough decisions.

Following her run for president, Schroeder continued to serve in Congress. She served on several House committees, including the National Security Committee (previously the Armed Services Committee), the Judiciary Committee, and the Post Office and Civil Service Committee. She also chaired the House Select Committee on Children, Youth, and Families, which identified ways to improve the lives of America's families. Some of her recent legislative accomplishments include the Violence Against Women Act, which strengthened the efforts of law enforcement agencies to fight violence against women; the Economic Equity Act, which focused on workplace issues for women, including job discrimination, day care, and opportunities for women business owners; the Breast and Cervical Cancer Mortality Prevention Act, which funded medical procedures for low-income women; the Child Support Responsibility Act, which ensured that divorced parents would provide financial support for their children; and the National Child Protection Act, which allowed child care providers and service organizations to do background checks on potential employees to identify those with any history of harming children. Schroeder summarized many of her views in her book *Champion of the Great American Family* (1989), in which she discussed a family policy agenda for the United States into the 21st century.

Retiring from Congress

On November 29, 1995, Schroeder announced that she would not run for re-election, but instead would retire from the House at the end of her term in 1996. In her mid-50s, she wanted an opportunity to try something new while she still had time. "My feelings are very mixed about leaving Congress," Schroeder explained. "I have had a very wonderful time being there. I never wanted to be a lifer, but every two years I talked myself into running for re-election. If I don't get out now, I'm going to be nearly 60 after another term. So if I am really going to do anything else except be in Congress, the time has come. Ageism [prejudice based on age] is alive and well, especially against women. I don't want to wait until I'm too old to do other things with my life.

"I really hate to leave Congress because it's been my whole adult life," she continued. "I have gone from toilet training my children to menopause while serving in Congress. On the other hand, there is the excitement of 'Wow, now what am I going to do with the rest of my life?' I feel a mingling of regret and optimism."

Although she is leaving Congress, Schroeder has made it clear that she isn't leaving the national stage. Instead, she was ready for a new stage to discuss what she sees as the three top issues facing the nation: the inequality of women in the workplace, the deteriorating state of the family, and the erosion of American communities. For the immediate future, she has agreed to teach a course in "The Politics of Poverty" at Princeton University. But she only committed to one year there, saying that she just might run for office again in 1998—perhaps for the Senate, perhaps for governor of Colorado.

MARRIAGE AND FAMILY

Pat and Jim were married on August 18, 1962. They have two children, Scott and Jamie, who are both now grown. Throughout her years in Congress, the family split their time between their homes in Washington, D.C., and Denver, Colorado.

WRITINGS

Champion of the Great American Family: A Personal and Political Book, 1989

HONORS AND AWARDS

Woman of Distinction (American Newswomen Club): 1982
Mother of the Year (National Mother's Day Committee): 1982
Commendation for Distinguished Service against Hunger (Bread for the
    World): 1984
Friend of Family Award (Family Law Section, American Bar Association):
    1992
10 Best Politicians for Women (*McCall's*): 1992
Robert C. Knapp Award (Harvard Medical School): 1992
Ryan White Award (WACHIVIY): 1993

FURTHER READING

Books

Almanac of American Politics, 1994
Fireside, Bryna J. *Is There a Woman in the House . . . or Senate?* 1994
Schroeder, Pat. *Champion of the Great American Family: A Personal and
    Political Book,* 1989
Who's Who in America, 1996
Who's Who in American Politics, 1995-1996

Periodicals

Boston Globe Sunday Magazine, Nov. 1, 1987, p.14
Current Biography Yearbook 1978
Los Angeles Times Magazine, Nov. 15, 1987, p.10
McCall's, Jan. 1980, p.28; June 1990, p.59
Ms., Feb. 1988, p.44
New York Times, Nov. 30, 1995, p.A13
New York Times Magazine, July 1, 1990, p.12
People, Sep. 7, 1987, p.48
Savvy, Dec. 1987, p.42
Vogue, Apr. 1986, p.176
Washington Post, Sep. 29, 1987, p.A1; Nov. 30, 1995, p.A12; Dec. 1, 1995, p.F1
Working Woman, Apr. 1996, p.42

ADDRESS

U.S. House of Representatives
2307 Rayburn House Office Building
Washington, D.C. 20515-0601

BRIEF ENTRY

Rebecca Sealfon   1983-
American Winner of the 1997 National Spelling Bee

EARLY YEARS

Rebecca Sealfon was born in New York City on July 8, 1983. Her father is Dr. Stuart Sealfon, a neurologist and neurobiologist who does research at Mount Sinai Medical Center in New York. Her mother is Celia Gelernter Sealfon, who has a master's degree in social work but is currently staying at home with the children. Rebecca, the oldest of their three kids, has a sister, Rachel, and a brother, Adam. They live on a quiet street in Brooklyn Heights, a part of New York City.

EDUCATION

Rebecca Sealfon has had a different type of education than most kids. Early on she attended St. Ann's School in Brooklyn Heights. But for the past five years, instead of attending school, she has been home schooled. Her mom does most of the teaching, but her dad also participates in the evening. The city school district requires families that do home schooling to submit a teaching plan and to send in academic results four times each year. So Stuart and Celia Sealfon met with the teachers at the local school to learn about the curriculum and to develop a study plan.

Families decide to home school their kids for different reasons: because of religion, or because they object to the subjects studied in the schools, or because they're looking for a different educational environment for their kids. The Sealfons felt that Rebecca was a bright, unusual student with a long attention span. They wanted her to be able to study a subject for longer than the usual class period of 45 minutes. They also wanted her to be able to move at her own pace and to have the freedom and flexibility to pursue independent projects. For Rebecca, spelling soon became one of those projects.

MAJOR ACCOMPLISHMENTS

The National Spelling Bee

The National Spelling Bee is sponsored by the Scripps Howard media organization. Spellers can compete through eight grade. Each year, regional contests include more than nine million students from the United States, Mexico, Guam, Puerto Rico, the Virgin Islands, and Defense Departments schools overseas. Over 200 winners of these regional contests go on to compete in the national championships. In all these events, each participant is given a word to spell. With a correct spelling, the student advances to the next round; with an incorrect spelling, the student is eliminated from the spelling bee. Participants are given lengthy lists of practice words that are used in first few rounds of the spelling bee; after that, the words are unfamiliar and difficult.

Rebecca first participated in the National Spelling Bee in 1996. She finished in eighth place that year, after misspelling "erythema" (a skin condition that causes small, tender red spots under the skin). When she decided to compete in the contest the following year, she began studying the word lists as much as three hours a day. According to Rebecca, "I studied spelling rules and the roots of words and how letters sound in foreign languages. I could guess the words I wasn't sure of because I knew the roots." All that studying paid off when she became one of two winners of the state contest in New York in March 1997. With that, she earned a trip back to the national championships, which finished up in Washington, D.C., on May 28 and 29, 1997.

It was a tough contest. By the end of the 14th round, it was down to just two contestants, Sealfon and Prem Murthy Trivedi, an 11-year-old from New Jersey. Sealfon became so nervous that she had to wait offstage between rounds. And her behavior onstage was rather distinctive, too. She spelled extremely slowly, saying each letter to herself, into her hand, before saying it out loud. She appeared very nervous, fidgeting with her hair and clothes. As she got each word right, she would pump her arms in the air before bounding offstage. Here are just a few of the words she spelled correctly: "vaporetto," "hippogriff," "desquamate," "vernissage," "nomothetic," "deliquesce," and "bourgade."

Sealfon and Prem battled through nine rounds, and then he misspelled "cortile" (a courtyard). Rebecca's final word was "euonym" (a name well-suited to a person, place, or thing). Although she didn't know the word, she was able to figure it out because she recognized its Greek root. She shouted each letter into the microphone, and then jumped for joy as she won the contest. As the national spelling champion, her prizes included $5,000 in cash, a large trophy, a laptop computer, an encyclopedia, and other gifts.

Rebecca has a lot of interests other than spelling. She enjoys writing stories, playing piano, using computers, and reading, both fiction and nonfiction. She especially likes fantasy books, including *The Lord of the Rings* by J.R.R. Tolkein and *The Chronicles of Prydain* by Lloyd Alexander. Lately she has been trying to teach herself to play chess. She also enjoys swimming, biking, kayaking, skiing, and hiking. For the future, Rebecca plans to attend Stuyvesant High School in New York, she says, because "that school has a more diverse environment than home schooling. There are more different people there."

FURTHER READING

New York Daily News, May 30, 1997, News Section, p.3; May 31, 1997, News
    Section, p.3
New York Times, May 30, 1997, p.B4; May 31, 1997, Section 1, p.23
Philadelphia Inquirer, May 30, 1997, p.A25
Washington Post, May 30, 1997, p.A9

ADDRESS

Scripps Howard National Spelling Bee
P.O. Box 5380
Cincinnati, OH 45201

WORLD WIDE WEB SITE

http://www.spellingbee.com

Tupac Shakur 1971-1996

American Rapper
Creator of *2Pacalypse Now, Strictly 4 My N.I.G.G.A.Z.,
Me Against the World,* and *All Eyez on Me*

BIRTH

Tupac Amaru Shakur was born on June 16, 1971, in the Bronx, a borough of New York City. He was known to his fans as 2Pac, the name under which he recorded. But the name Tupac Amaru, which comes from an Inca chief, means "shining serpent," while Shakur means "thankful to God" in Arabic. His mother was

Afeni Shakur, and his father was Billy Garland. Tupac had one sister, Sekyiwa, and a brother, Maurice.

YOUTH

Shakur had a very tough start on life. His mother, Afeni Shakur, was a political activist and member of the Black Panthers. This militant black group, which was active primarily during the late 1960s and early 1970s, rejected the call for nonviolent civil disobedience that characterized the Civil Rights Movement. Instead, the Black Panthers believed that violent revolution was the only way for black people to achieve their freedom. They called for all blacks to take up arms, and various Black Panther groups around the country responded with violent confrontations and legal conflicts. Afeni Shakur was a member of one such group, later known as the "New York 21."

Before Tupac's birth, Afeni and other members of her group had been arrested for allegedly conspiring to bomb several public places around New York City, including department stores and police stations. While she was out on bail awaiting trial, she got pregnant with Tupac. But some of the other members of the group decided to jump bail. Rather than wait around for the trial, they left the country and fled to Algeria. To prevent her from leaving also, the authorities revoked her bail and locked her up in prison. The conditions there were tough for a pregnant woman—so bad, in fact, that she was afraid that her baby wouldn't survive. "I had a million miscarriages, you know," she recalls. "This child stayed in my womb through the worst possible conditions. I had to get a court order to get an egg to eat every day. I had to get a court order to get a glass of milk every day—you know what I'm saying. I lost weight, but he gained weight. He was born one month and three days after we were acquitted. I had not been able to carry a child. Then this child comes and hangs on and really fights for his life." Afeni was acquitted on the bombing charges in May 1971, and Tupac was born one month later.

His father, Billy Garland, was around briefly during the first couple years of his son's life. He and Afeni had split up by the time Tupac was born, and Garland saw him only occasionally until he was about five. After that, Garland moved to New Jersey, and he didn't see his son again until 1994. Shakur grew up not knowing who his father was; he always hoped it was a neighborhood drug dealer named Legs.

Tupac and his family moved around a lot, and they were very poor. They lived in the ghetto in the Bronx and Harlem, in homeless shelters, and with friends and relatives. For a time his mom was hooked on drugs, too. It was Legs, the man who Tupac thought was his father, who first introduced her to crack cocaine. Afeni struggled with drug addiction through much of the 1980s. Legs eventually died of a drug-induced heart attack. Tupac was devastated when he died, feeling that he had lost his father.

Tupac struggled to grow up in this environment. Early on he showed a love of the theater and poetry, which brought him a fair amount of teasing from the other kids in the neighborhood. Looking for a creative outlet for her son, Afeni signed him up for a Harlem theater group when he was 12. In 1984 he won his first acting part, as Travis in *A Raisin in the Sun* by Lorraine Hansberry. The production, which took place at the Apollo Theater in Harlem, was a fundraiser for Jesse Jackson's 1984 presidential campaign. "I remember thinking," Shakur later said, "'This is something that none of them kids can do.' I didn't like my life, but through acting I could become somebody else." During rehearsals for the play Shakur turned 13, and the cast gave him a surprise birthday party. One of the presents appeared to be a box of fancy chocolates, but inside were 13 one-dollar bills, each tied with a ribbon. Shakur used the money to buy food for his family.

EDUCATION

Shakur started out attending public schools in New York. But Afeni wanted to escape her troubles there, so in the mid 1980s, when Tupac was a teenager, they moved to Baltimore, Maryland. Tupac was accepted into Baltimore's prestigious High School for the Performing Arts, where his artistic talents were recognized and encouraged. He joined the school's drama productions and wrote poetry as well; he even studied ballet. "That school was saving me, you know what I'm saying'?" Shakur later said. "I was writing poetry . . . and I became known as MC New York because I was rapping, and then I was doing the acting thing. It was a whole other experience for me to be able to express myself—not just around black people but also around white people and other kinds of people. It was the freest I ever felt in my life."

But that period soon came to an end. In 1988, when Shakur was 17, the family moved again, this time to Marin City, California, a town north of San Francisco. His life changed drastically there. He started out attending Tamalpais High School near Marin City, but he soon dropped out (although he later earned his GED, or General Equivalency Diploma). Dropping out would prove to be the beginning of a downward spiral. It would propel him into super-stardom as a rap artist—but at a huge cost. He would become a gangster and a thug, would lead a life filled with violence and legal problems, and would die much too young.

FIRST JOBS

After dropping out of school Shakur spent the next few years just hanging around. He crashed with friends, hustled on the streets, and sold drugs in a Marin City housing project nicknamed "the Jungle." But he was also doing some rapping around the Bay Area with Vallejo MC Ray Luv in the group The

One Nation MC's. "He wasn't a gangster when he lived out here with us," a member of the group later recalled.

In 1989 he met Shock-G, the leader of the funky hip-hop group Digital Underground. He started working for the group as a dancer and on the road crew. The following year he appeared on Digital Underground's "Same Song" from their *This Is an EP Release*. This hit single and video, along with his work on their next release, *Sons of the P*, garnered a lot of national attention, and ultimately won him a solo recording contract.

CAREER HIGHLIGHTS

Shakur was a contradictory and controversial figure. His career ran the gamut from best-selling albums and critically acclaimed movie roles to violent run-ins with the police. He was an accomplished writer and rapper, but he was also a convicted sex offender. He varied between macho bragging about his gangster lifestyle and bemoaning the desperation and self-destructive violence of life on the streets. It's hard to make sense of all these facets of his image and his career.

Gangsta Rap

Shakur came to rap at a time when it was going through a change. Rap music had started out on the East Coast, and much of it there was either lighthearted party music or testaments to black pride. As it moved to the West Coast, though, it began to change. Both the music and the lyrics became more aggressive, often glorifying violence and degrading women. This was gangsta rap. It portrayed a very dark view of urban black life, depicting a landscape where violent gangs control the streets and the police are the enemy. The music has become very controversial. Its opponents say that gangsta rap helps perpetuate violence by glamorizing it. But its supporters feel that it just reflects the harsh, desperate reality of life in the ghetto for many blacks.

For gangsta rappers, their image became as important as their music. Many felt that their credibility on the street was key to their reputation as rappers. For that reason, it has seemed that many have taken on a whole gangsta persona. Shakur was no exception; it often seemed that his image was as important as his music. He even proclaimed it on his body. A large tattoo across his abdomen spelled out "THUG LIFE," with the "I" in the form of a bullet. "[As] his popularity grew," Charisse Jones wrote in the *New York Times*, "his life began to mirror the swaggering bravado and violence that is so much a part of his art, and it became more and more difficult to distinguish between the . . . performer and the troubled characters that he rapped about and portrayed in films."

Early Credits

Shakur was living in northern California when he first got started as a rapper and actor. His work with Digital Underground had earned him a recording contract with Interscope Records. His first solo release was *2Pacalypse Now* (1991), which sold a very respectable half a million copies. It included two hit singles, "Trapped" and "Brenda's Got a Baby." His second release, *Strictly 4 My N.I.G.G.A.Z* (1993), produced the hits "Holler If Ya Hear Me," "I Get Around," and "Keep Ya Head Up." Both of these releases grimly depicted life on the streets, showing all its poverty, despair, and violence. Throughout, Shakur alternated moments of compassion and tenderness, political and social observation, and expressions of rage and brutality. These contradictory impulses continued throughout much of his work and are part of the reason, critics agree, that Shakur's work was so moving, so real, and so important.

At the same time, Shakur was beginning his acting career. In his first movie, *Juice* (1991), set on the streets of Harlem, he played the violent and unpredictable Bishop, who goes on a crime spree. While the movie was not a great success, critics thought that his performance was spellbinding. He went on to appear as the intense and complex postman Lucky in the male lead opposite Janet Jackson in *Poetic Justice* (1993) and as the neighborhood heavy and drug dealer Birdie in a supporting role in *Above the Rim* (1994). While none of these films proved to be a huge success at the box office, Shakur consistently won praise as a gifted performer.

Legal Problems

Throughout these artistic triumphs, though, Shakur was faced with a host of legal problems. In the spring of 1992, a Texas state trooper was killed by a teenager who was listening to *2Pacalypse Now*, which contains songs about killing the police. That same year, Shakur attended an outdoor festival where a fight broke out. He was armed, and when he dropped his gun, a stray bullet from it killed 6-year-old Qa'id Walker-Teal. A wrongful death suit brought by Walker-Teal's parents was settled in November 1995, when Shakur's recording company paid them just under half a million dollars. Shakur's legal problems multiplied in 1993, when he was arrested for allegedly attacking a limousine driver who took him to a taping of "In Living Color." The charges were dropped later. He was also arrested for assaulting director Allen Hughes on a video shoot. For that offense, Shakur was sentenced to 15 days in jail and 45 days of community service. In October 1993, he was arrested in Atlanta, Georgia, for allegedly shooting at two off-duty cops. Police claimed they were in the middle of a traffic argument when Shakur fired a gun, although the rapper said he was aiding a black motorist being harassed by police. He was later cleared of shooting charges. In April 1994 he was arrested during a traffic stop in Los Angeles when police found two 9-mm pistols in the car. And in

Shakur in Gridlock'd

August 1994, Shakur was convicted on misdemeanor assault and battery charges for beating a rapper in Michigan.

The gravity of these charges, though, was overshadowed by a much more serious offense. In November 1994 Shakur went on trial to face charges that he had forced a 20-year-old woman to have sex with him in a New York hotel back in November 1993. Shakur denied the charges. But during the trial, when the jury was deliberating on the verdict, Shakur was shot. On November 30, 1994, he and several associates entered the lobby of a building in New York, planning to take the elevator to a recording studio on an upper floor. They were followed to the elevator by three men, who told them to lay on the floor. Shakur resisted, and he was shot numerous times, including twice in the head, once in the left arm, once in the thigh, and once in the groin. He was also robbed of $40,000 worth of jewelry. The police believed that it was a straightforward robbery, but Shakur was convinced that he had been set up. When he returned to the courthouse for the continuation of his trial, he was found guilty of sexual assault and sentenced to serve one-and-a-half to four-and-a-half years in prison.

For eight months, Shakur was imprisoned in upstate New York while awaiting his chance to appeal the verdict. In October 1995, he was freed on $1.4

million bail. His bail was posted by Marion "Suge" Knight, the chief executive and producer of Death Row Records. (Knight is often called Suge, pronounced "Shoog," which is short for Sugar Bear, his nickname from his days as a college football player.) Well known in the rap world, Knight is considered powerful, mysterious, successful, notorious, and dangerous. His ties to Los Angeles gang life are an ongoing question for industry observers, who claim that he flaunts his own image as a gangsta, wearing gang colors and symbols. His label, Death Row Records, was one of the principal players in a feud that had developed between some East Coast and West Coast rappers— a feud that many believed could become violent. After Shakur's release from jail, he and Knight announced that he had signed a deal with Death Row.

More Music

After being tried for sexual assault, shot, left virtually bankrupt from legal fees, and incarcerated in prison, Shakur's attitudes began to change. While in prison he made several remarks to reporters about his regrets and his plans to quit the gangsta lifestyle. His recording *Me Against the World* (1995), which was released while he was still in prison, seemed to confirm these plans. Written in a confessional and intimate tone, many of the raps seemed to reflect on his own troubled past and on his role in promoting ghetto violence. "*Me Against the World*—by and large a work of pain, anger, and burning desperation —is the first time 2Pac has taken the conflicting forces tugging at his psyche head-on," Cheo H. Coker concluded in *Rolling Stone* magazine. "Whether he leaves prison with a new sense of direction or is consumed by the same forces that chased him as a ghetto child running wild remains to be seen. But love him or hate him, 2Pac remains one of the most compelling characters in black popular culture—and a stint in jail is unlikely to change that."

As soon as Shakur left prison and signed with Death Row Records, though, he returned to his gangsta image and violent, confrontational lifestyle. His first recording on Death Row, *All Eyez on Me* (1996), was also his final release during his lifetime. The first double CD in rap, it immediately flew to the top of the charts. On this CD, Shakur rejected the reflective stance of his previous release. Seemingly unreformed by prison, he flaunted his success, raged against the world, and seemed to foresee his own death. *All Eyez on Me* is considered Shakur's greatest work. "*All Eyez* is an epic expression of single-minded, narcissistic bravado, stretched out over loping beats and top-shelf samples . . . and delivered by 2Pac with gritty, cock-strut authority. It's like a Cali thug-life version of Pink Floyd's *The Wall*—pure gangsta ego run amok over two CDs, wounded pride on a nonstop vengeance kick," said David Fricke in *Rolling Stone*.

Tupac's Death

On September 7, 1996, Tupac Shakur was in Las Vegas, Nevada, to attend a heavyweight title match between Mike Tyson and Bruce Seldon. Shakur was there with a group from his label, Death Row Records, that included chief executive Suge Knight. He and Shakur left the match together in a black BMW, with Knight driving and Shakur in the front passenger seat. When they were stopped in traffic, a white Cadillac pulled alongside. Two men got out and began shooting. Knight suffered only minor injuries, but Shakur was hit four times. He suffered massive chest wounds, plus injuries to the pelvis and hands. Shakur was rushed to the hospital, where doctors performed multiple emergency surgeries. For six days he remained in a coma in critical condition, with his mother at his bedside.

There was much conjecture afterward about the intent of the drive-by shooting. No one seemed to be sure who the gunmen were, why they were shooting, or who they were aiming at. Many believed that the ambush was actually intended for Knight. Some thought it derived somehow from Knight's alleged involvement with the Bloods, a Los Angeles street gang. Others said it was the result of the continuing feud between East and West Coast rap acts. And Knight's group wasn't talking. His car was part of a convoy of about ten cars filled with an entourage of friends and bodyguards from Death Row Records. Yet all claimed that they hadn't seen anything and that they couldn't help the police track down Shakur's killers.

Shakur never regained consciousness after the shooting. On September 13, 1996, Tupac Shakur died of complications from gunshot wounds. He was 25 years old. Shakur was deeply mourned. Many grieved about his early death, lamenting that he had been caught up in the violence that he so accurately portrayed. Jesse Jackson seemed to say it best: "Sometimes the lure of violent culture is so magnetic that, even when one overcomes it with material success, it continues to call. Tupac couldn't break the cycle."

Final Works

At the time of his death, Shakur had completed several unreleased works. *The Don Killuminati/ The 7-Day Theory* was his first posthumous release. It was recorded under the pseudonym Makaveli, a reference to Niccolo Machiavielli, the 16th-century Italian author and statesman who wrote *The Prince*, an essay on acquiring and maintaining power. Despite occasional moments of compassion and introspection, much of the CD is unrepentant and ruthless. It debuted at No. 1 on the charts, although it was not highly regarded by critics. Shakur recorded other cuts that may well be released on future CDs.

Shakur also acted in several movies to be released posthumously. The first was *Bullet,* filmed in 1994 but released direct-to-video in 1997, in which

Shakur had a small roll as a gangsta. His next release was *Gridlock'd* (1997), a buddy picture about two addicts who try to get off drugs when another member of their jazz trio overdoses on heroin and ends up in a coma. While the two are trying to get help to kick drugs, they keep running into constant problems with the system: with rigid rules that are confusing and contradictory and bureaucratic social-service agencies that are indifferent and unhelpful. Despite the serious theme, it's a funny movie. Shakur's performance won rave reviews from critics, who praised his charm, sincerity, sensitivity, vulnerability, wit, power, and promise. One final film, *Gang Related*, finished filming before his death. It's scheduled to be released in late 1997.

Tupac's Legacy

"I don't know whether to mourn Tupac Shakur or to rail against all the terrible forces—including the artist's own self-destructive temperament—that have resulted in such a wasteful, unjustifiable end," Mikal Gilmore wrote in a moving tribute in *Rolling Stone* magazine. "I do know this, though: whatever its causes, the murder of Shakur, at 25, has robbed us of one of the most talented and compelling voices of recent years. He embodied just as much for his audience as Kurt Cobain did for his. That is, Tupac Shakur spoke to, and for, many who had grown up within hard realities—realities that mainstream culture and media are loath to understand or respect. His death has left his fans feeling a doubly sharp pain: the loss of a much-esteemed signifier and the loss of a future volume of work that, no doubt, would have proved both brilliant and provocative."

"But listen to Tupac Shakur before you put his life away," Gilmore continues. "You will hear the story of a man who grew up feeling as if he didn't fit into any of the worlds around him—feeling that he had been pushed out from not only the white world but also the black neighborhoods in which he grew up. You will also hear the man's clear intelligence and genius: his gifts for sharp, smart, funny perceptions, and for lyrical and musical proficiency and elegance. And, of course, you will hear some downright ugly stuff—threats, rants, curses and admitted memories that would be too much for many hearts to bear. Mainly, though, you will hear the tortured soul-searching of a man who grew up with and endured so much pain, rancor, and loss that he could never truly overcome it all, could never turn his troubled heart right-side up despite all his gifts and all the acceptance he eventually received."

MARRIAGE AND FAMILY

In mid-1995, Shakur married Keisha Morris, his long-time girlfriend. He and Morris were already engaged when he was convicted of sexually abusing a 20-year-old woman. They were married at Clinton Correctional Facility in

New York, where Shakur was serving his prison term. The marriage was later annulled, although the two remained friends. At the time of his death, Shakur was engaged to Kidada Jones, the daughter of music producer Quincy Jones.

CREDITS

Recordings

This Is an EP Release, 1990 (with Digital Underground)
Sons of the P, 1991 (with Digital Underground)
2Pacalypse Now, 1991 (this and all following are solo recordings)
Strictly 4 My N.I.G.G.A.Z., 1993
Thug Life, Vol. 1, 1995 (recorded with other rappers)
Me Against the World, 1995
All Eyez on Me, 1996
The Don Killuminati: The 7 Day Theory, 1996 (posthumously released under name Makaveli)

Films

Juice, 1991
Poetic Justice, 1993
Above the Rim, 1994
Bullet, 1997 (filmed in 1994, but released on video only)
Gridlock'd, 1997

HONORS AND AWARDS

American Music Awards: 1997, Favorite Rap/Hip Hop Artist

FURTHER READING

Periodicals

Entertainment Weekly, Apr. 8, 1994, p.24; Dec. 6, 1996, p.34
Esquire, Dec. 1996, p.78
Essence, Dec. 1996, p.38
Independent (London), Sep. 17, 1996, p.16
Interview, July 1995, p.52
Jet, Sep. 30, 1996, p.62
Los Angeles Times, Sep. 9, 1996, p.A1; Sep. 14, 1996, p.A1
New York Times, Dec. 1, 1994, p.A1; Sep. 14, 1996, p.A1; Sep. 16, 1996, p.A1
Newsweek, Dec. 12, 1994, p.62; Sep. 23, 1996, p.66

People, Dec. 12, 1994, p.159; Sep. 23, 1996, p.75; Sep. 30, 1996, p.80
Premiere, Aug. 1993, p.84
Rolling Stone, Oct. 31, 1996, pp.38 and 49
Source, Nov. 1996, pp.14 and 100
Spin, Dec. 1996, p.57
Vanity Fair, Mar. 1997, p.244
Village Voice, Dec. 13, 1994, p.75

Tabitha Soren   1967-

American Television Journalist
Political Reporter and Anchor for MTV News,
Co-Host for "The Week in Rock"

BIRTH

Tabitha Sornberger was born August 19, 1967, in San Antonio,
Texas. Her father, Air Force Lt. Colonel John Thomas
Sornberger, is a career military officer. Her mother, Mary Jane
(Quinn) Sornberger, chose her daughter's name from the
Bible — not, as many people think, from the popular television
show, "Bewitched." Tabitha has one younger sister.

YOUTH

As a "military brat," Tabitha spent much of her childhood moving around the world. In addition to Texas, she and her family have lived in California, Arizona, Florida, Rhode Island, Virginia, Nevada, Germany, and the Philippines. Looking back on those years, Tabitha believes that moving around so much taught her to be more adaptable and relaxed about meeting new people—skills that proved valuable when she became a television journalist. Moving around had another effect, too. "Tabitha has seen a lot of the world," her mother says, "so maybe she appears a little older."

CHOOSING A CAREER

Soren never watched much television when she was growing up, but living in different countries awakened her interest in politics and gave her an opportunity to observe different political systems from an outsider's point of view. By the time Ronald Reagan became president of the United States, she had already developed a strong sense of cynicism about politics in this country.

While she was living in Manila under the dictatorship of Ferdinand Marcos, Soren had an experience she will never forget. She was on her way to a swim meet one day when her school bus passed Marcos's luxurious palace, surrounded by slums. She found the contrast between the wealthy dictator's lifestyle and the poverty of his people very troubling. "I saw how people without a democracy lived," she says. "It was very sad." Soren says this is what made her want to be a reporter.

EDUCATION

Tabitha decided to attend New York University because she was tired of the "homogenized" life she'd led on the various Air Force bases where she'd grown up. She majored in journalism, graduating cum laude in 1989. While she was a college student, she worked as an intern at ABC's "World News Tonight" and at CNN, the Cable News Network.

FIRST JOBS

After graduating from college, Tabitha landed a job as a news reporter for the ABC affiliate in Burlington, Vermont. She served as anchor for the 11 p.m. news broadcast and covered events at the statehouse in Montpelier, often filming her own stories as well as reporting them. It was her station manager in Burlington who persuaded Tabitha to shorten her last name to Soren.

Tabitha's social life suffered in Vermont, however, and she felt uncomfortable on camera trying to dress and act like someone much older. By 1991

she had moved back to Manhattan. While freelancing there, she met Dave Sirulnick, the news director for MTV, whom she had known when she was a college intern at CNN. Sirulnick asked her to help anchor his network's nightly news broadcast.

CAREER HIGHLIGHTS

Since arriving at MTV News in 1991, Soren has re-defined political reporting. As the cable television channel that ushered in the 1980s music video revolution, MTV was known primarily for its focus on the music industry and popular culture. But with the 1992 presidential election coming up, the network decided to cover the campaign from the perspective of "Generation X"—young people in their late teens and 20s who were eligible to vote, but who had a reputation for being apathetic about the political process. Soren was chosen to interview and profile the candidates, and then to report on the conventions and the election itself.

MTV's "Choose or Lose" election coverage targeted the 18 to 30 age group and offered 18 daily news broadcasts as well as in-depth political reports and features. All were produced in the network's characteristic style, with lots of quick cuts, flashy graphics, and rock music in the background. It made Tabitha Soren, with her disarmingly casual approach to interviewing, a recognized celebrity. Although President George Bush initially refused to be interviewed by what he called the "teenybopper station," Soren persuaded candidate Bill Clinton to appear on an MTV forum with 200 young people— an event that Clinton feels made a real difference in his popularity among young voters. After Clinton's inauguration, it was Soren who held the first one-on-one interview with the newly elected President. For her work on "Choose or Lose" during the presidential campaign, Soren won the prestigious Peabody Journalism Award.

"The MTV Interview"

December 1995 marked the debut of "The MTV Interview," an hour-long show featuring Soren talking with well-known personalities from politics, music, television, and the movies. Her first three guests were notorious for being difficult, but Soren handled them with her customary cool, posing tough and often very personal questions. She asked controversial PLO leader Yasir Arafat about his views on American youth and his own days as a young bachelor. She also interviewed actor-director Sean Penn, known for his hostility to the press, and rapper Tupac Shakur, who was free on bail awaiting his appeal on sexual assault charges. Unlike other television journalists, who typically interview people sitting in a studio, Soren had the camera follow her as she took her subjects out for a drive or for a walk along the beach.

Asked to describe her interviewing style, Soren says, "I think I act differently than a lot of reporters. When I interview someone, it's more casual, and there's not a lot of posturing. I ask different questions; they are caught off guard, and they seem more human because they have to think of an answer on the spot."

Spokesperson for a Generation

With her bright red hair, blue nailpolish, and unconventional wardrobe, Tabitha Soren has become widely known as the spokesperson for Generation

X. She dislikes the label, though, because she doesn't think it gives young people enough credit for their accomplishments. But her reputation as the voice of the post-Baby-Boom generation has won her a number of prestigious jobs. In an effort to attract younger viewers, NBC's "Today" show hired Soren in 1992 to contribute twice-monthly reports on politics and pop culture. She is also a contributor to *Elle* magazine.

In her bi-monthly column for the *New York Times* syndicate called "Something to Think About," Soren has discussed subjects ranging from gay rights to computer bulletin boards. Syndicate executive editor Gloria Brown Anderson comments, "I think Tabitha is an aware and intelligent young person with a special perspective on what's going on in this country and the world. . . . I don't think anyone can speak for an entire generation, but Tabitha does share and reflect the interests of people in their 20s." *Newsweek* magazine highlighted Soren in 1994 as one of the 19 most influential members of Generation X.

Current and Future Plans

Most recently, Soren covered the 1996 presidential campaign, in which politicians made more of an effort to appeal to young voters. She held a

Soren with presidential candidate Bob Dole

roundtable discussion featuring Speaker of the House Newt Gingrich and presidential candidates Bill Clinton, Bob Dole, and Ross Perot.

In addition to being the chief reporter on politics and national affairs for MTV News, Soren co-hosts (with Kurt Loder) "The Week in Rock," a half-hour roundup of news from the world of rock music.

Soren has had offers to do everything from commercials to writing her auto-biography. But she is concentrating on being a journalist. Because she is still regarded as a "lightweight" by many older, more established television journalists, Soren is aware of the risks involved in moving beyond MTV. For the time being, she'd like to stay at her current job because it enables her to combine her two major passions in life: music and politics. Her ultimate goal is to work on a long-term documentary series like those done by Bill Moyers.

HOME AND FAMILY

Soren lives in Brooklyn with her cocker spaniel, who is named Vegas be-cause "she acts like a show girl." Although Soren has had two major rela-tionships — one lasting four years, the other three — she describes herself as being "more boy crazy than I've been in my entire life."

MAJOR INFLUENCES

Soren appears to be following in the footsteps of Barbara Walters, one of the first "celebrity journalists"—a term used to describe journalists who are as famous as the people they interview. Although the two women are nearly four decades apart in age, Soren looks up to Walters: "She's done so much. Barbara Walters is a maverick for women in terms of journalists."

Soren also admires journalist Linda Ellerbee, co-producer of "The MTV Interview." She describes Ellerbee as "someone who has always paved her own way. She doesn't seem to have abandoned her soul."

HOBBIES AND OTHER INTERESTS

In her free time, Soren enjoys going to music clubs with her friends to listen to new bands. "I've always felt that music was a very passionate form of communication and inspiration," she says. "It got me through a lot of diffi-cult times in high school. It still does."

Soren hates shopping in stores, but confesses that she likes to catalog-shop. She describes the "perfect evening" as staying at home to watch "Seinfeld" and "The Simpsons" on television.

HONORS AND AWARDS

Peabody Journalism Award (University of Georgia): 1993, for "Choose or
   Lose" coverage of 1992 presidential election
Leadership Award (National League of Women Voters): 1993

FURTHER READING

Periodicals

Boston Globe, Aug. 19, 1994, p.A8
Harper's Bazaar, Apr. 1996, p.120
New York Times, Mar. 14, 1993, Section 9, p.1
People, Oct. 19, 1992, p.75
Seventeen, Nov. 1993, p.82
US, May 1996, p.93
USA Today, Apr. 14, 1993, p.D10
Wall Street Journal, Dec. 4, 1995, p.A10
Washington Post, Dec. 3, 1995, p.Y4

ADDRESS

MTV News
1515 Broadway
New York, NY 10036

WORLD WIDE WEB SITE

http://www.MTV.com

BRIEF ENTRY

Herbert Tarvin   1985-

American Student
Returned Money to Bank after Brinks Truck Accident

EARLY YEARS

Herbert Alexander Tarvin was born on July 19, 1985, in Miami, Florida. His mother is Valencia Stovall, his father is Herbert Habersham, and his step-father is Paul Stovall. He has two brothers, Herbert Lee and Jon-Paul, and one sister, Simoneoni. They live in Liberty City, a poor neighborhood in Miami. Herbert is a sixth-grade student at St. Francis Xavier Elementary School. His favorite subject there is math.

MAJOR ACCOMPLISHMENTS

Before January 1997, Herbert Tarvin was a pretty typical kid. He liked playing the saxophone and singing in the choir at his church. He also enjoyed taking karate classes, playing football, and watching TV, especially his favorite shows, "Matlock" and "Goof Troop." He certainly wasn't famous.

That soon changed, though. On Wednesday, January 8, 1997, a Brinks truck got in an accident in Miami. Brinks trucks are armored cars that transport large sums of money from stores to banks. Early that Wednesday morning, at 7:25 a.m., the truck lost control on an overpass while entering a major freeway. The truck, which was filled with $3.7 million in cash and food stamps, hit a guard rail and split open. "The car literally opened like a sardine can, and money literally showered down to the street below as well as onto the highway," according to Lt. Bill Schwartz, a spokesman for the Miami police department. The two Brinks guards were slightly injured, but they have recovered.

The accident took place in Overtown, a predominately African-American neighborhood in Miami. It's also one of the poorest sections of the city. Many of the people there earn less than $5,000 a year. Some of the homes have dirt floors and no running water. As reports of the accident spread, the area was soon swarming with people—some from the neighborhood, some driving through on their way to work, and even some who heard about it on the news and headed right over. And all were scrabbling around on the ground, trying to pick up as much cash as they could find. "It was pandemonium," Lt. Schwartz recalled. "People were climbing over fences, climbing over each other. They put it in their pockets, in paper bags, wherever they could until they couldn't carry any more."

Herbert Tarvin walked through the area on his way to school that morning. He stopped and picked up 85 cents and then continued on his way. When he got to school, he told his teacher, Ardie Edwards, about picking up the money, and she talked to him about making the right decision. "It was a big temptation," Herbert admits. "But my teacher inspired me and told me to make a choice: keep it or give it away. It wasn't mine, and I gave it back." Facing this choice, his decision was clear. "I knew it was wrong for me to keep anything and I knew if I kept it, I would have been stealing. It doesn't belong to anyone, except maybe the bank." So Herbert and his teacher arranged to turn the money in to the police.

"I'm so proud of him I'm overwhelmed," said his mother, Valencia Stovall. "No one made him turn in the money that morning. He did this all on his own."

The overturned truck created a big controversy in Miami. People considered it a moral dilemma. Did the residents of Overtown have the right to keep the

Tarvin with his class at Disney World

money, some people wondered, because they are poor? But Herbert never doubted what was the right thing to do. He just called it stealing.

Only a few other people returned the money that they picked up. One was a woman named Faye McFadden. A mother of six, McFadden was ashamed to see herself on a TV news report picking up money at the accident scene. She knew she wasn't setting the right kind of example for her kids. She returned $19.53.

Their honesty touched a lot of people. Many offered money and other awards, both to McFadden and to Herbert, as a way of rewarding their honest behavior. According to Lt. Schwartz, "We're so desperate in this society to believe in simple values such as honesty that when somebody does it, it renews our faith in humanity." Jack Lau, pastor at St. Francis Xavier, would agree. "It's an education for everybody in the community. If you do right, it pays," Father Lau said. "What has made this an issue is that people are looking for hope and honesty. They are looking to a child to tell them what's true." At the Miami police station, calls poured in from people all over the country who wanted to send in money. One school in Virginia collected 85 cents from each student to send to Herbert. He also received a financial award from the Brinks company, as well as a paid trip to Disney World for his family and all his classmates!

Herbert has said that he is saving all the money for college. He had previously mentioned that he hopes to attend Morehouse College in Atlanta, and he wants to become a lawyer. Recently, he was offered a full scholarship to St. Thomas University in Miami. Now Herbert knows that he'll have a chance for a college education.

"What Herbert learned from this is that honesty is a part of the real world and good things happen to people who are honest," according to his teacher, Ardie Edwards. "The children see that there is a positive side of being a good person."

For many people, children and adults, Herbert Tarvin has become a powerful role model for honesty and for doing the right thing. He is a hero. His friend Samuel Patterson explained it like this: "Some people thought he shouldn't say anything—you know, like 'Finders keepers, losers weepers.' But that changed because of Herbert. He is a role model for kids. Maybe if they found money, maybe they'd think of him and give it back instead of keeping it."

FURTHER READING

Periodicals

Ft. Lauderdale Sun Sentinel, Jan. 9, 1997, p.A1; Jan. 14, 1997, p.B3; Jan. 28, 1997, p.E8
Miami Herald, Jan. 9, 1997, p.A1; Jan. 16, 1997, p.C3; Feb. 12, 1997, p.D8
New York Times, Jan. 12, 1997, Section 1, p.13

ADDRESS

P.O. Box 540794
Opa-Locka, FL 33054

Merlin Tuttle   1941-

American Mammalogist
Founder of Bat Conservation International

BIRTH

Merlin Devere Tuttle was born in Honolulu, Hawaii, on August 26, 1941. His father, Horace L. Tuttle, was a biology teacher, while his mother, Myrna June Tuttle, was a businesswoman. The oldest of three children, Tuttle has a brother, Arden, and a sister, Myrna.

YOUTH

"By the time I was nine years old, I already had decided to be a mammalogist," Tuttle once remarked. Fascinated by animals since early child-hood, Tuttle spent many of his early days studying the various members of the animal kingdom, from those in his backyard to more exotic creatures that he read about in books. He credits his interest in animals to his parents, who were big animal lovers themselves. His father was an avid bird-watcher who kept reptiles and amphibians as pets, and his mother happily nurtured Tuttle's early enthusiasm for the natural world.

In 1951, when Tuttle was ten years old, his family moved to Bakersfield, California. His love of the outdoors was undiminished by the move, and soon he was raising Monarch butterflies and recording observations about the be-havior of his pets and the neighborhood wildlife. He also helped his father with a nature education program that he was teaching at Yosemite National Park. The program used a variety of animals to teach students about the nat-ural world. Young Tuttle was a willing assistant to his father, tending to the owls, hawks, vultures, magpies, and badgers that his father used in the nature program.

By the fifth grade, Tuttle had become entirely committed to studying wildlife. He spent as much time as he could studying the mammals of California and learning their scientific names. His schoolwork suffered as a result, and he actually received failing marks in the fifth grade. Still, his teachers knew that he was a bright student who simply needed to pay more attention to his studies, and they allowed a relieved Tuttle to continue on to the sixth grade.

In 1957, the Tuttle family moved from California to Knoxville, Tennessee, and Tuttle's life soon changed dramatically. While still in high school, he learned that a bat cave was located only two miles from his home. The cave was a roost for thousands of gray bats, and the teenager settled into a routine of studying the winged creatures. The gray bats that Tuttle observed were con-sidered to be a nonmigratory species—that is, a species that lives in the same area year round. After spending some time observing them, though, he decid-ed that the reference books he had read might be wrong. He noticed that the bats roosted in the cave only in the spring and the fall, and that they disap-peared at other times of the year. This suggested that the animals actually were migratory, spending the winter in some other location. During his senior year of high school, Tuttle convinced his parents to take him to the Smithsonian Institution in Washington, D.C. There he sought out the bat ex-perts and presented them with three years of field notes on the gray bats. The bat specialists were impressed with the young man's research. Before leaving the Smithsonian Institution, Tuttle was given several thousand bat bands (identifying tags) and was told to use them to prove his theory.

Over the next few months, the entire Tuttle family became involved in his re-search. They helped Merlin capture and band the bats he was trying to track, but the mystery of the bats' wintertime home continued. He knew that migratory species of bats head south to spend the winter months in a warmer climate, but Tuttle was unable to locate any such southern destination. It was only through a stroke of good luck that Tuttle was able to find the gray bats' winter roost. After hearing about a bat cave 100 miles north of his home, he traveled there with his father. Inside they found their banded bats. Tuttle had discovered that not only were the bats migratory, but that they migrated north instead of south. Over the next few months he compiled his discovery and other observations into scientific papers. By the time he graduated from high school, he had published three articles in the prestigious *Journal of Mammalogy.*

EDUCATION

After graduating from high school in 1959, Tuttle enrolled in college, but once again his passion for studying animals caused his grades to suffer. "I was almost thrown out of the University of Tennessee my freshman year," he admitted. "I spent so much time working with authorities in the field and doing my own thing that I didn't make it to many classes." He eventually transferred to Andrews University, in Berrian Springs, Michigan, where he learned to balance his college coursework with his own studies of bats and other mammals.

Tuttle graduated with a degree in zoology in 1965 and returned to Washington, D.C., where he had been hired to co-direct a Smithsonian Institution mammal project. He spent the next three years leading expeditions to the Venezuelan rain forests to study mammals. After returning to the United States Tuttle began to work on his doctoral degree at the University of Kansas. There, as in the past, he concentrated his studies on the gray bat, an animal for which he was developing an increasing fondness. His doctoral dissertation on the population ecology of those animals is still regarded as a classic treatise on cave bats. He received his Ph.D. from the University of Kansas in 1974.

CAREER HIGHLIGHTS

Life of Adventure

In 1975 Tuttle became curator of mammals at the Milwaukee Public Museum. By this time, he had become so well known in the field of bat study that he was nicknamed "Batman." His job allowed him to continue traveling around the world to study mammals, but he spent the majority of his field research time studying bats.

During the next several years, Tuttle traveled to places where few people ever go. Loaded down with such gear as a nightscope (an instrument for viewing

Tuttle with associate roping in a cave

objects in the dark), ropes for climbing into caves, and a "bat detector," a device that allows him to listen to the ultrasonic sounds that bats use to navigate, Tuttle bravely ventured into many mysterious and unfamiliar places.

These adventures sometimes turned dangerous. In South America, Tuttle was chased by local tribesmen wielding poison arrows, and in Thailand, he was pursued by gun-toting Communist rebels. Whether eluding angry people or skulking through tiger- and cobra-infested jungles, though, Tuttle kept his wits about him. Still, once in a while, he found himself in a situation that tested even his steady nerves. On one occasion, while searching for bats in Peru, he embarked on a difficult journey that included hiking over mountains and down cliffsides, crossing a pond "that was full of piranha and electric eels," and lowering himself into a cave so small that he had to crawl on his belly to get through. When the cave finally got too small for him to go any farther, he stopped and began to crawl backward the way he had come. It was then that he noticed that the ceiling of the cave was covered with hundreds of deadly scorpions, their poisonous tails dangling only inches from his body. "I just about wore a groove in the bottom of the rock trying to keep away from the scorpions," he later said.

By this time, Tuttle was well aware that most people did not share his love for bats, and he was concerned about their dwindling numbers in many areas. But it was not until 1976, when he discovered that a 250,000-member bat colony making its home in an Alabama cave had been destroyed by vandals, that he became an activist determined to protect bats and educate the American public about their true nature. He points out that much of the mythology surrounding bats is false; they are not blind, for instance, nor do they tangle in people's hair. He even notes that bats are far less likely than dogs or cats to contract rabies. "The odds that you will ever be harmed by a bat," remarked Tuttle, "are on a par with the odds that you will be run over in bed by a Mack truck at 3:00 on Sunday morning."

The Truth About Bats

Tuttle launched a series of speeches and papers that explained to skeptical people that bats actually were good to have around in many respects. "Of the world's nearly 1,000 species of bats, 44 sweep across the night skies of North America," he wrote. "North American bats are essential to keeping populations of night-flying insects in balance. Individual bats can catch hundreds hourly, and large colonies eat tons nightly, including countless beetles and moths that cost farmers and foresters a fortune, not to mention mosquitos in our backyards. A colony of just 150 big brown bats can eat enough cucumber beetles each summer to protect local farmers from 18 million of their rootworm larvae. This pest alone costs U.S. growers a billion dollars annually." Tuttle also pointed out that bats are important pollinators of many plants, including avocados, bananas, cashews, agaves, and figs. Noting that the agave plant is used to make tequila, Tuttle once said, "I know a lot of people who think they don't like bats but would hate to lose their margaritas."

Tuttle also decided to learn how to photograph bats. Traditionally, most photographs of bats were taken when the bats were being held by their wings. In this position, bats will snarl in self-defense. Tuttle wanted to show bats in their natural habitats, and he soon emerged as one of America's most noted animal photographers. His pictures, which have appeared in magazines and museum exhibits around the world, have captured bats in the full range of their natural activity, from hunting to sleeping to suckling their young.

Bat Conservation International

In 1982, Tuttle founded Bat Conservation International (BCI), an organization dedicated to educating people about the value of bats. The group also pushes for the preservation of bats and engages in ongoing bat research. Tuttle had founded BCI only after his pleas for help received scant attention from wildlife organizations and government agencies nominally responsible for bat protection. "It would have been a lot easier to raise money to kill bats than to save them," he said, contending that up to $50 million was spent on an annual basis to kill bats in the United States in the early 1980s. "Existing organizations were largely unaware of the importance or plight of bats, and in any event, considered them too hopelessly unpopular to be helped."

Determined to change people's ideas about bats, Tuttle made guest appearances on such television shows as "Good Morning America," the "Today Show," "Late Night with David Letterman," and "Newton's Apple." On those visits he typically presented trained bats that performed tricks in response to his voice or hand signals. "When you see them as they really are," explained Tuttle, "they're just as inquisitive, comical, and cute as other animals."

In 1986, the work at BCI became so overwhelming that Tuttle quit his job at the Milwaukee Public Museum. A short time later he moved the organization's headquarters to Austin, Texas, where a major bat controversy had been brewing. Austin was home to between 750,000 and 1.5 million Mexican free-tailed bats, who had taken up residence under the city's massive Congress Avenue Bridge. "At night they emerged to hunt insects, creating swirling skeins visible for miles around—a spectacle as grand as Carlsbad Cavern's famed New Mexico colony, which has declined to less than a million," said Tuttle. "At first the people of Austin saw a nightmare instead of a spectacle. As the bats took wing, all the old bat bugaboos arose from the populace." Townspeople demanded that the bats be exterminated, and various plans to evict the creatures were discussed. To Tuttle, though, "the situation represented a tremendous opportunity. In 1986 I moved BCI to Austin and began trying to reduce fear with reason. Skeptics abounded. . . . But as I introduced Austinites to their bats through lectures, talk shows, and audiovisual programs for schools, people quickly changed their minds." Tuttle proudly notes that now, when the great colony of bats emerges from under the bridge in the early evening, townspeople spread blankets on the riverbanks to watch the spectacle, and the windows of nearby restaurants are jammed with onlookers. Since Tuttle's arrival, the town has come to call itself the Bat Capital of America, and city planners are even preparing to erect additional bat-friendly bridges.

Tuttle photographing bats in a cave

Bat Conservation International continued to grow throughout the late 1980s and 1990s, and it became recognized around the world as an important conservation organization. In 1991 BCI was given the Society for Conservation Biology's Distinguished Achievement Award in recognition of its efforts. The Society cited BCI's "contributions to the understanding and protection of biological diversity" and its valiant efforts to protect one of nature's most misunderstood creatures.

By 1995 the membership in BCI had reached 13,000, and Tuttle commented that the organization shows no sign of slowing down. In recent years BCI has maintained its strong bat research presence while simultaneously purchasing key pieces of land that serve as home to bat colonies. Such purchases included Bracken Cave, a cave 60 miles southwest of Austin that is home to 20 million Mexican free-tailed bats, the world's largest colony of bats. BCI also sponsors nationwide workshops to teach wildlife managers and conservationists how to protect bats, and the group has learned to work closely with state and federal agencies. BCI has also opened lines of communication with the Mexican government to discuss protection for the millions of bats that migrate to that country during America's winter months. Bat Conservation International even publishes special bat-house plans that can be constructed to provide homes for bats in backyards across the country. Tuttle notes that some farmers who have constructed such bat-houses have seen crop damage from insects drop dramatically due to the presence of their flying neighbors.

Tuttle, meanwhile, has published articles and photographs in popular magazines like *National Geographic, Smithsonian,* and *International Wildlife,* and he has written a number of books on bats over the years as well. Perhaps the best known of these are *America's Neighborhood Bats,* a 1988 book that proved tremendously popular. Two other major titles are *Bats of North America,* and *Bats of the World.* Tuttle was also featured in a CBS science documentary called *The Secret World of Bats,* a 1992 film that was broadcast around the world and received many awards and prizes.

But while the efforts of Tuttle and Bat Conservation International have made a difference in the public's understanding of bats, Tuttle knows that there is still a lot of work to do. "Serious threats remain," Tuttle has cautioned, "including outright killing of bats, destruction or disturbance of their cave habitats, and recently, increased closing of abandoned mines. Six bat species in the U.S. are endangered, and 18 others are candidates for addition to the endangered species list. With 24 species out of 44 in such dire straits, bats as a group rank as the most endangered land mammals in the U.S.—even though a few individual colonies number in the millions."

MARRIAGE AND FAMILY

Tuttle was married in 1975, but his marriage ended after seven years, in 1982. He notes, though, that he and his ex-wife remain friendly, and that she is even a member of Bat Conservation International. "Everybody who knows me knows I'm married to BCI," Tuttle remarked.

SELECTED WRITINGS

The Amazing Frog-Eating Bat, 1982
Gentle Fliers of the African Night, 1986
America's Neighborhood Bats: Understanding and Learning to Live in Harmony with Them, 1988
Photographing the World's Bats: Adventure, Tribulation, and Rewards, 1988
Texas Bats: A Resource in Peril, 1989
Batman: Exploring the World of Bats, 1991 (with Laurance Pringle)

HONORS AND AWARDS

Gerrit S. Miller Jr. Award: 1986, "in recognition of outstanding service and contribution to the field of chiropteran [bat] biology"

FURTHER READING

Books

Almanac of Famous People, 1993
Bat Conservation International. *Bats: Gentle Friends, Essential Allies,* 1988
Cooper, Gale. *Animal People,* 1983

Periodicals

Chicago Tribune, Oct. 29, 1987, p.5
Current Biography Yearbook 1992
Dallas Morning News, Oct. 25, 1992 p.A57
Life, Nov. 1994, p.132
National Geographic, June 1991, p.130; Aug. 1995, p.36
Natural History, Oct. 1987, p.66; Oct. 1988, p.66
New Yorker, Feb. 29, 1988, p.37
Popular Science, Nov. 1996, p.52
Scientific American, Dec. 1991, p.150
Time, Oct. 13, 1986, p.116; Aug. 21, 1995, p.58
Washington Post, July 2, 1989, p.A3; Sep. 20, 1994, p.A19

ADDRESS

Bat Conservation International
P.O. Box 162603
Austin, TX 78716-2603

BRIEF ENTRY

Mara Wilson   1987-
American Actress
Co-Starred in the Films *Matilda* and *Mrs. Doubtfire*

EARLY LIFE

Mara Wilson was born on July 24, 1987, in Burbank, California. Her father, Mike, is a broadcast engineer with a TV station in Los Angeles. Her mother, Suzie, was a full-time homemaker until her death from cancer in April 1996. Mara is the fourth of their five children, with older brothers Danny, John, and Joel, and younger sister Anna. She attends public school, where her favorite subject is reading. At home, Mara is treated like all the other kids. She has chores to do around the house, she is expected to clean up her room, and she receives just 75 cents a week for an allowance. The money that she has earned from acting is put in the bank to be saved for when she's an adult.

Mara decided that she wanted to act by the age of four. She was inspired by her oldest brother, Danny, who had landed parts on a few TV commercials. Her parents thought she was too young, though. They worried about her ability to handle the rejection that she would face if she started trying out for parts. But Mara was determined. So her parents set up a series of mock auditions with her older brothers acting as casting directors. Mara would come in and pretend to try out for a part, and her brothers would critique her performance. But each time they told her she didn't get the job, she was upbeat, optimistic, and determined to try again. Her parents finally gave in, and her mom started taking her to real auditions. Within a few weeks of signing with an agent, she was cast in commercials for Oscar Mayer, Texaco, Bank of America, and Marshalls.

MAJOR ACCOMPLISHMENTS

Mara Wilson got very lucky early on. Her first real role was in the hit film, *Mrs. Doubtfire* (1993), starring Robin Williams. Mara played Natalie Hillard, the youngest daughter. The movie was a huge success, and Wilson won rave reviews for her performance. She next appeared in the television movie *A Time to Heal* (1994). She went on to star in *Miracle on 34th Street* (1994), a remake of the 1947 film starring Natalie Wood. Winning that role was really an accomplishment, because the filmmakers had decided to write the part for a boy. But Mara's audition impressed them so much that she beat out thousands of other young actors for the role. She plays a very practical young girl, Susan, who has to be convinced that Santa Claus exists. For Mara, that's not a big issue. Her family is Jewish, so they don't celebrate Christmas.

Matilda

Mara's next big role was in the movie *Matilda* (1996). Based on the classic children's book by Roald Dahl, *Matilda* tells the story of an exceptionally intelligent little girl who develops special powers. Matilda's parents are neglectful and stupid and her school principal is mean and hateful. But her teacher, Miss Honey, is a treasure who loves and protects the children.

The movie, like all of Roald Dahl's work, has a dark edge to it. Many parents disliked the cruelty and thoughtlessness of the adults in both the book and the film, and some questioned the story's appropriateness for children. But

not Danny DeVito and Rhea Perlman, married actors who played Matilda's parents. Parents themselves, they have both commented on how much they have enjoyed Dahl's works and how much they have enjoyed reading his books to their own children. In fact, DeVito had this to say: "No matter how extreme the situations are in his books, the kids get it. Kids know it's a fantasy, they know the characters are outrageous and excessive, and they know that, in real life, there are repercussions from cruelty and physical violence. In other words, they know that *Matilda* is a fantasy."

The movie *Matilda* proved to be a huge hit with children and adults. In particular, Wilson was praised for her precocious and endearing performance. But by the time the movie came out, her life had undergone a tremendous change. Her mother, who had always stayed with Mara on the set during all her movies, had been diagnosed with breast cancer. She went through several rounds of surgery and other treatments, but she died on April 26, 1996. DeVito described her presence on the set of *Matilda* like this: "Mara's mom was with us through the whole filming of *Matilda*," he says. "She carried this great spirit through the whole thing, even though she was going through a lot of heavy-duty stuff. She and Mara had a wonderful relationship, and she was just a shining light during [the] film."

Mara is currently filming her next picture, *The Fairy Godmother*, in which she co-stars with Francis Capra, Martin Short, and Kathleen Turner. She enjoys acting and hopes to continue. And indeed, her colleagues on past films have often commented on her professionalism, her intelligence, her concentration, and her commitment to work. But Mara also likes to write, and she has talked about writing screenplays or directing movies. "I don't know if I'm always going to acting. Maybe when I grow up, I will be a scriptwriter. I always have a few scripts in my head," she says. "But for now, I like acting, because it feels like I'm pretending. It's not exactly like playing . . . because when you act, you can't say what you want to say; you have to say what [the director] wants you to say."

CREDITS

Mrs. Doubtfire, 1993 (feature film)
A Time to Heal, 1994 (TV movie)
Miracle on 34th Street, 1994 (feature film)
Matilda, 1996 (feature film)

FURTHER READING

Daily News of Los Angeles, Nov. 19, 1994, p.L1; Nov. 29, 1994, p.L1
Newsday, Nov. 18, 1994, p.B45
Los Angeles Times, July 26, 1994, p.F1
People, Apr. 29, 1996, p.61
Seattle Post-Intelligencer, Nov. 7, 1994, p.C1

ADDRESS

Gold/Marshak
3500 West Olive Avenue, Suite 1400
Burbank, CA   91505

Photo and Illustration Credits

Madeleine Albright/Photos: UN/DPI photo by Evan Schneider, copyright United Nations; *State* magazine.

Gillian Anderson/Photos: Michael Lavine/FOX; Ken Staniforth/FOX.

Rachel Blanchard/Photos: George Lange; Copyright © ABC.

Zachery Ty Bryan/Photos: E.J. Camp.

Claire Danes/Photo: *Little Women*/Joseph Lederer.

Celine Dion/Photos: AP/Wide World Photos; Grant W. Martin Photography. Copyright © 1997 CARAS.

Jean Driscoll/Photos: FAYFOTO/Boston 1997; AP/Wide World Photos.

Louis Farrakhan/Photos: AP/Wide World Photos.

Ella Fitzgerald/Photos: AP/Wide World Photos.

Harrison Ford/Photos: *Air Force One*/Claudette Barius.

Bryant Gumbel/Photos: Tony Barboza; C. Blankenhorn; Al Levine.

John Johnson/Photos: Reprinted with permission of *The Chicago Sun-Times*, copyright © 1996. Reprinted with permission of *The Chicago Sun-Times*, copyright © 1996/Bob Black.

Michael Johnson/Photos: AP/Wide World Photos.

Maya Lin/Photos: Darryl Estrine Photography; AP/Wide World Photos; Mark Wright Photography, Montgomery, Ala.

George Lucas/Photos: Copyright © 1991 Lucasfilm Ltd. All rights reserved/ Greg Gorman; Copyright © 1988 Lucasfilm Ltd./Keith Hamshere.

John Madden/Photo: Aaron Rapoport/FOX; UPI/Corbis-Bettmann.

Bill Monroe/Photos: Jim DeVault; © Jon Sievert/Michael Ochs Archives/ Venice, CA

Alanis Morissette/Photos: Michele Laurita; Greig Reekie/*Toronto Sun*; Mark O'Neill/*Toronto Sun*.

PHOTO AND ILLUSTRATION CREDITS

Samuel Morrison/Photo: Fort Lauderdale *Sun-Sentinel.*

Rosie O'Donnell/Photos: Copyright © 1996 Warner Bros.; Copyright © 1994 by Universal City Studios, Inc. All rights reserved.; Rosie O'Donnell in Nickelodeon Movies' *Harriet the Spy.*

Muammar Qaddafi/Photos: AP/Wide World Photos.

Christopher Reeve/Photos: AP/Wide World Photos; Dirk Halstead/Gamma Liaison.

Pete Sampras/Photos: Tommy Hindley.

Pat Schroeder/Photos: AP/Wide World Photos.

Tupac Shakur/Photos: Copyright © 1996 Gramercy Pictures/Nicola Goode.

Tabitha Soren/Photos: Michael Lavine; AP/Wide World Photos.

Herbert Tarvin/Photos: Marlene Quaroni

Merlin Tuttle/Photos: Merlin D. Tuttle, Bat Conservation International.

Mara Wilson/Photos: Francois Duhamel.

Appendix

This Appendix contains updates for individuals profiled in Volumes, 1, 2, 3, 4, 5, and 6 of *Biography Today.*

* YASIR ARAFAT *

As 1997 draws to a close, Arafat's hold on power within the Palestinian community in the West Bank and Gaza areas of Israel is in question. The militant Palestinian group Hamas staged three suicide bombings in Jerusalem and Tel Aviv in 1997, killing and injuring Israelis and threatening the tenuous peace between the Israeli and Palestinian communities. Israeli Prime Minister Benjamin Netanyahu escalated the tensions between the two groups by allowing Israelis to build homes within a part of Jerusalem that the Palestinians had hoped to establish as a capital. This caused a breakdown in the peace talks between the Israelis and the Palestinians that stretched from February to October. U.S. Secretary of State Madeleine Albright visited Israel in September 1997. She was clear in her message to Netanyahu and Arafat: that the two groups needed to settle their differences and rededicate themselves to the peace process that had been hammered out by the late Israeli leader Yitzhak Rabin and Arafat in the mid-1990s. Tensions flared again in late September when it was disclosed that Israel had tried to assassinate a leader of Hamas in neighboring Jordan. As Netanyahu and Arafat met again in October to resume their talks, the political situation in the Middle East was less stable than it has been in years.

* BILL CLINTON *

In 1997 President Clinton has worked on a federal balanced budget and child health care programs and focused his attention on national standards for education. The most serious political problems he has faced are allegations that he was involved with illegal fundrasing during his 1996 reelection campaign. Republican congressional sources allege that Clinton used the phones in the White House to solicit money for his reelection campaign, which is illegal under the law. According to more serious allegations, congressional Republicans charge that the Clinton administration accepted large and illegal contributions from foreign governments, as well as donations from supporters that were channeled through another source to conceal the identity of the donor. Clinton hosted a series of "coffees" at the White House where the contributors met with him; in October, tapes of these meetings became part of the evidence in determining whether or not to pursue a further investigation. Based on the evidence, the Senate Committee on Governmental Affairs failed to find any evidence of wrongdoing. However, Attorney General Janet Reno is considering whether the allegations warrant the appointment of an independent council to investigate the matter.

* CHELSEA CLINTON *

Chelsea Clinton started college in the fall of 1997. Accompanied by her parents, she moved into her dorm at Stanford University. The editor of the school paper promised to respect Chelsea's need for privacy, and the students in her dorm were getting used to the presence of Secret Service agents.

* JACQUES COUSTEAU *

Jacques Cousteau, the world-famous oceanographer, died in Paris, France, on June 25, 1997, at the age of 86. Cousteau became known to millions of Americans for his films depicting the life of ocean plants and animals that he produced from the 1950s through the 1980s. Although he is best known for his television documentaries, Cousteau's greatest achievement was the development of the Aqua-lung, and underwater breathing device known as "scuba." "Scuba" is actually the acronym of the device, "self-contained underwater breathing apparatus." Cousteau developed the scuba so that he could examine the undersea world he came to love and pledged to protect. Through his documentaries, he presented the beauty and wonder of the ocean depths, while alerting the world to the dangers of undersea pollution. Cousteau was a passionate defender of the ocean plants and animals who were endangered by what Cousteau saw as their exploitation by greedy human interests. At his death, the chairman of the National Geographic Society, Gilbert Grosvenor, said, "The ocean environment has lost its greatest champion." Cousteau's son Jean-Michel said, "The work of my father was a hymn to life. On the wall of my office there is a quotation from my father: 'The happiness of the bee and the dolphin is to exist. For man it is to know that and to wonder at it'."

* DIANA, PRINCESS OF WALES *

On August 31, 1997, Diana, Princess of Wales, was killed in a car accident in Paris. She was the former wife of Prince Charles, heir to the British throne, and the mother of Prince William and Prince Harry. Diana was killed with Emad Mohamed al-Fayed, the son of a wealthy Egyptian businessman, along with the driver of the car. Diana's bodyguard was the only survivor of the crash. According to reports in the press, the car was traveling at high speeds to avoid photographers for tabloid newspapers, who had followed and hounded Diana for years. Her death brought an outpouring of sympathy for the princess and worldwide condemnation of the members of the press who disturbed Diana's privacy. The photographers who allegedly caused the crash are under investigation in France and may be charged in the deaths.

Biography Today will present a full, updated entry on Diana in the January 1998 issue.

* AL GORE *

Vice President Al Gore, who hopes to run for president in 2000, saw his chances diminish as he became the center of a probe into possible illegal fundraising practices. According to allegations, Gore used his phone at the White House to call possible donors and ask for money for the Clinton-Gore reelection campaign in 1996, which is against a federal law. In October 1997, Attorney General Janet Reno had not yet decided if she would appoint an independent counsel to further investigate the matter. Gore was also in the news regarding a Democratic event that took place at a Buddhist temple in California during the reelection campaign. Gore insisted that the event was not a fundraiser, but three Buddhist nuns who attended the event described fundraising activities linked to the event to a Senate hearing into the matter. How this will effect Gore's chances if he does indeed decide to run for the presidency in 2000 remains to be seen.

* JACKIE JOYNER-KERSEE *

Jackie Joyner-Kersee, called the "world's greatest athlete," announced that she will retire from sports in September 1998. She made the announcement in September 1997, saying she will continue to compete in events in the U.S. and Europe, ending with the Grand Prix events in Europe in the summer of 1998.

* CARL LEWIS *

Carl Lewis retired from track and field competition in September 1997, at the age of 36. His final competitive race took place on August 26, 1997, in Berlin, Germany. In that race, he ran the anchor leg of the 4 x 100 meter relay, which his team won. A crowd of 60,000 gave Lewis a standing ovation. Back in the United States, Lewis ran his final race at his alma mater, the University of Houston. Once again, he anchored the 4 x 100 meter relay, taking his final lap around the track he funded as a gift to the University. Lewis retires as one of the most decorated figures in American track and field history, with nine gold medals from the Olympics and eight gold medals from the World Championships. "Physically, I feel I could still jump well and run well," Lewis said after his final run. "Mentally, I feel it's time to move on. The desire to compete isn't there anymore." Lewis said his future plans include "conducting track clinics for kids, acting, writing fitness books, promoting an indoor-outdoor mountain bike, and my own line of dress clothes."

* MOBUTO SESE SEKO *

Ousted as President of Zaire in May 1997, Mobuto Sese Seko fled to exile in Morocco, where he died of prostate cancer on September 7, 1997. He was 66 years old. Zaire has been renamed the Republic of the Congo by its new leader, Laurent Kabila, who is now president of the nation. Kabila had been one of Mobuto's strongest opponents, and he had led a rebellion against Mobuto's rule that was eventually successful in removing him from power. By the time he was deposed, Mobuto had lost the support of previously friendly African and European countries. Kabila has been unable to bring peace to Congo, and the nation continues to suffer from factional fighting.

Name Index

Listed below are the names of all individuals profiled in *Biography Today*, followed by the date of the issue in which they appear.

General Index

This index includes subjects, occupations, organizations, and ethnic and minority origins that pertain to individuals profiled in *Biography Today*.

Places of Birth Index

The following index lists the places of birth for the individuals profiled in *Biography Today*. Places of birth are entered under state, province, and/or country.

Alabama
Aaron, Hank – *Mobile* . . . . Sport 96
Barkley, Charles – *Leeds* . . . . Apr 92
Jackson, Bo – *Bessemer*. . . . . Jan 92
Jemison, Mae – *Decatur* . . . . Oct 92
Lewis, Carl – *Birmingham* . . . . Sep 96
Parks, Rosa – *Tuskegee* . . . . Apr 92
Whitestone, Heather – *Dothan* . . . . . Apr 95

Algeria
Boulmerka, Hassiba – *Constantine* Sport 96

Angola
Savimbi, Jonas – *Munhango* . . . . ModAfr 97

Arizona
Chavez, Cesar – *Yuma* . . . . Sep 93
Morrison, Sam – *Flagstaff*. . . . . Sep 97
Strug, Kerri – *Tucson*. . . . . Sep 96

Arkansas
Clinton, Bill – *Hope*. . . . . Jul 92
Clinton, Chelsea – *Little Rock* . . . . . . Apr 96
Grisham, John – *Jonesboro* . . . . . . Author 95
Johnson, John – *Arkansas City* . . . . . Jan 97
Pippen, Scottie – *Hamburg*. . . . . Oct 92

Australia
Norman, Greg – *Mt. Isa, Queensland* Jan 94
Travers, P.L. – *Maryborough,*
  Queensland . . . . Author 96

Bosnia-Herzogovina
Filipovic, Zlata – *Sarajevo*. . . . . Sep 94

Brazil
Mendes, Chico – *Xapuri, Acre* . . . . . . Env 97
Pelé – *Tres Coracoes, Minas Gerais* Sport 96

Bulgaria
Christo – *Gabrovo* . . . . Sep 96

Burma
Aung San Suu Kyi – *Rangoon* . . . . . . Apr 96

California
Abdul, Paula – *Van Nuys* . . . . Jan 92
Adams, Ansel – *San Francisco*. . . . . Artist 96
Aikman, Troy – *West Covina* . . . . Apr 95
Allen, Marcus – *San Diego* . . . . Sep 97

Babbitt, Bruce – *Los Angeles* . . . . Jan 94
Bergen, Candice – *Beverly Hills* . . . . . Sep 93
Bialik, Mayim – *San Diego*. . . . . Jan 94
Breathed, Berke – *Encino*. . . . . Jan 92
Brower, David – *Berkeley* . . . . Env 97
Cameron, Candace. . . . . Apr 95
Coolio – *Los Angeles* . . . . Sep 96
Evans, Janet – *Fullerton* . . . . Jan 95
Fielder, Cecil – *Los Angeles*. . . . . Sep 93
Fields, Debbi – *East Oakland*. . . . . . . Jan 96
Fossey, Dian – *San Francisco* . . . . Science 96
Garcia, Jerry – *San Francisco* . . . . Jan 96
Gilbert, Sara – *Santa Monica* . . . . Apr 93
Griffith Joyner, Florence – *Los*
  Angeles . . . . Sport 96
Hammer – *Oakland* . . . . Jan 92
Hanks, Tom – *Concord* . . . . Jan 96
Jobs, Steven – *San Francisco* . . . . Jan 92
Kistler, Darci – *Riverside* . . . . Jan 93
LeMond, Greg – *Los Angeles*. . . . . . Sport 96
Locklear, Heather – *Los Angeles* . . . . Jan 95
Lucas, George – *Modesto* . . . . Apr 97
Nixon, Joan Lowery – *Los*
  Angeles. Author 95
Nixon, Richard – *Yorba Linda* . . . . . Sep 94
O'Dell, Scott – *Terminal Island* . . . Author 96
Oleynik, Larisa – *San Fancisco* . . . . . Sep 96
Olsen, Ashley . . . . Sep 95
Olsen, Mary Kate . . . . Sep 95
Ride, Sally – *Encino* . . . . Jan 92
Thiessen, Tiffini-Amber – *Modesto* . . . Jan 96
Werbach, Adam – *Tarzana* . . . . Env 97
White, Jaleel – *Los Angeles* . . . . Jan 96
Wilson, Mara – *Burbank* . . . . Jan 97
Woods, Tiger – *Long Beach* . . . . Sport 96
Yamaguchi, Kristi – *Fremont* . . . . Apr 92

Canada
Blanchard, Rachel – *Toronto, Ontario* Apr 97
Candy, John – *Newmarket, Ontario* . . Sep 94
Carrey, Jim – *Newmarket, Ontario* . . . Apr 96

355

Morrison, Toni – *Lorain*. . . . . Jan 94
Perry, Luke – *Mansfield*. . . . . Jan 92
Rose, Pete – *Cincinnati* . . . . Jan 92
Shula, Don – *Grand River* . . . . Apr 96
Spielberg, Steven – *Cincinnati* . . . . . . Jan 94
Steinem, Gloria – *Toledo* . . . . Oct 92
Stine, R.L. – *Columbus* . . . . Apr 94

Oklahoma
Brooks, Garth – *Tulsa* . . . . Oct 92
Duke, David – *Tulsa* . . . . Apr 92
Ellison, Ralph –*Oklahoma City*. . . Author 97
Hill, Anita – *Morris* . . . . Jan 93
Hinton, S.E. – *Tulsa* . . . . Author 95
Mankiller, Wilma – *Tahlequah*. . . . . . Apr 94
Mantle, Mickey – *Spavinaw* . . . . Jan 96
McEntire, Reba – *McAlester*. . . . . . . Sep 95

Oregon
Cleary, Beverly – *McMinnville*. . . . . . Apr 94
Groening, Matt – *Portland* . . . . Jan 92
Harding, Tonya – *Portland*. . . . . Sep 94
Hooper, Geoff – *Salem* . . . . Jan 94
Pauling, Linus – *Portland* . . . . Jan 95
Phoenix, River – *Madras* . . . . Apr 94
Schroeder, Pat – *Portland* . . . . Jan 97

Pakistan
Bhutto, Benazir – *Karachi*. . . . . Apr 95
Masih, Iqbal . . . . Jan 96

Palestine
Perlman, Itzhak – *Tel Aviv* . . . . Jan 95
Rabin, Yitzhak – *Jerusalem* . . . . Oct 92

Pennsylvania
Abbey, Edward – *Indiana*. . . . . Env 97
Anderson, Marian – *Philadelphia* . . . . Jan 94
Berenstain, Jan – *Philadelphia* . . . Author 96
Berenstain, Stan – *Philadelphia* . . Author 96
Bradley, Ed – *Philadelphia* . . . . Apr 94
Calder, Alexander – *Lawnton* . . . . . Artist 96
Carson, Rachel – *Springdale*. . . . . . . Env 97
Cosby, Bill. . . . . Jan 92
Duncan, Lois – *Philadelphia*. . . . . . . Sep 93
Gingrich, Newt – *Harrisburg*. . . . . . . Apr 95
Griffey, Ken, Jr. – *Donora* . . . . Sport 96
Iacocca, Lee A. – *Allentown*. . . . . Jan 92
Jamison, Judith – *Philadelphia* . . . . . Jan 96
Marino, Dan – *Pittsburgh* . . . . Apr 93
McCary, Michael – *Philadelphia* . . . . Jan 96
Montana, Joe – *New Eagle*. . . . . Jan 95
Morris, Nathan – *Philadelphia* . . . . . Jan 96
Morris, Wanya – *Philadelphia*. . . . . . Jan 96
Pinkney, Jerry – *Philadelphia* . . . . Author 96
Smith, Will – *Philadelphia* . . . . Sep 94

Stockman, Shawn – *Philadelphia* . . . . Jan 96
Thomas, Jonathan Taylor
　– *Bethlehem* . . . . Apr 95
Van Meter, Vicki – *Meadville* . . . . Jan 95
Warhol, Andy. . . . . Artist 96
Poland
John Paul II – *Wadowice*. . . . . Oct 92
Sabin, Albert – *Bialystok* . . . . Science 96
Puerto Rico
Lopez, Charlotte. . . . . Apr 94
Novello, Antonia – *Fajardo* . . . . Apr 92
Russia
Asimov, Isaac – *Petrovichi* . . . . Jul 92
Chagall, Marc – *Vitebsk* . . . . Artist 96
Fedorov, Sergei – *Pskov* . . . . Apr 94
Gorbachev, Mikhail – *Privolnoye* . . . . Jan 92
Nevelson, Louise – *Kiev* . . . . Artist 96
Nureyev, *Rudolf*. . . . . Apr 93
Yeltsin, Boris – *Butka* . . . . Apr 92
Senegal
Senghor, Léopold Sédar – *Joal* . . ModAfr 97
Serbia
Seles, Monica – *Novi Sad* . . . . Jan 96
Somalia
Aidid, Mohammed Farah . . . . . ModAfr 97
South Africa
de Klerk, F.W. – *Mayfair* . . . . Apr 94
Mandela, Nelson – *Umtata, Transkei*. . Jan 92
Mandela, Winnie
　– *Pondoland, Transkei* . . . . ModAfr 97
South Carolina
Childress, Alice – *Charleston* . . . . Author 95
Daniel, Beth – *Charleston* . . . . Sport 96
Edelman, Marian Wright
　– *Bennettsville* . . . . Apr 93
Gillespie, Dizzy – *Cheraw* . . . . Apr 93
Jackson, Jesse – *Greenville* . . . . Sep 95
Spain
Domingo, Placido – *Madrid*. . . . . . . Sep 95
Ochoa, Severo – *Luarca*. . . . . Jan 94
Sanchez Vicario, Arantxa
　– *Barcelona*. . . . . Sport 96
Tanzania
Nyerere, Julius Kambarage . . . . ModAfr 97
Tennessee
Andrews, Ned – *Oakridge* . . . . Sep 94
Doherty, Shannen – *Memphis*. . . . . . Apr 92
Fitzhugh, Louise – *Memphis* . . . . Author 97
McKissack, Fredrick L. – *Nashville* Author 97
McKissack, Patricia C. – *Smyrna* . . Author 97
Rudolph, Wilma – *St. Bethlehem* . . . . Apr 95

Birthday Index

November (continued)

		Year
12	Andrews, Ned	1980
	Harding, Tonya	1970
13	Goldberg, Whoopi	1949
14	Boutros-Ghali, Boutros	1922
15	O'Keeffe, Georgia	1887
16	Baiul, Oksana	1977
17	Fuentes, Daisy	1966
18	Driscoll, Jean	1966
	Mankiller, Wilma	1945
19	Strug, Kerri	1977
21	Aikman, Troy	1966
	Griffey, Ken, Jr.	1969
	Speare, Elizabeth George	1908
24	Ndeti, Cosmas	1971
25	Grant, Amy	1960
	Thomas, Lewis	1913
26	Pine, Elizabeth Michele	1975
	Schulz, Charles	1922
27	White, Jaleel	1977
29	L'Engle, Madeleine	1918
	Lewis, C. S.	1898
	Tubman, William V. S.	1895
30	Jackson, Bo	1962
	Parks, Gordon	1912

December

		Year
2	Macaulay, David	1946
	Seles, Monica	1973
	Watson, Paul	1950
3	Filipovic, Zlata	1980
7	Bird, Larry	1956
8	Rivera, Diego	1886
12	Bialik, Mayim	1975
	Frankenthaler, Helen	1928
13	Fedorov, Sergei	1969
15	Aidid, Mohammed Farah	1934
	Mendes, Chico	1944
16	McCary, Michael	1971
18	Sanchez Vicario, Arantxa	1971
	Spielberg, Steven	1947
19	Morrison, Sam	1936
21	Evert, Chris	1954
	Griffith Joyner, Florence	1959
22	Pinkney, Jerry	1939
23	Avi	1937
25	Sadat, Anwar	1918
26	Butcher, Susan	1954
27	Roberts, Cokie	1943
28	Washington, Denzel	1954
30	Woods, Tiger	1975

People to Appear in Future Issues

Actors
Trini Alvarado
Richard Dean
   Anderson
Dan Aykroyd
Tyra Banks
Drew Barrymore
Levar Burton
Cher
Kevin Costner
Courtney Cox
Tom Cruise
Jamie Lee Curtis
Patti D'Arbanville-
   Quinn
Geena Davis
Ozzie Davis
Ruby Dee
Michael De Lorenzo
Matt Dillon
Michael Douglas
Larry Fishburne
Jody Foster
Morgan Freeman
Richard Gere
Tracey Gold
Graham Greene
Mark Harmon
Michael Keaton
Val Kilmer
Angela Lansbury
Joey Lawrence
Martin Lawrence
Christopher Lloyd
Kellie Martin
Marlee Matlin
Bette Midler
Alyssa Milano
Demi Moore
Rick Moranis
Tamera Mowry
Tia Mowry
Kate Mulgrew
Eddie Murphy
Liam Neeson
Leonard Nimoy
Sean Penn
Phylicia Rashad
Keanu Reeves
Jason James Richter

Julia Roberts
Bob Saget
Arnold
   Schwarzenegger
Alicia Silverstone
Christian Slater
Taran Noah Smith
Jimmy Smits
Wesley Snipes
Sylvester Stallone
John Travolta
Mario Van Peebles
Damon Wayans
Bruce Willis
B.D. Wong
Malik Yoba

Artists
Mitsumasa Anno
Graeme Base
Yoko Ono

Astronauts
Neil Armstrong

Authors
Jean M. Auel
John Christopher
Arthur C. Clarke
John Colville
Paula Danziger
Paula Fox
Jamie Gilson
Rosa Guy
Nat Hentoff
Norma Klein
Lois Lowry
Stephen Manes
Norma Fox Mazer
Anne McCaffrey
Gloria D. Miklowitz
Marsha Norman
Robert O'Brien
Francine Pascal
Daniel Pinkwater
Louis Sachar
John Saul
Amy Tan
Alice Walker

Jane Yolen
Roger Zelazny

Business
Minoru Arakawa
Michael Eisner
David Geffen
Wayne Huizenga
Donna Karan
Phil Knight
Estee Lauder
Sheri Poe
Anita Roddick
Donald Trump
Ted Turner
Lillian Vernon

Cartoonists
Lynda Barry
Roz Chast
Greg Evans
Nicole Hollander
Art Spiegelman
Garry Trudeau

Comedians
Billy Crystal
Steve Martin
Eddie Murphy
Bill Murray

Dancers
Debbie Allen
Mikhail Baryshnikov
Gregory Hines
Twyla Tharp
Tommy Tune

Directors/Producers
Woody Allen
Steven Bocho
Tim Burton
Francis Ford Coppola
Ron Howard
John Hughes
Penny Marshall
Leonard Nimoy
Rob Reiner
John Singleton
Quentin Tarantino

Environmentalists/
Animal Rights
Kathryn Fuller
Linda Maraniss
Ingrid Newkirk
Pat Potter

Journalists
Tom Brokaw
John Hockenberry
Ted Koppel
Jim Lehrer
Dan Rather
Nina Totenberg
Mike Wallace
Bob Woodward

Musicians
Ace of Base
Babyface
Basia
George Benson
Bjork
Clint Black
Ruben Blades
Mary J. Blige
Bono
Edie Brickell
James Brown
Ray Charles
Chayanne
Natalie Cole
Cowboy Junkies
Sheryl Crow
Billy Ray Cyrus
Melissa Etheridge
Aretha Franklin
Green Day
Guns N' Roses
P.J. Harvey
Hootie & the Blowfish
India
Janet Jackson
Michael Jackson
Jewel
Winona Judd
R. Kelly
Anthony Kiedis
Lenny Kravitz
Kris Kross
James Levine

LL Cool J
Andrew Lloyd Webber
Courtney Love
Lyle Lovett
MC Lyte
Madonna
Barbara Mandrell
Branford Marsalis
Paul McCartney
Midori
Morrissey
N.W.A.
Jesseye Norman
Sinead O'Connor
Luciano Pavoratti
Pearl Jam
Teddy Pendergrass
David Pirner
Prince
Public Enemy
Raffi
Bonnie Raitt
Red Hot Chili Peppers
Lou Reed
L.A. Reid
R.E.M.
Trent Reznor
Kenny Rogers
Axl Rose
Run-D.M.C.
Paul Simon
Smashing Pumpkins
Sting
Michael Stipe
Pam Tillis
TLC
Randy Travis
Terence Trent d'Arby
Travis Tritt
U2
Eddie Vedder
Stevie Wonder
Trisha Yearwood

Dwight Yoakum
Neil Young

Politics/World Leaders
Harry A. Blackmun
Jesse Brown
Pat Buchanan
Mangosuthu Buthelezi
Violeta Barrios de Chamorro
Shirley Chisolm
Jean Chretien
Warren Christopher
Edith Cresson
Mario Cuomo
Dalai Lama
Mike Espy
Alan Greenspan
Vaclav Havel
Jack Kemp
Bob Kerrey
Kim Il-Sung
Coretta Scott King
John Major
Imelda Marcos
Slobodan Milosevic
Mother Theresa
Ralph Nader
Manuel Noriega
Hazel O'Leary
Leon Panetta
Federico Pena
Simon Peres
Robert Reich
Ann Richards
Richard Riley
Phyllis Schlafly
Donna Shalala
Desmond Tutu
Lech Walesa
Eli Weisel
Vladimir Zhirinovsky

Royalty
Charles, Prince of Wales
Duchess of York (Sarah Ferguson)
Queen Noor

Scientists
Sallie Baliunas
Avis Cohen
Donna Cox
Stephen Jay Gould
Mimi Koehl
Deborah Letourneau
Philippa Marrack
Helen Quinn
Barbara Smuts
Flossie Wong-Staal
Aslihan Yener
Adrienne Zihlman

Sports
Jim Abbott
Muhammad Ali
Michael Andretti
Boris Becker
Barry Bonds
Bobby Bonilla
Jose Canseco
Jennifer Capriati
Michael Chang
Roger Clemens
Randall Cunningham
Eric Davis
Clyde Drexler
John Elway
George Foreman
Zina Garrison
Anfernee Hardaway
Rickey Henderson
Evander Holyfield
Brett Hull
Raghib Ismail
Jim Kelly

Petr Klima
Willy Mays
Paul Molitor
Jack Nicklaus
Joe Paterno
Kirby Puckett
Pat Riley
Mark Rippien
Daryl Strawberry
Danny Sullivan
Vinnie Testaverde
Isiah Thomas
Mike Tyson
Steve Yzerman

Television Personalities
Andre Brown (Dr. Dre)
Katie Couric
Phil Donahue
Kathie Lee Gifford
Ed Gordon
Arsenio Hall
Ricki Lake
Joan Lunden
Dennis Miller
Diane Sawyer
Alison Stewart
Jon Stewart
Vanna White
Montel Williams
Paul Zaloom

Other
James Brady
Johnnetta Cole
David Copperfield
Jaimie Escalante
Jack Kevorkian
Wendy Kopp
Sister Irene Kraus
Jeanne White